Law and Islam in the Middle East

Law and Islam in the Middle East

Edited by Daisy Hilse Dwyer

Bergin & Garvey Publishers
New York • Westport, Connecticut • London

Library of Congress Cataloging-in-Publication Data

Law and Islam in the Middle East / edited by Daisy Hilse Dwyer.
p. cm.
Includes bibliographical references.
ISBN 0-89789-151-1 (lib. bdg. : alk. paper)
1. Islamic law—Middle East. I. Dwyer, Daisy Hilse.
LAW <ISLAM 7 Law 1990>
340.5'9'0956—dc20 89-18545

British Library Cataloguing in Publication Data is available.

Library of Congress Catalog Card Number: 89-18545
ISBN:0-89789-151-1

First published in 1990

Bergin & Garvey, One Madison Avenue, New York, NY 10010
An imprint of Greenwood Publishing Group, Inc.

Printed in the United States of America

The paper used in this book complies with the Permanent Paper Standard issued by the National Information Standards Organization (Z39.48-1984).

10 9 8 7 6 5 4 3 2 1

CONTENTS

Acknowledgments vii

1. Law and Islam in the Middle East: An Introduction 1
   Daisy Hilse Dwyer

2. Women and Criminal Justice in Egypt 15
   Safia K. Mohsen

3. Litigant Strategies in an Islamic Court in Jordan 35
   Richard T. Antoun

4. Literacy and the Law: Documents and Document Specialists in Yemen 61
   Brinkley Messick

5. Islam and the Struggle over State Law in Turkey 77
   June Starr

6. Reinstating Islamic Criminal Law in Libya 99
   Ann Elizabeth Mayer

7. Legal Postulates in Flux: Justice, Wit, and Hierarchy in Iran 115
   Michael M. J. Fischer

8. Working the Law: A Lebanese Working-Class Case 143
   Suad Joseph

Index 161

About the Editor and Contributors 167

ACKNOWLEDGMENTS

This volume grew out of a seminar which was funded by the Exxon Education Foundation and was held at Columbia University in 1980 under the auspices of the Middle East Institute of the Columbia University School of International Affairs and the Parker School of Foreign and Comparative Law of the Columbia School of Law. I wish to thank each of the aforementioned entities for its gracious support. I also wish to thank the seminar's participants for the valuable insights provided by them at that time and the volume's contributors for their attention in reflecting pertinent new developments in the Middle East in their chapters. Special thanks are also owing to editor Ann Gross and word processor Yvonne Illich for their attentive, professional work in connection with the publication of this volume.

1

LAW AND ISLAM IN THE MIDDLE EAST: AN INTRODUCTION

Daisy Hilse Dwyer

A striking element in the cultural configurations that are grounded in Islam is the primary place that law has within them. In Islam, law consists of a comprehensive set of rules for human conduct as provided through Allah's command, with those rules being instrumental in controlling negative social and political tendencies.[1] As the fourteenth-century Arab philosopher ibn Khaldun asserted: "Man is by nature a domineering being; and his desire to overcome . . . others, and subdue and coerce them is the source of wars and trespassing" (Mahdi 1957:178). Responding to this force, "the Law . . . is designed to preserve and protect human society" (Mahdi 1957:193).

The central position accorded to law in Islam has long been recognized by Muslim jurisprudents and by Western legal scholars. The internationally renowned Islamic law scholar Joseph Schacht, for example, concluded: "Islamic law is the epitome of Islamic thought, the most typical manifestation of the Islamic way of life, the core and kernel of Islam itself" (1964:1).

But the relation of Islam in and to law-related behavior also needs to be closely examined, especially at a time when Islamic fundamentalism is flourishing. While law is a key component in the fabric of Islamic thought, when and where Islam is evoked in law-related behavior, among individuals and among groups, remains to be considered and contrasted within the region. To what degree is the law-related behavior of Middle Easterners—the way in which they approach, utilize, conceptualize, and articulate law and legal institutions—distinctive because of the Islam-in-law relation? To what degree does Islamic law constitute a set of alternatives that litigants, judges, and government leaders adhere to, magnify, ignore, or reject according to situational context? Indeed, to what degree are existing legal processes—those that apply Islamic law and those that do not—used by Muslims in the region?

This volume takes an intensive look at Middle Eastern law as Muslims actually practice it in a diversity of Middle Eastern nations. It looks at the dynamics of dispute settlement, the interaction of court personnel with litigants, the content of legislation, and the promulgation of public policies about law. It examines the power dynamics of law's interpersonal, intergroup, and international sides. In doing so, the volume pinpoints spheres of flexibility in contemporary Middle Eastern legal systems, as they are shaped by and respond to demands from within and without. It also charts the many-faceted pertinence of the Islamic legal strain in an age in which Islamic fundamentalism provides a popular social and political paradigm in what are intricate and multistranded legal configurations. Focusing on the specifics of contemporary politics and social life, this volume provides a baseline for understanding how, and the degree to which, the legal principles and the legal ethos that came to be elaborated in Islam many centuries back continue to provide a vital dynamic in legal behavior and thinking today.

SOURCES OF LAW

The law that Muslim Middle Easterners utilize has often been discussed in terms of sources or origins, most prominent among them being Islamic law, local customary law, and those laws of European origin that were imposed or adopted from the colonial period onward in various Middle Eastern nations.

Of these, Islamic law (*shari'a*) is taken by Muslim jurisprudential theory to be generated from certain divine sources. These include four so-called roots: the Quran, the Sunna (the model behavior of the Prophet), analogic reasoning (*qiyas*), and the consensus of the community (*ijma'*) (which has come to mean the consensus of the community of Muslim legal scholars). Additional sources have been recognized by Muslim legists depending upon the region whose law is considered and include, for example, seeking the most equitable solution (*istihsan*) and seeking the best solution for the general interest (*istislah*). Coupled with the Sunna (which itself changed and developed over time) and the Quran, the other sources permitted Muslims in the early centuries of Islam to adapt their law to social context before the independent inquiry of jurists became more restricted as exhaustive legal manuals were amassed.[2]

As to the law that is associated with custom and usage, elements of so-called customary law continue to this day in the various regions of the Middle East (e.g., in the law of water rights in the Yemen [Maktari 1971] and Morocco [Hammoudi 1985]; in marriage and divorce law in Jordan [see Antoun, this volume]). Indeed, to the degree that it did not conflict with Islamic law, customary law (*'urf*) itself was recognized by certain Muslim legists as a source, albeit a subsidiary one, of Islamic law. In the contemporary period certain references to custom and usage have been introduced into law codes (e.g., the provision that recognizes local custom in setting marital support obligations in Morocco [Colomer 1963:184]), and certain nations in the region specify custom as a source to be utilized in determining what law is to apply when legislation is lacking.

As the previously cited examples of existing customary law—water rights and marriage and divorce law—imply, customary law often covers important ground. It is important to note, however, that customary law becomes a marked category of law in discussions about Middle Eastern law largely by virtue of how it is different from Islamic law. Differences from Islamic law, however, do not necessarily make local customary law un-Islamic in a broader sense. The French and British frequently encouraged local allegiance to customary law in their efforts to separate so-called "tribes" from more Islamized populations. In Morocco the French attempted to do this in 1930 by recognizing the judicial competence of the customary courts in the Berber regions. Their tactic was founded on erroneous suppositions as Moroccan history indicates: many Moroccans mobilized against this Christian attack on Islam and the Moroccan nationalist movement gained momentum.

As to Western legal principles, these entered the region primarily as a product of the colonialist enterprises of the French and British and, to a lesser degree, other Europeans, and came to predominate in civil, commercial, and criminal law. In many Middle Eastern nations, these legal spheres came to be handled in Westernized courts while "traditional" religious courts were left to handle personal status law (the laws of marriage, divorce, succession, child custody, and guardianship, for instance). A unified national court system often ensued. In certain nations such as Iran and Libya, as this volume shows, the influx of Western legal principles has been substantially rolled back.

As the actualities of judicial and legislative behavior show, however, any analysis of Middle Eastern law in terms of discrete sources or origins does violence to our sense of the adaptiveness and flexibility of the relevant legal systems as wholes. Much of what is deemed Islamic originated in pre-Islamic custom and the incorporation of customary or European law into legal corpuses that are labeled as Islamic on their home ground continues to this day (see Messick, 1983, on the development of a public prosecutor in the Yemen). Moreover, the transformational devices or rationales that are used in this process are sometimes specifically denoted as Islamic (e.g., citing the Islamic requirement that co-wives are to be treated equally as a basis for the abolition of polygyny, equal treatment being construed as impossible), although the substantive legal provisions that result from the transformation, such as monogamy in Tunisia, might be radically different from their Islamic legal roots. Indeed, throughout Islamic history, specific Muslim institutions, like the religious (*shari'a*) courts, have been maintained alongside, and likely by virtue of, other institutions whose officials responded to immediate exigencies and operated without the full panoply of Islamic law's constraints and safeguards (extensive evidential requirements).

The tendency for amalgamation from diverse sources has been pinpointed as a major dynamic by legal historians who have focused on the Islamic law configuration in the Middle East. Noel Coulson, for example, cites the fusion of religiously introduced standards and precepts with customary law as central to the general process of legal development in Islam (1971:2f). Joseph Schacht also reminds us that Muslim jurisprudence worked on both popular and administrative practice, imbuing it with religious and ethical emphasis, the result being Islamic law (1950:283).

The dynamic of amalgamation that those scholars describe joins the considerable variability in how disputes and law cases are handled, which numerous anthropologists have noted with respect to the Middle East. Examination of the latter tendency reaffirms the point that context rather than source or origin is most likely the core phenomenon to be delineated in understanding the handling of disputes and law cases. Some theorists tie such variability to the importance of personal ties in determining legal outcomes in the region (see Joseph, this volume), while others have noted the general "open-textured" nature of concepts relating to social relationships (Rosen 1984), which allows individual actors to define and redefine behavior and relationships, including law-related behavior and relationships, according to context.

It is debatable whether specific sources and origins of law can be easily traced given the changing contexts in which law operates and given the fact that the creation of a unified legal system itself entails considerable differential forgetting of history, including origins. When Middle Easterners themselves attribute origins to the law that they practice, however, this volume explores the phenomenon (see chapter 6, this volume). Variability in how law is conceptualized and applied and in how disputes and law cases are handled, however, is a major topic that this volume explores. In particular, differences of approach to law and premises about law frequently occur by class, sex, sect, and subregion, and these differences are especially noted herein. Moreover, the institutional mechanisms through which new law is created, be they legislative, administrative, or other, must be contrasted as regards their power implications.

This volume underlines the central role that a changing Islam has played and continues to play in the formal organization of Middle Eastern legal systems and in the shaping of the region's renditions of its legal pasts, presents, and futures. It reiterates, however, that the actual form and impact of Islam may be different according to the specific community, region, nation, subgroup and issue involved (see Geertz, 1968, for a discussion of Islam's contrastive forms in Morocco and Indonesia) and that the diverse fashions in which Islamic law is emphasized or muted in the legal equation are part of the continuingly complex viability of the legal systems in the region.

THE COURTROOM PROCESS

While Middle Eastern legal processes may involve numerous participants at different stages (e.g., *'ulama* or religious scholars who make pronouncements about law; scribes who draw up legal documents; mediators who engage in alternative dispute settlement), litigants and judges are the focal actors in most Middle Eastern courtrooms. In contradistinction to the United States, where lawyers are focal in presenting court cases, litigants rather than lawyers are active participants in most courts in the Middle East. Even though lawyers have a complex history in the region (Ziadeh 1968) and are increasingly being utilized, they continue to act only occasionally as advocates in many regional courts, and many *qadis* continue to encourage direct litigant input even when lawyers are present (Rosen 1979, 1989).

The often-limited involvement of lawyers in day-to-day judicial affairs in the Middle East has a major implication: the focus of courtroom activity shifts from the bar to the bench. Middle Eastern law has often been characterized by Westerners as functioning through *qadi*'s justice, a pejorative term that emphasizes arbitrary decisionmaking. *Qadi*'s justice, however, is an accurate depiction in the sense that the judge (*qadi*) is typically focal in factfinding and decisionmaking. (No jury system exists under Islamic law). Judges, in conjunction with court scribes and police, for example, explained the intricacies of law to prospective litigants at the pretrial phase in the regional court in Morocco where this anthropologist-lawyer did research. In the courtroom, they drew out opponents' arguments and occasionally cross-examined. Certain anthropologists (Rosen 1981) have noted that judges often agonize over the equity of the opinions they render, especially in nations like Morocco, where the creative element in judgeship is strong (Toledano 1981). Their goal is to get litigants back on track for the purposes of negotiating their own permissible relationships (see Rosen 1989), again quite contrary to the stereotype.

Because of the relatively high level of litigant involvement in courtroom processes in the Middle East, any analysis of courtroom behavior compels us to consider the complex legal lives of lay people with a particular thoroughness. Given the importance of social ties and relationships in how decisions are made in legal arenas in the Middle East, an anthropological approach that looks at the actualities of law in the eyes of the entire folk, not only legal professionals, provides a particularly appropriate analytic framework, which is adopted herein.

THE LETTER OF MIDDLE EASTERN LAW: PERSONAL STATUS LAW REVISITED

Personal status law remains the bastion of Islamic law in Middle Eastern nations.[3] With many of its origins in sacred sources, Middle Eastern laws of marriage, divorce, succession, child custody, guardianship—to wit, what has been called personal status law—comprise those parts of the region's legal corpuses that certain Muslims take to be immutable. While these corpuses have come to be revised in many ways in the contemporary period, the revisions have also tended to be guarded.

Principles of classical Islamic law have been maintained to a substantial degree on the personal status front in the Middle East's law codes, but varyingly according to the nation. In the face of Quranic stipulations that guarantee the polygyny option (a Muslim man may be simultaneously married to four wives), for example, only Turkey, South Yemen, and Tunisia have passed legislation prohibiting polygyny. The polygyny right has, however, come under the supervision of the courts in many nations in which it continues to exist, with the equal and just treatment of wives being a concern of many *qadis*. In certain nations that right may also be limited by virtue of the wife's rights: in Morocco, for example, a wife may stipulate in the marriage contract that she will gain the right to divorce her husband if he takes a second wife. Shifts in the Islamic laws of succession have also occurred (Coulson 1978) but have frequently involved changes that are of limited controversy or that have had their impact chiefly on non-Muslims (Ziadeh 1979:38). The principle that is found in the Quran that gives certain female heirs only a half-share of inheritance in comparison to male heirs who are in a parallel kin position to the deceased, for example, has not been equivalently touched by legislative reform. As to child custody, the idea that a mother's rights to her children extend largely to the children's earlier years continues to be found in many contemporary Middle Eastern law codes, although some codes, such as Iraq's 1978 code, have also come to stress the notion of a child's best interest. And as to divorce law, a man's right to repudiate his wife unilaterally remains substantially in force in the region although restrictions as to how and when the repudiation may occur sometimes have been added. In an effort to realign the preexisting power balance between men and women with respect to divorce, however, women's divorce options have generally been expanded, in some cases substantially, such as in Tunisia where a wife, like a husband, obtained the right to insist upon a divorce. In sum, many Middle Eastern nations have preserved certain core Islamic law principles, while revising the legal corpuses that surround them by stressing certain ethical principles, some of which (e.g., the equal treatment of co-wives) are grounded in the *shari'a*.

At the same time, close observation of actual law-related behavior in various Middle Eastern nations demonstrates that substantial maneuvering occurs with respect to personal status law beyond the changes that have been implemented in law codes (see White, 1978, and Esposito, 1982, for overviews). In some cases the actualities of law-related behavior go beyond the limits of legislative reform, while in many other cases actual behavior reveals that traditional practices—Islamic and customary—continue despite certain legislative reforms. Contrary to Islamic law, which imposes no specific minimal age requirements for marriage, most Middle Eastern nations have enacted minimum age requirements at which males and females may marry (in certain nations these age requirements may be superseded in specified circumstances). Such requirements are themselves frequently circumvented, however, by families wishing to marry daughters off early. And while most nations have opted to retain many provisions of the Islamic law of succession, certain have reinterpreted other statutes that could be used to by-pass some of these laws, such as the law of bequest (Coulson 1969:98) and certain other principles in the Islamic law of succession tend not to be followed (for instance, females are frequently disinherited entirely, especially when real property is at issue). Moreover, even in nations in which women may obtain divorces under only limited circumstances, numerous women can and do precipitate divorces by returning to their natal families.

In this volume, the authors who deal with the on-the-ground intricacies of the law of family relations underscore the social, political and economic factors that support stasis or change in this crucial sphere. In particular, they detail the complex blend of options and constraints that Middle Easterners experience in confronting personal status issues and also note that the laws governing family relations cannot be viewed in terms of personal status law alone.

In her analysis of criminal law as applied to Egyptian women, Mohsen (chapter 2) stresses that the legal status of women is not only determined by personal status law; criminal law is increasingly relevant. Mohsen notes the social pressures that push increasing numbers of Egyptian women to commit various crimes inside and outside their families. She also documents the responses and attitudes of courts and police. Mohsen makes several important points. First, while Egyptian criminal law is largely Western in content, the way in which it is implemented is culture-specific. Second, with respect to women who are charged with crimes as well as women who are victims, police, prison personnel, and the courts tend to respond distinctively, in large part because of the protective attitude that Egyptian society maintains toward women generally, women being regarded as private rather than public personages. Hence, while the letter of the law sometimes discriminates against women, this disadvantage is, in Mohsen's view, often counter-balanced by the greater protection that women can expect to receive. Mohsen's analysis also finds variability in court and police responsiveness to female criminals by class.

Antoun (chapter 3) examines the relationship of Islamic law and customary law with respect to the personal status issues that Jordanian peasants bring to court. As Antoun puts it, local custom recognizes consanguine relations, as evidenced in the parent-child tie, as fundamental, while Islamic law recognizes the fundamental integrity of the conjugal family within a consanguine structure. By examining the strategies of Jordanian villagers in marriage, divorce, and child custody cases as they occurred in the Islamic court of a Jordanian village during the period before the 1973 petroleum crisis, Antoun finds that both paradigms were manipulated by litigants. Indeed, consanguine allegiances tended to take priority over conjugal concerns, although Islamic legal principles were also stressed during the court cases. The preeminence of consanguine concerns was often achieved through the court's acknowledged commitment to reconciliation (which it also emphasized to be a value grounded in Islam), which often obviated any explicit decisionmaking based on Islamic law by the court. In Antoun's view, the emphasis on consanguine priorities generally worked in women's best interests. Antoun also sees women's interests as having been served by their evoking certain Islamic rules (e.g., women's right to appear in court; their right to *mahr* or bridal payment), and he reminds us that both Islamic law and customary law can be and have been used by women against both consanguine and conjugal relatives.

In chapter 4 Messick focuses on the law of evidence and social relations. As Messick reminds us, written legal documents were not recognized in the Islamic law of evidence, early Muslim jurists denying the validity of such written proof. Nonetheless, the use of documents triumphed more or less completely among jurists, depending upon the region of the Middle East considered. In the present day in highland Yemen, the region of Messick's research, legal documents are in wide use but are, as Messick shows in his sociological analysis, of varying cruciality in guaranteeing a transaction, with a key determining factor being the type of kin relationship, business tie, or friendship existing between the disputants. Messick's analysis shows that legal documents are less essential and are made less ironclad when adequate assurance exists in the form of positive personal bonds that the parties will engage in the agreed-upon behavior. As to legal organization in highly contentious Yemeni society, document writers, who may provide successive drafts of documents and thereby work toward the settlement of disputes, are as common as are court judges and arbitrators as settlement agents.

Starr's material (chapter 5) on Turkish Muslims indicates that commitment to religious versus secular law is generally not at issue when litigants decide how to handle personal status and other disputes. Multiple options for conflict resolution exist at the local level in Turkey, which is formally a secular state, but litigants activate these options or other alternatives according to which system (the informal, local-level, more customary system of social control or the nominally secular state system) provides them greater advantage and leverage. In the village of her fieldwork, Starr found that litigants chose carefully if and when to voice their complaints before (1) the national courts, the village council, or the village headman, or (2) traditional village mediators. Village women, for example, generally brought their cases to the national courts in order to benefit from a less constraining (and less Islamic) system. Indeed, they filed twice as many routine suits in the district court, and subsequently won more cases than men. According to Starr, the national courts provide relief to litigants from local interests that have an Islamic association, while the local-level system continues to flourish because it more often supports other subgroups, most prominent among them being males, landowners, and seniors.

The aforementioned chapters underscore the need to think of the Islamic law component as but one strain among a number of alternatives that disputants can more or less implement according to case and context. They additionally demonstrate how Islamic law provisions can be redefined and occasionally evaded. A major conclusion in these chapters also concerns the legal/social dynamic: Muslim Middle Easterners' choices of legal arenas and their ways of handling their disputes become understandable only through close attention to the interpersonal power dynamic in which disputants engage (see also Mayer, 1985, with respect to property law).

LAW AND FUNDAMENTALISM

While the most enduring principles of Islamic law involve personal status, the most striking recent reassertions of Islamic law have occurred with respect to other legal corpuses. The reintroduction of certain Quranic criminal law provisions in Libya, Pakistan, Iran, and the Sudan, particularly those involving the corporal punishment of offenders, provides a prominent example. This tendency has extended the geographical range of fundamentalism in criminal law matters far beyond the Persian Gulf states where such provisions traditionally held sway. Other revivals have occurred in the commercial law context. Banks have been established, for example, in various Middle Eastern nations, which implement a "zero interest" policy that responds to the Islamic prohibition of usury.

Mayer and Fischer examine how and the degree to which Islamic fundamentalism has been revived in the legal domain in Libya (chapter 6) and Iran (chapter 7). It is a domain in which fundamentalist commitments have been strongly voiced by those governments. Each author finds that fidelity to Islamic law takes a form that is consistent with nation-specific histories. Each author also finds that Islamic legal fundamentalism provides a powerful validating ethos for those governments in the eyes of their citizenries.

Mayer details the key elements of the Islamic fundamentalism that Libya has implemented under Qaddafi. She notes the political intricacy of a process that is both fundamentalist and not. Specifically, she documents the differential reinstatement of Islamic law principles in criminal law versus commercial, contractual, and property law and the divergence that exists between Libya's Islamic legislation and its implementation by a judiciary trained along Western lines. Her analysis is that Qaddafi's fundamentalism focused on Islamic criminal law as derived, with certain subsequent changes, from one primary source of Islamic law—the Quran—and that Qaddafi thereby avoided instituting other fundamentalist revisions that would stymie the commercial growth and economic development of his oil-rich economy. Mayer also notes that reinstating Islamic law in Libya responded to the government's attempt to become associated with goals that are meaningful to the masses.

Fischer's interpretation of legal-political developments before and during the early years of the revolution in Iran seeks, in part, to distinguish general developments that are an inextricable part of any political revolution from those historical developments grounded in Islam. In his view, much of what Westerners associate with an Islamic fundamentalist revolution reflects general revolutionary tendencies. Moreover, many of the moments in which Islamic legal fervor has waxed strongest in Iran occurred during deep struggles for power by Muslim clerics. Through his analysis of the relationship of the judicial system and power, Fischer's material supports the argument that an Islamic emphasis in law is more responsive to context than many observers think. He also traces the attempts, which were both clerical and secular, to reform the earlier political system and to eliminate injustices within the legal system, a system that was used increasingly under the Pahlavis to marshall political power.

The law-related behavior of Muslim Middle Easterners cannot be considered from the vantage point of Muslim-Muslim relations alone. Joseph's Lebanese fieldwork (chapter 8) especially provides indicators of how Middle Eastern Muslims have developed intricate involvements with Middle Easterners of other ethnic groups, sects, classes, and regional backgrounds in a world in which, as Joseph puts it, "the law neither protected individuals automatically nor operated independently by formal rules." As part of the process Sunnite and Shi'ite working-class Beirutis traditionally maintained patron-client relations with Armenian Catholic, Maronite, Greek Orthodox, and other Christians, they activated those ties in handling their legal and administrative affairs, and they drew upon kin morality to cut across class lines. Indeed, a Muslim's optimal conflict strategy likely involved multiple inroads into worlds other than his own. In the face of internecine war Joseph notes that these options are still utilized by (and in some cases have become more critical to) the Lebanese working class.

VARIABILITY IN MIDDLE EASTERN LEGAL SYSTEMS

Legal scholarship increasingly recognizes the need for precise portrayals of law. In particular, legal scholars focusing on other legal systems stress the need to detail differences in law-related behavior by group and trace the intergroup dialectic (Dwyer 1979). Legal historian Lawrence Friedman (1975), for example, argues that multiple "legal cultures" exist in any society, and these legal cultures rarely coïncide with formal depictions in law codes and law manuals.

The scope of differences between de facto and de jure law remains to be explicated for the contemporary Middle East, but the distinctions that certain legal theorists have noted provide useful beginnings toward such an analysis. Legal sociologist Donald Black (1976) emphasizes that societies may have "more law" or "less law," more law, in his view, meaning a greater use of legal institutions, more legal knowledge, and starker punishments. Legal economist Marc Galanter (1974) has focused on the socioeconomic side of law's variability, stressing the differences that are experienced in the legal involvements of the "haves" and "have nots." And as legal anthropologists Laura Nader (Nader and Todd 1978) and Lawrence Rosen (1984), and legal sociologist Richard Abel (1973) remind us, the specificities of the disputing process (in the sense of how disputes are conducted, whether they are resolved, if they are handled in court, and whether disputes in court reach final judgment) are themselves critical to our understanding of legal processes. These distinctions are relevant throughout this volume, where they are fleshed out with examples from Middle Eastern law as it is actually practiced.

As this volume indicates, the legal predilections, treatment, and judicial access of Middle Easterners often vary along class, national, subregional, occupational, gender, and sectarian lines. For the men and women considered in Starr's article on Turkey, women were found less often to use local mediators in family law cases. The two sexes commit crimes that are distinctively evaluated by court personnel and police in Egypt. As to class, working-class Lebanese are found to have substantial gaps in their knowledge of administrative law and practice, and accurate knowledge cannot be assured to them through their social networks, a circumstance that distinguishes them from the nation's elite. The class origins of female criminal offenders in Egypt also correlates with the relative presence or absence of police sympathy and support. And as a vulnerable minority group, Zoroastrians in Iran pursued their grievances with differential vigor than the Shi'ite majority, and they expected lesser returns under both the Pahlavi and earlier regimes. Moreover, the discontent of particular occupational groups dramatically fanned the flames of fundamentalism in Iran and elsewhere. Finally, differences can be marked among legal personnel themselves: a Western-trained judicial elite limited the implementation of the Quranic punishments that Islamic scholars advocated in Libya.

One correlate of such differences is that Islamic fundamentalism has taken divergent legal forms (Dessouki 1982). While pan-Islamic universalism is a goal that certain political leaders (Nasser, Qaddafi) have striven to implement, each nation that has gone the route of fundamentalism has obtained its support from certain groups more than others, and the process has been marked by features deriving from distinctive national pasts (Ayubi 1980; Fluehr-Lobban 1987). This results in contrasts in personnel and leadership, variability in the tonality of change, and differences in the legal sources cited by those fundamentalist movements.

Note that a substantial number of political leaders in the Middle East testify to their personal allegiances to Islamic law as proof of their political worth. Libya's Qaddafi, for example, points to the enactment of his versions of Islamic criminal law as validation for his regime; his Islamic legal purity proves that he is more religious than his predecessor, King Idris, himself a devout. Khomaini's Iran implemented Islamic law with varying intensity, often according to the persistence of the onslaught of political competitors. Sudan's Nimeiry similarly cited his reinstatement of Islamic law as a validation, and he used it for more than a decade to quiet the opposition of other law-focused fundamentalist groups such as the Muslim Brotherhood.

These leaders' fundamentalist programs resonated with the needs and demands that a substantial number of subgroups are experiencing during the present period of rapid change. These subgroups may include local artisans and shopkeepers who have to compete with large-scale producers and suppliers; students faced with critical shortages of white-collar jobs; migrant laborers from poor Middle Eastern regions (e.g., Jordan, Palestine, Yemen, Egypt, Morocco) who experience Islamic fundamentalism as the key to affluence similar to that of the Persian Gulf.

But, as one scholar has noted (Ayubi 1980: 494), while movement back to Islamic law is a major concern of fundamentalist groups, their lay memberships are sometimes not equipped to provide the requisite legal content. Using the imagery and values of Islam when the letter of Islamic law cannot easily be replicated is one means of accomplishing the task.

As this circumstance reminds, and as this volume documents, a commitment to enhance Islam-in-law is not necessarily synonymous with the reestablishment of some version of what Islamic law was in classical times (see Ayoob 1981). Rather, Islamic law is often embraced not so much for its specific provisions, but as a core institution and a key symbol (Abel 1978) that recall a dynamic past and that carry the vision of an improved future. Having embraced the symbol, a broad range of legal alternatives sometimes becomes available for use in the eyes of the users.

The variable spirit of Islamic law is as much to be explored (Gellner and Vatin 1981), then, as is the variable letter of Islamic law in the contemporary Middle East. As the case of each nation described in this volume reminds us, the spirit of Islamic law and the letter of Middle Eastern law—Islamic law or not—interrelate in diverse ways that must be carefully delineated if the Islam-in-law relation is to be understood.

Documenting that variability as it occurs in key nations across the Middle East is this volume's task.

NOTES

1. Within an Islamic framework law consists of a Muslim's duties to Allah and to man, as provided through Allah's command. Classical Muslim jurisprudence also attached a scale of values to human behavior such that "reprehensible," "permissible" and "recommended" join "obligatory" and "prohibited" as categories for evaluating human acts. The breadth of scope of law in Islam that is implied in the foregoing descriptions is also apparent in the term *shari'a* itself, which is generally translated as "straight way," meaning the comprehensive path for living that a Muslim should pursue. Only a portion of law in this sense, however, is applicable by courts. In general, religious practices and recommended, permissible, and reprehensible acts are not regulated by legally applicable rules.

2. Several versions of *shari'a* are significant from the standpoint of the application of Islamic law today. There are four so-called schools applicable to the Sunnite population, namely the Hanafi, Maliki, Shafi'i, and Hanbali schools. Sunnites compose the vast majority of Muslims in the Middle East. The Shi'a variant of Islam distinguishes itself on certain fundamental theological questions and itself splits into three (the Ithna' Ashari, Isma'ili, and Zaidi) branches. An additional major variant of Islamic law is represented by the Ibadi sect. In most of the Middle East the Hanafi school of Islamic law is generally applied, but other schools are applicable chiefly in the following geographical areas: Maliki law in North Africa, Shafi'i law in the southern part of the Arabian peninsula, Hanbali law in Saudi Arabia, Shi'a law in Iran and portions of Iraq, Zaidi law in the Yemen, and Ibadi law in Oman and small enclaves in Algeria. It is also significant to note that according to Islamic legal theory, a Muslim court should apply the school of law that an individual chooses. This does not occur in fact in the region's courts, but one route to the reform of law codes in the region has been to select appropriate provisions from the laws that other schools offer and to incorporate such principles into the relevant law code.

3. In 1924, the *shari'a* courts were abolished in Turkey. In 1926, Turkey replaced Islamic law, including personal status law, with a code of Swiss origin and became a secular state. Only Turkey, however, has undertaken such a radical course of action among Middle Eastern nations. And as Starr demonstrates in this volume, Islamic laws of personal status continue to be applied in Turkey alongside secular law in certain contexts.

REFERENCES

Abel, Richard L. 1973. "A Comparative Theory of Dispute Institutions in Society." *Law and Society Review* 8(2): 217–47.

———. 1978. "Comparative Law and Social Theory." *American Journal of Comparative Law* 26: 219–26.

Ayoob, Mohammed (ed.). 1981. *The Politics of Islamic Reassertion.* New York: St. Martin's Press.

Ayubi, Nazih N. M. 1980. "The Political Revival of Islam: The Case of Egypt." *International Journal of Middle Eastern Studies* 12: 481–99.

Black, Donald. 1976. *The Behavior of Law.* New York: Academic Press.

Colomer, Andre. 1963. *Droit Musulman: La Succession, Le Testament.* Rabat: Editions la Porte.

Coulson, Noel J. 1969. *Conflicts and Tensions in Islamic Jurisprudence.* Chicago: University of Chicago Press.

———. 1971. *Succession in the Muslim Family.* Cambridge: Cambridge University Press.

———. 1978. "A Comparison of the Law of Succession in the Islamic and British Legal Systems." *American Journal of Comparative Law* 26: 227–32.

Dessouki, Ali E. Hillal (ed.). 1982. *Islamic Resurgence in the Arab World.* New York: Praeger Special Studies.

Dwyer, Daisy H. 1979. "Substance and Process: Reappraising the Premises of the Anthropology of Law." *Dialectical Anthropology* 4: 309–20.

Esposito, John L. 1982. *Women in Muslim Family Law.* Syracuse, N.Y.: Syracuse University Press.

Fluehr-Lobban, Carolyn. 1987. *Islamic Law and Society in the Sudan.* London: Frank Cass and Company, Limited.

Friedman, Lawrence. 1975. *The Legal System: A Social Science Perspective.* New York: Russell Sage Foundation.

Galanter, Marc. 1974. "Why the 'Haves' Come Out Ahead: Speculations on the Limits of Legal Change." *Law and Society Review* 9(1): 95–160.

Geertz, Clifford. 1968. *Islam Observed.* New Haven: Yale University Press.

Gellner, Ernest, and Jean-Claude Vatin (eds.). 1981. *Islamic Resurgence in the Arab World.* Paris: Centre National de la Recherche Scientifique.

Layish, Aharon. 1975. *Women and Islamic Law in a Non-Muslim State.* Jerusalem: Israel Universities Press.

Mahdi, Muhsin. 1957. *Ibn Khaldun's Philosophy of History.* Chicago: University of Chicago Press.

Maktari, A.M.A. 1971. *Water Rights and Irrigation Practices in Lahj: A Study of the Application of Customary and Shari'ah Law in South-West Arabia.* Cambridge: Cambridge University Press.

Messick, Brinkley. 1983. "Prosecution in Yemen: The Introduction of the Niyaba." *International Journal of Middle East Studies* 15: 507–18.

Nader, Laura, and Harry F. Todd, Jr. 1978. "The Disputing Process." In L. Nader and H.F. Todd, Jr. (eds.). *The Disputing Process—Law in Ten Societies.* New York: Columbia University Press.

Rosen, Lawrence. 1979. "Social Identity and Points of Attachment." In Clifford Geertz, Hildred Geertz, and Lawrence Rosen. *Meaning and Order in Moroccan Society:*

Three Essays in Cultural Analysis. New York: Cambridge University Press.

———. 1981. "Equity and Discretion in a Modern Islamic Legal System." *Law and Society Review* 15: 217–45.

———. 1984. *Bargaining for Reality: The Construction of Social Relations in a Muslim Community*. Chicago: University of Chicago Press.

———. 1989. *The Anthropology of Justice: Law as Culture in Islamic Society*. Cambridge: Cambridge University Press.

Schacht, Joseph. 1950. *The Origins of Mohammedan Jurisprudence*. Oxford: The Clarendon Press.

———. 1964. *An Introduction to Islamic Law*. Oxford: The Clarendon Press.

Toledano, Henry. 1981. *Judicial Practice and Family Law in Morocco*. New York: Columbia University Press.

White, Elizabeth. 1978. "Legal Reform as an Indicator of Women's Status in Muslim Nations." In Nikki Keddie and L. Beck (eds.). *Women in the Muslim World*. Cambridge: Harvard University Press.

Ziadeh, Farhat J. 1968. *Lawyers, the Rule of Law, and Liberalism in Modern Egypt*. Stanford: Hoover Institution on War, Revolution, and Peace.

———. 1979. *Property Law in the Arabic World*. London: Graham and Trotman.

2

WOMEN AND CRIMINAL JUSTICE IN EGYPT

Safia K. Mohsen

Whenever anthropologists have looked at the legal basis of women's status in the Middle East, they have viewed law almost exclusively in terms of personal status and family law. With its roots in the *shari'a* (Islamic law), family law has commonly been regarded as a repository of traditional values, reflective of the more "authentic" aspects of Middle East cultures. In addition, family law deals more directly with the types of activities and relationships most closely associated with women.

This preoccupation with personal status and family law has obscured the existence of other significant forms of law in the Middle East. Of these, criminal law has been particularly under-represented in the literature on Middle East women. Derived for the most part from foreign sources, it continues to be viewed in many countries in the area as an alien institution or as a remnant of Western domination. In recent years this has given rise to movements aimed at revising criminal law and other secular laws to reflect the more Islamic character of these societies. In May, 1980, for example, Egyptians voted overwhelmingly to establish Islamic law as the major source of legislation in Egypt. Pressure to "islamize" the law has continued, fueled, on the one hand, by the growing power of the Islamic movements, and, on the other, by the increasing dissatisfaction of the public with the inability of the current criminal law to deal with the wave of crime that has accompanied the petroleum era in Egypt and other Muslim countries. In the 1987 Egyptian parliamentary elections, islamization of law in one form or another was part of the platform of practically all the political parties. When and how this commitment to Islamic law will affect the Egyptian Criminal Code is not yet clear.

This chapter looks at some aspects of Egyptian criminal justice as it concerns women. The emphasis is upon how women, both as victims and as offenders, are treated at the various stages of the criminal justice process.

Data gathered from interviews with police, judges, prison administrators, and female prisoners point to the fact that while the content of the law is largely

Western, its transformation through implementation in real-life situations is culture-specific. In general, there appears to be a contradiction between viewing the criminal justice process as an impersonal and public process on the one hand, and the cultural perception of women as private entities whose problems should be handled informally and privately on the other. Moreover, the criminal behavior that activates the relevant law enforcement procedures reflects the rapid social transformations that are taking place in Egyptian society today.

Both as victims and as offenders, Egyptian women today are implicated in the criminal process with rising frequency and with new kinds of criminal acts. As offenders, women are subject to harsher treatment in some contexts but greater leniency in others, so that the effect of gender on the application of criminal law is not easily predicted. This lack of consistency is also reflected in the treatment of female victims of criminal acts, both on the part of the criminal justice system and the public at large.

CRIMINAL LEGISLATION IN EGYPT

While personal status and family law has retained its close reliance on Islamic law as a source of legislation, criminal law has for the most part severed its connections to the Islamic idea of criminal justice.

The law's essentially non-Islamic form is the outcome of a long series of legal revisions that gradually, but persistently, introduced provisions from foreign sources into the criminal code. Criminal law had remained Islamic from the Muslim invasion of Egypt in 640 through the mid-nineteenth century. Minor modifications were carried out during that period, but Islamic law remained the main source of criminal legislation, especially for crimes against persons and crimes of "honor." The first major departure from Islamic law with regard to "crimes" was introduced by Ottoman law, which represented a mixture of French and Islamic law. Further borrowing from French sources was reflected in the 1875 revisions, which established the Mixed Laws and court system to deal with cases involving foreigners. In 1882, legislation produced the modern Egyptian Criminal Code. It represented the first coherent criminal code covering both the substantive and the procedural aspects of criminal justice. Despite its origin in French law, however, the 1882 Criminal Code lacked basic elements of modern criminal law such as a clear description and specification of crimes and a guarantee of equality under the law for all individuals regardless of their social or economic background.

An attempt to correct some of the deficiencies in the law led to further revisions in 1904. The revised law drew on a wider base as its source, including Belgian, Italian, and Indian law. It also included provisions suggested by the Egyptian Legal Advisory Council which was formed to oversee the revisions.

In 1937 the jurisdiction of the Egyptian Penal Code was extended to foreigners and that necessitated further adjustments. Revisions have continued since then, but these have been more on the order of updating the law rather than generating major changes in content. Additional revisions involved criminalizing some acts that were not previously covered in the law (e.g., prostitution in 1949), decriminalizing others (e.g., the rape of a wife by her husband), and changing the penalties for certain crimes (e.g., trafficking in illegal drugs).

WOMEN AND THE CRIMINAL CODE

Most of the crimes connected with women and their activities are grouped under what the Criminal Code refers to as "Crimes Against Honor" (*gara'm el 'rd*). They are defined as those acts which "violate the sexual freedom of individuals or offend their sense of sexual modesty" (Ramadan 1979: 282). Included in this category are rape, sexual assault, indecent public exposure, adultery, and public solicitation for immoral acts (prostitution). Other crimes, such as homicide, also tend to be viewed distinctively when women are involved. The sexuality of women colors the handling and outcomes of such cases, whether women are offenders or victims, as the following discussion of certain of these crimes attests.

Homicide

Homicide committed for reasons of "honor," one of the most common motives for murder in Egypt, is committed for the most part against women. According to the 1981 Public Security Reports of the Ministry of Interior, women were the victims in 92% of all homicide cases committed for reasons of honor during that year. This trend is observed even when the offender is a woman. Women carry the burden of responsibility for family honor both in their own behavior and in that of their female relatives, especially those in their care. Especially in the conservative Upper Egyptian region, it is not uncommon for a mother to participate in the murder of her own daughter if the reputation of the latter becomes tarnished, in some cases carrying out the murder herself. In 1982, I interviewed two women in el Kanater Maximum Security Prison for Women who had killed their daughters to protect the family honor. In both cases, the charges of sexual impropriety of the daughters were later found to be untrue. Women are also more frequently victims of homicide motivated by domestic difficulties. Men and women tend to kill members of the opposite sex for "domestic" reasons, but since men commit proportionately more murders in all categories, women are more likely to be victims of domestic violence.

Infanticide, on the other hand, is almost always a female crime. Defined as the willful killing of children, usually infants, it is one of the most under-reported crimes in Egypt. Even when reported, infanticide is rarely prosecuted. Many law enforcement officers view such a crime as more the result of the woman's ignorance than of malicious intent. As one police officer put it,[1] "No woman in her right mind would knowingly or voluntarily kill her own child even if it is an illegitimate child. Her punishment is the loss of the child and the guilt over it. Any additional legal punishment does not serve the interest of anyone." In a highly publicized case in 1986, a woman from the poor Cairo district of Bulaq killed her newborn infant by throwing him in the river. Arrested and charged with murder, she was later released and the charges dropped. The District Attorney's office justified the action on the grounds that the woman, whose husband had abandoned her with two other children and no source of income, was under pressure that reduced her ability to exercise sound judgment. In addition, her two other children needed her care. The District Attorney's decision was generally supported by the public.

Not all infanticide cases go unprosecuted however. In the same year a woman who killed her six-month old son to punish her husband for seeing other women was charged with murder. Her trial is still pending, and no one expects the charges to be dropped. The crime is somehow viewed as a violent crime against the husband for which the woman should be punished. This view is held by both men and women.

Closely related to the crime of infanticide is abortion. The Penal Code's treatment of abortion reflects the ambivalent attitude of the legislature toward abortion. While it does not define what constitutes abortion, it assigns penalties for "anyone who intentionally causes a pregnant woman to abort her fetus by hitting or injuring it. . . . " (Article 260), or by "using drugs and other non-violent methods, or by helping the woman locate such drugs or methods" (Article 261). Acts specified under Article 260 are considered felonies, while those under Article 261 are treated as misdemeanors. The assumption is that abortion is inflicted in the first case without the woman's consent and therefore deprives her of her right, or rather social duty, to bear children. The second case, on the other hand, involves the woman's private decision to terminate her pregnancy, an important but less serious offense.

As is the case with infanticide, abortion is rarely reported to the police and when reported is difficult to prosecute successfully. The general view among law enforcement agencies in Egypt is that abortion is and should be a private matter and that bringing the case to the attention of the authorities is an unnecessary interference in the private lives of individuals. In practice they have treated it as such, thus rendering almost useless those articles of the law related to abortion. "We look at it this way," said a police officer, "If the woman is married and is going through with the abortion against her husband's wishes or without his knowledge, then she is foolish and obviously jeopardizing her own marriage. The risk she is taking with her marriage is enough of a penalty for her. If, on the other hand, she is doing this with her husband's knowledge and consent, who are we to tell them that they should have the child? That is up to the man to decide. A man has to have a good reason to prevent his wife's having his children. If the woman is not married, then abortion is the only way to prevent a scandal. Bringing a legal proceeding against her or whoever helped her is likely to make the pregnancy known, thus subjecting the woman to the anger of her family and that of society. That would be more penalty than the crime calls for. Luckily we do not get many cases of abortion. Only when such complications as the death of the woman occurs while undergoing the abortion are we sometimes notified. And even then, the evidence is usually insufficient to send the case for prosecution."

Certain aspects of the legal treatment of homicide especially discriminate against women. Among the six conditions under which murder would carry the death penalty is the use of poison as the weapon in the crime. Article 233 of the Penal Code specifies that "anyone causing the death of a human being by deliberately using substances that are capable of causing death, whether sooner or later, is punishable by death."

Despite the recent decrease in the number of homicides by poisoning, that method remains the one most commonly used by women. In effect, then, the provision makes murder by women more harshly punished than those commonly committed by men. Legal authorities argue that the original aim was not to single out women for harsh treatment but to protect the victim from a method that does not provide him with any warning. Moreover, they argue, the crime represents betrayal, usually by a close relative or someone close enough to be entrusted with the preparation of food. In many cases the crime claims the lives of more than the intended victim or victims.

While the harsh treatment of those convicted of homicide by poisoning unintentionally discriminates against women, Article 237 of the Penal Code seems deliberately to put women at a disadvantage vis-a-vis men. Article 237 states that a man who surprises his wife in the act of adultery and kills her and/or her partner is punishable with a maximum sentence of six months in prison. The provision, however, does not apply to the wife who surprises her husband in the same condition and commits a similar act. In this case, the act is considered murder.

Article 237 is the only case in the Egyptian penal system in which "provocation" by the victim or victims changes the legal description of the crime. The provision finds many defenders among jurists who argue that nothing is more humiliating to the husband than finding his wife in bed with another man. Being in bed, however, is not a necessary condition. What constitutes provocation is left to the discretion of the judge. In one case the judge ruled that a murder is justified under Article 237 if a man finds his wife in circumstances that leave no doubt that adultery has been committed. Such circumstances were achieved, in the judge's estimate, when the husband found his wife in sleeping attire and acting suspiciously, with a strange man in the house. The ruling was upheld by the Supreme Court (December 6, 1975).

A wife in the same circumstances, however, is denied the same right to lenient penalty. The assumption is that if the husband can marry a second wife under the law, finding him in bed with another woman should not be devastating. The right of the man to his wife's sexual activity, on the other hand, is exclusive. It is further maintained that the judge can always take into consideration the conditions of the crime and therefore can grant the wife leniency under the same circumstance. The difference is that in the first case the judge does not have discretionary power over the legal definition of the crime and sentence (although he has the right to determine whether the legal condition has been fulfilled), whereas in the second case he has both the right to define what constitutes provocation and the discretion as to whether to use it as a basis for reducing the sentence.

It should be added that the law denies the husband the right to benefit from the provocation clause if he himself has been convicted of adultery. The man is supposed to set an example for his wife and family to follow (Supreme Court ruling, January 3, 1965). The husband is also restricted by the condition of "surprise": a man who has known about his wife's affairs and who plans to catch her in the act is not protected under the provisions of Article 237. Limitations on the use of the Article are thus so restricting that some jurists maintain that it is questionable whether it provides a particular advantage to the husband.

Adultery

Adultery itself is another example in which criminal law discriminates against women. The penalty for a guilty husband is a maximum sentence of six months but for a women it is two years. The law considers adultery a crime against the private right of the husband; thus he can stop the sentence against his wife anytime by simply agreeing to resume marital relations. In justifying the practice, jurists maintain that adultery is the kind of offense in which the sanctity of marriage and the family is more important than the assertion of society's right against criminals. Such sanctity is best assessed by the husband, whose rights are the subject of protection in the first place.

The emphasis on the rights of the husband does not mean that a wife cannot bring charges of adultery against her husband. There are certain differences, however, between the right of the husband and that of the wife. A husband can charge his wife with adultery no matter where she commits the crime. A wife, on the other hand, cannot accuse her husband of adultery unless the act was committed in the marital residence. This has been rationalized on the grounds that a husband's right to his wife's sexual activities is exclusive, while a wife's right over her husband's sexual activities is not. If a man can legally marry a second wife, he can have sexual relations with another woman as long as he does not violate the wife's right to privacy and dignity within her domestic domain.

Rape and Sexual Assault

Not all the inequities in the law work to the disadvantage of women. Nowhere is this more evident than in cases of rape and sexual assault. Article 276 of the Criminal Code states that "a man who has sexual intercourse with a woman without her consent is punished by imprisonment at hard labor." Further, if the offender is a member of her immediate family, someone with authority over her, someone entrusted with her care or supervision, or a domestic in her service, the sentence is increased to life at hard labor.

Rape is therefore a crime. committed against women only. Sexual attacks against males are dealt with under the provisions for "Sexual Assault" which do not make distinctions between men and women as victims. Despite reference to rape as an assault against the sexual freedom of the woman, however, the law emphasizes the protection of the sexual rights of the husband and the reputation of the family.

The key issue in the crime of rape is establishing the woman's lack of consent. Unlike the United States, in which the burden of proving the absence of consent has often been shifted to the woman, in Egypt law makes it easy to establish proof. The Criminal Code defines the absence of consent broadly enough to cover any condition in which the woman's will to resist is weakened. This includes threats of physical harm as well as any psychological pressure or deceit that makes a woman vulnerable to the sexual demands of the offender. In one case the element of surprise at finding someone in her room, even in the absence of any threats by the rapist, was judged as sufficient to negate the woman's consent. In another case a man was convicted on rape charges when he gained sexual access to a female domestic worker by threatening to accuse her of stealing his gold watch.

In addition, the law makes it possible for the woman to bring charges of attempted rape in cases in which the sexual assault was interrupted for one reason or another. Thus a man who pulled a woman by the arm and started to reach for her undergarments, fleeing when the woman screamed for help, was convicted of attempted rape (Criminal Court Records: June 3, 1981).

Acts that cannot be classified as rape or attempted rape can still be prosecuted under the sexual assault provision of the Penal Code. Unlike rape, sexual assault does not require sexual intercourse, completed or aborted. Instead, any act of a sexual nature that results in the "sexual humiliation" of a victim may be prosecuted under these provisions. Thus a man who embraced a female acquaintance against her will, pinning her to the floor, was convicted of sexual assault even though he made no attempt to undress her and he himself was fully clothed (Supreme Court: January 28, 1979).

Obviously, what constitutes humiliating behavior differs from one individual to another. The law gives the judge the power to assess the circumstances in each case, taking into account the victim's age and background, and prevailing social norms. In one case a man who took advantage of a crowded bus to expose himself and touch a woman passenger was convicted of sexual assault. In a similar situation in which the woman was found to have a previous conviction for prostitution, the man was acquitted of sexual assault but was fined for indecent public exposure (a misdemeanor).

Law enforcement officers are generally sympathetic to victims of rape and sexual assault, relieving them of much of the trauma of public exposure. Rape cases get a great deal of attention from the police, and judges have tended to hand down fast and harsh penalties for the crime. In 1985, in response to several highly-publicized cases in which the woman was kidnapped and gang-raped, the

Legislature made rape in which more than one perpetrator are involved a capital offense. Under the new legislation, five men involved in a kidnap/rape case in 1986 were sentenced to death and are currently awaiting execution.

Yet despite legal and law enforcement attitudes that favor the rape victim, rape remains one of the most under-reported crimes in Egypt. Family reputation or that of the victim is the main reason. This is especially true in cases in which the offender is a close relative of the victim. Many view rape in these cases as a family matter that should be handled without police intervention.

Fear for the woman's reputation stems from the general view that women embody the honor of the family and that rape somehow reduces a woman's value. It jeopardizes not only her chances for marriage but her sisters' and that of other close female relatives. This is illustrated in a case reported by a Cairo newspaper, of a young girl who was raped by her uncle (al-Akhbar, May 10, 1979). When the rape was discovered by her older brother, he conspired with the uncle to kill his sister. In the trial he maintained that he was defending the honor of the family and of his sister and was being kind to her by sparing her a life of shame and loneliness. Similarly, describing his experience as a police officer, Tal'at Nagub Ahmad (1979) refers to a case in which a young woman living with her old father was preparing to get married to her cousin, a well-educated government employee. One week before her wedding while alone in the house, she was raped by one of the workers hired to make the wedding arrangements. Despite the fact that her fiance was her cousin and in love with her, he left her immediately after the rape, refusing even to see her. Knowing that her future chances for marriage were ruined, the police officer felt sorry for the girl. He convinced one of his undercover agents to marry the girl for a short time to remove the stigma. Despite the difference in backgrounds, the girl and her father agreed immediately to the marriage as the only way to save the woman's reputation.

GENDER, CLASS AND SPECIAL CONSIDERATIONS IN CRIMINAL CASES

Although some of the cases mentioned above seem to point toward general discrimination against woman in Egyptian criminal law, this conclusion might not be justified. True, some provisions in the law do tend to put women at a disadvantage, but they are balanced by others that give women an edge in terms of legal protection. In the case of rape, for instance, the law offers more protection for women than do the laws of many Western countries. Women also seem to benefit in sentencing. The law exempts women from serving in hard-labor camps for crimes in which such a sentence is otherwise specified. Instead, women serve these sentences in regular prisons, performing ordinary prison work such as laundry and embroidery. Women with small children are even allowed to have their children with them in prison if no adult relative is willing to care for the children outside prison.

Special consideration is frequently given to women by law enforcement agencies. It is not uncommon for police officers to let a female offender go free if they believe that arrest and prosecution could jeopardize her reputation or harm her family. Judges often give women relatively light sentences when there is evidence to indicate that they were taken advantage of or that they were victims of circumstance.

Special consideration for women by law enforcement officers, however, is sometimes overshadowed by social class considerations. A middle class man might get better treatment than a woman from a lower socioeconomic background. And while social class privilege is more likely to play a role in minor offenses, preferential treatment concerning major crimes is not unknown. For women, however, the impact of class is not easily predictable. With the rising frequency of crimes committed by middle class women, class advantage is frequently overshadowed by the officials' indignation over criminal acts committed by women who do not appear to be driven by economic needs. This is especially evident in the case of prostitution where the perceived threat to morality is greater the higher the status of the woman.

Yet it remains true that the general attitude of both the legislature and law enforcement agencies is that women are less capable of taking care of themselves and that it is the responsibility of society to protect them. Criminal violations by women are viewed more as a product of women's ignorance and mental incapacity than of malice. As such, women are considered less culpable than men.

Case 1

My dreams were simple: having what other women had. A four-story house, living in one apartment and renting the rest, a car we operate as a taxi cab, gold bracelets and rings, and beautiful clothes. I wanted to be envied by other women and admired by men. And why not? My husband was not less of a man than our neighbors Hassounsh or l-Hut or Hussein Zeinah. They all started poor like him; then they went to Kuwait and came back with money, lots of it. They started their own business, and now their wives were draped in silk. All those skinny, ugly wives! I am a hundred times more beautiful than they and yet I have the one husband who cannot make it. He isn't stupid; he just isn't ambitious. Whenever I nagged him about going to the Arab countries to work, he would laugh at me and tell me that I was dreaming and that his only hope was to get a job as a factory worker in the new industry at the nearby town of Helwan and to leave the back-breaking agricultural work that didn't pay enough for us to eat. When he got the job at the factory, it was a day of celebration.

Then we moved to Helwan, and he started his work at the factory. But the fifteen pounds a month he made was barely enough for us to live on. No money for clothes, even the cotton ones, and certainly no money for gold bracelets. As for the house and car . . . forget it. But I was not about to abandon my dreams. I kept nagging him to go to the Arab countries and ridiculed him for not being able to give me what my neighbors had.

Finally he left for Libya. But he could not find a high-paying job there and was finally deported because he had no steady job. He came back emptyhanded. There was no hope for him. He was a born loser. It was at this point, that I decided to take matters in my own hands. It was up to me to find a way to fulfill my dreams. I found myself thinking of Zaki, the door-to-door jewelry merchant who comes to the neighborhood every few days to sell gold to the women of the area.

I kept thinking about him and visualized him with his yellow coat, his silk *jalaba* and above all his suitcase full of gold. There must be enough gold in that suitcase to at least buy the car, if I could only get my hands on it. I remembered the way he looked at me the first time he saw me and how he once put his hands on my knee when my husband was away in Libya. I had resisted his advances at that time. Now things are different. I started to encourage him to come to the house when my husband was working in the factory. When he became a regular visitor, the time was ripe to carry out my plans. When I told my husband of my plans he was horrified. "You want me to kill a man so you can get his money? That is insane. I can't do it. I can't do it," he kept shouting.

But I insisted and kept ridiculing him and accusing him of not being a man. He finally agreed, and I had everything ready. I invited Zaki to the house, pretending that I wanted to buy a gold bracelet. This way I was sure he would bring his suitcase with him. My husband was to leave his work unnoticed, come back to the house, kill Zaki and return to the factory before anyone noticed his absence. The plan worked. When my husband entered the room, Zaki was sitting on the edge of the bed showing me some gold earrings.

When he saw my husband coming toward him with an iron pipe in his hands, he closed the suitcase and held it close to his chest. My husband kept coming toward him. Then he swung the pipe at him but missed him. Zaki started to move away from the bed, but my husband hit him again. This time the blow landed on Zaki's head, and I heard a faint scream and Zaki fell to the floor. My husband became crazy and kept hitting him even after the body was not moving anymore. By the time he stopped, Zaki's head was a mess of blood, flesh and broken bones. The suitcase was now lying in the pool of blood at the foot of the bed. I grabbed it and emptied its contents on the blanket. We then dragged the body to the courtyard, poured kerosene on it and set it afire. We were terrified at the amount of smoke and foul smell that began to spread and we were afraid the neighbors might notice it, so we poured water on the fire and decided to dispose of the body some other way.

The above excerpt from a lengthy interview with Shifiqa, a twenty-six-year-old inmate of el Kanater Maximum Security Prison for Women who is serving a life sentence for murder, illustrates some of the new pressures to which women are subjected under the impact of the rapid social change and urbanization taking place in Egypt today. Pressures developed out of a heightened emphasis on consumption and aspirations for a Western style of life. The main message is carried out by the mass media. With the development of popular radio and television, the message is now reaching a very wide audience.

But while the consumption message is carried uniformly throughout Egyptian society, economic and social factors have not provided equal access for achieving affluence by legitimate means. Women from the lower socioeconomic strata, in particular, seem to suffer most. But middle class women are not immune to pressure. Their increased participation in the work force has placed additional demands upon them. The jobs middle class women hold and the nature of their social networks require them to maintain a certain lifestyle unlike poorer women. Yet the incomes that they obtain from their jobs are not much higher than that of lower class women.

This should not imply that female crimes are a recent phenomenon in Egypt. The notorious female duo of Rayah and Sekinah, who reportedly had killed hundreds of their wealthy clients in Alexandria over several years, goes back to the 1920s. Egyptian women have been part of the criminal pool since records on crime have been kept. Not only were they involved in such traditionally feminine crimes as prostitution and infanticide but also murder, smuggling, and kidnapping.

Recent economic pressures, however, have created additional incentives for women to break the law and have provided additional opportunities for them to carry out their crimes. As men become more geographically mobile, seeking higher wages in cities or overseas, many abandon their responsibilities to their wives and children. Although no adequate statistics exist on the subject, both law enforcement agencies and social welfare departments agree that the incidence of desertion by husbands has increased dramatically.

Although part of the rise might be due to a greater willingness on the part of women to report desertion, they hoping to get help from the government, it is a fact that an increasing number of women find themselves in a position in which they have to support themselves and their children without the help of men. Many of these women lack marketable skills for legitimate work. This is a recurrent theme in interviews I have had with women who broke the law over the past few years.

New economic demands are also breaking down the isolation of women. As more women seek employment outside the home, they acquire more freedom of movement and become less subject to the close supervision of family and relatives. Moreover, an increase in level of education, especially for middle class women, has enabled women to hold responsible positions with access to valuable resources and with greater temptation, at the same time that social contacts lower the risk of prosecution.

Work patterns for lower class women have also changed. Traditionally, these women sought employment in the informal sector of the economy mainly as helpers in tailors' shops, in small family operated stores, or as domestic servants. The relationship that these women had with their employers was close and personal. Domestics were considered members of the family, and their employers frequently took a personal interest in their welfare, seeking husbands for them and arranging marriages. While such close relationships never prevented these women from stealing from their employers, their sense of personal loyalty kept such violations within limits, restricting theft to little items that were not likely to be noticed. Even when noticed, these minor thefts were rarely reported to the police and were handled on an informal basis.

Many of these women now work in factories or in large government stores for remote and impersonal employers to whom they owe no personal loyalty and where supervision is generally lacking. The new employers have no hesitation reporting and prosecuting offenders when caught. While these social changes have affected the patterns of female criminality in general, drug trafficking and prostitution have been particularly reflective of the new changes.

Drug Trafficking

After the penalties for drug trafficking were increased in 1958, many drug smugglers used women to carry and distribute drugs. The assumption was that women were not likely to arouse the suspicion of the police and therefore were less likely targets for arrest. Smugglers have used women with no criminal records to smuggle illegal drugs into the country as well as to distribute the drugs to customers.

Women's involvement in the illegal drug trade is by no means new. In a survey of female prisoners carried out by the National Center for Social and Criminological Research in 1959,[2] women convicted on narcotics charges constituted the largest single group in the prison population: of the 717 inmates, 212 (25.8%) were serving sentences for drug smuggling. The proportion becomes even greater if we add the fifty-six who were serving sentences for using illegal drugs.

Many of the women interviewed for that study stated that they had voluntarily participated in distributing the drugs in order to reduce the risk of their husbands getting arrested. Their rationale was that their husbands were more capable of supporting the family than they were and that if one parent was to be arrested, it was better for the children to have the mother rather than the father go to prison.

The incidence of women smuggling narcotics has dramatically increased in recent years. Smugglers have continued to find women who are willing to take the risk. Many of these women are lured into the drug trade by promises of money, marriage, or both. Some are even used without their knowledge or consent. The following cases provide a sample of differing motivations.

Case 2

I was singing in a small night club in Beirut, waiting for my chance to go to Cairo to perform in the Pyramid Street night clubs. This is where the real money is. Customers there tip the singers and dancers no less than ten pounds, and the clubs pay very well. Then I met this man who said he was an agent for a big recording company. He told me that I was Pyramid Street material. He said he had connections and that he was on a trip to find talented performers for television and night clubs and that I was promising. He told me that the important thing is to have the right image. Big cars and signs of affluence are what the nightclub owners look for. They don't know anything about singing or dancing, and therefore they rely on the appearance of importance to guide them in their selections. He said he would provide me with very expensive clothes and a big car to take back with me to Cairo and that he would join me later.

He told me that the owner of the club would be waiting for me at the airport. When I saw the car I almost fainted. It was a big Mercedes with air conditioning and everything. I couldn't believe it. He said I could pay him for it from my income over a 5-year period. I flew to Cairo, and the car was shipped by boat the next day. I was met at the airport by a man who told me he was the owner of an important nightclub and took me to a luxurious apartment in Zamalek district. When the ship with the car arrived in Alexandria, I went to get it out of the customs area. As I cleared the customs I was met by a group of people who said they were from the Narcotics Squad. They took the tires off the car and found opium and hashish. I cried and told them I had nothing to do with the whole thing and was innocent, but they did not believe me. I am serving a life sentence for smuggling, but I am submitting a petition to the President, and I hope they believe it this time. The agent is sending me notes saying that he would kill me if I did not compensate him for the car that was confiscated by the police. Even if I get out of here, I am going to be dead.

Case 3

Admitting her guilt in smuggling narcotics, B. M. justified it as the only way she could have been able to help her daughter achieve her goal of marrying the distinguished suitor who had asked for her hand. A widow of a government employee, she had to raise four children

> on a limited pension. All four children were in school. The oldest, the daughter in question, was a freshman in college. "When my daughter came back from the university that day and told me that one of her instructors was interested in marrying her, it was like a dream come true. I had worked so hard after my husband's death to raise the children and to give them a good life and a good education. Believe me, it wasn't easy. I wanted my daughters to find decent, financially able husbands so that they would not have to live the kind of life I have lived. The following day, the man brought his mother and sister to visit us and to ask officially for my daughter's hand. He even agreed to furnish the apartment. All he required was that we find a suitable apartment for them to live in. For weeks we looked for a suitable apartment until I found a really nice one that was also close to the university where he works. The problem was that the owner of the apartment wanted 12,000 pounds key money. Where could I get that money?
>
> That was more money than I've ever had. I was crying and telling my troubles to one of my neighbors when she suggested that I go and see a man she said would help. She said the man worked in import/export and that he frequently employed people, especially women, to carry out his business abroad. It didn't take me too long to realize what his business really was. I knew he was a smuggler and that what he wanted me to do was to bring smuggled goods for him into the country. Being a woman and with no previous record, he told me my chances of getting caught were slim. I agreed. I thought my luck would hold and I would have achieved my dream of helping my daughter. It was my first time. I wasn't lucky. I got caught in Cairo Airport and I was sentenced to life imprisonment."

Judges are not always harsh in their sentencing of women convicted on drug charges. Realizing that these women are themselves victims of the drug trade, judges have been reluctant to impose maximum sentences on women convicted on drug charges. Instead judges have tended to hand down relatively short prison terms in place of life sentences at hard labor.

Prostitution

It is the consensus of law enforcement agencies that prostitution is on the rise and has been for the past ten years. Yet crime statistics regarding both arrests and convictions point to a decline over the same period. The reasons are that the characteristics of the prostitutes themselves, the call clients, the methods used to attract clients, and the places where the services are rendered are all changing. In the old days, prostitutes were predominantly poor women from rural backgrounds who walked the streets and carried out their activities in cheap hotels or taxicabs, splitting the money with hotel managers or drivers, who frequently worked as their contacts and as pimps. Such women made up over 90 percent of the arrests in Cairo during 1958, according to a study by the National Center for Social and Criminological Research.

The pattern has changed in recent years. With the increase in the number of foreign visitors from the rich Arab countries, the activities of prostitutes have shifted from the street and from cheap hotels to the expensive apartments many of these visitors keep. The high fees they are willing to pay (up to 1,000 pounds, according to a member of the Vice Squad) have attracted a different class of women to prostitution. Some middle class women, whose appetites for consumption have been heightened but whose financial means have not been sufficient to satisfy their new needs, have turned to prostitution as a means of obtaining additional cash. The privacy of the clients' apartments has also lowered the risk for the women. The social connections and ability of rich clients to pay bribes and to influence law officers have made it almost impossible for these women to be convicted even if they get arrested.

Most of these women are part time or "target" prostitutes, seeing clients only to acquire money needed for a specific item they want to purchase. Many are university and high school students or middle class women who use work and school as an alibi for getting out of the home to perform their occasional activities as paid sex partners. The following is part of an interview with a first year university student who was caught in a raid on a bachelor's apartment:

Case 4

> I had never done this before and I had no intention of doing it again. All I wanted was to get enough money for an air ticket to Rome where I planned to spend the summer. My parents promised to give me enough money to live in Rome, but I was to work as a private tutor after classes so I could get money for the ticket.
>
> Then I met this friend of mine who was telling everyone that she was giving private lessons and that was how she got the money for all the expensive clothes she used to wear to the university. I asked her to find me a job similar to hers. The following day she called me and told me that I should meet her at the cafeteria at the college because she had found me a good job that would not take too much of my time. When I met her the following morning she told me that a friend of her sister's husband, a rich Saudi businessman, had seen me with her and that he was very attracted to me and wanted to see me. She said that he was very rich and that he would give me expensive presents, including clothes and perfume. When I told her that I had wanted a teaching job, she laughed and said, "You can teach him anything; he is open minded." Two days later I met him at Groppi. After having ice cream and lemonade, he said that his apartment was nearby and that it

> was more private so that we could talk without everyone staring at us. In his apartment there were two other men and an hour later two more men came in with a woman. We started drinking. After I was really drunk, the men suggested that I rest a little in bed before leaving for home. I heard a noise in the outside room and a police officer came to the bedroom and arrested me.

The shift toward part time prostitution has been the major change in that crime in recent years. The relative freedom of movement of prostitutes has also enabled them to have their own contacts, thus eliminating the need for the traditional pimp or madame of the old days.

Lower class prostitution still flourishes and still provides the bulk of arrests for prostitution in Egypt. But it too has been undergoing transformation. In addition to the young, rural women who are used by pimps in the old-fashioned way, many urban lower class women are entering the field. Many of these women are still working through pimps. But instead of the full time middlemen operating from such districts as Muhammad Ali Street in Cairo, many of today's pimps are doormen, owners of laundromats, or repairmen operating from their own shops or work places, which are usually located in middle class neighborhoods. Many of their clients are foreign students from the Arab countries who cannot afford the lavish spending required by the educated middle class part-time prostitutes who are patronized by their more affluent countrymen. Many of these women maintain a front as domestic workers for their clients, offering their sexual favors as extra services.

It is also interesting to note that these women, like their more educated sisters, generally refuse to offer their services to Egyptian men. One reason is a common belief that Egyptian men cannot afford to pay high fees or provide them with the kind of gifts that they receive from foreign customers. But the most significant factor is the anonymity that they are able to maintain when dealing with non-Egyptians. Such anonymity enables them to sell their sexual services while maintaining an appearance of respectability within their own permanent social networks. One such woman is So'ad. She is in her late twenties, slim and well-dressed. She comes from a small village outside of Alexandria.

Case 5

> I am not what you think. I am just a working mother who is trying to raise a kid on limited income and with no help from anyone. I don't get paid money by any of the men I know. They pay me only for the housework which I do very well. Anything else they give me is a gift. They give me nice clothes, perfumes, and cosmetics. I cannot get these things in Egypt. They get it for me from Kuwait and even France and England. They go to all these places. Once in a while they pay for the private tutor I have for my son. I want to raise my son to be an

important person and I want him to have the best education possible. His father was a medical student here. He was from Jordan. I came to work for him, and he married me. After he finished his studies he left Egypt without even telling me. One morning he left for work and never came back. He sent his son some money from Jordan but that didn't last long. I had to work to support myself and my son. My parents are dead, and I have no one to support me. I work cleaning houses for foreigners. They treat me like a human being and do not yell at me all the time. I have to keep my appearance and my son has to get educated. So whatever I get from my job I can certainly use.

Homicide

Not all crimes, however, have been affected by the recent changes in social life. Some have remained relatively stable in frequency of occurrence, although motives have changed somewhat. Homicide is such a crime. Of the serious crimes committed by women homicide is the most frequently committed crime. According to a Ministry of Justice Statistical Report, in 1972 women committed 163 serious felonies. Of these, 77 were murders or attempted murders and 26 were aggravated assault. Many of the latter might in fact have been attempted murder reduced to the lesser charge in plea bargaining.

Previously cited cases notwithstanding, homicide committed by women remains for the most part a crime motivated by domestic or personal considerations. Because of that factor, and of the limited nature of women's social associations and their relatively restricted mobility, the victims of women's domestic violence are almost always close relatives.

Women commit murder for a variety of reasons. The following case illustrates some of the personal pressures that women feel today and their translation into violent crime. Alya is a woman in her late twenties serving a fifteen-year sentence for the second-degree murder of her husband. Plump but attractive, she insists that she does not know how her husband was killed.

Case 6

I am not saying I didn't do it, it is just that I don't know how I could have done it. He was the only man in my life. He was the only person who made me feel wanted. Until I met him no one wanted me. When my father divorced my mother, we went to live with her sister. Her husband, who owned a spice shop, treated us like servants. My mother worked all day to take care of her sister's house and children, and I went to school. After school, I took care of the children. We lived in a small room outside the kitchen. Then my mother found herself a husband, but he was not interested in having me move in with them. My mother agreed to leave me with my aunt. But my aunt's husband did not want me to stay; so I moved to live with my father. His wife did not want me, and they were fighting about it all the time. When I graduated from elementary school and was at the top of my class, I decided to go to the school for midwives and paramedics. It was a way for me to live away from all those people who did not want me.

Besides, the government pays the students, in addition to room and board, some allowance. It was real independence for me. After graduation I was hired at one of the government hospitals. It was there that I found out how interested in death I was. When a patient died everyone felt sad except me. I felt envious, for death was the ultimate in comfort. I used to look at funerals in the streets with women wailing and crying, and smile in comfort. Several times I thought of taking my own life, but I did not have the courage. Poison was available to me at the hospital but I had seen how the patients who came to the hospital, with poisoning suffered, and I didn't want to go through the same pain. My dream was either to die or to become the head nurse on the floor so I could feel superior. Then I met him. He was an intern at the hospital and a very good doctor. He treated the nurses like human beings, not the way other doctors treated them, like servants. We fell in love and were married. That was the talk of the hospital for months. After all, it is not every day that a doctor marries a lowly midwife/nurse. Things like that happen only in novels. But we were married, and I moved to live in his nice apartment overlooking the river. I was happy but never felt secure. Every morning I looked around the apartment to see that he was still there, that he had not left me for someone of his own social class. I never understood why he would want me when everyone else did not. I did not expect it to last. I used to accuse him of infidelity every time he was late. Once in a while he got mad at me and fed up with my suspicions and beat me, but we made up. I still was insecure and was so depressed about the prospect of him leaving me that I kept thinking again about suicide. This time I had a better idea of how to do it and without the pain of poison. I decided to use his gun (he kept one in his drawer for protection).

That night I was really depressed and was angry for something that went wrong at the hospital. I went home and saw the gun, aimed it at myself and fired. The first shot hit my arm, but I did not feel any pain. He jumped out of bed to take the gun away from me. Before he could reach me, I fired again pointing at my chest. I did not feel any pain, but I saw him fall on the floor, with blood gushing out of his head. How it happened I couldn't really tell. Apparently the judge and district attorney thought I did it intentionally, and I was sentenced to fifteen years in prison. I don't see any difference between here and the outside world. This is a small prison, outside there is a big one. That is the only difference.

CONCLUSION

Modern Egyptian society is undergoing rapid social change, with the lifestyles and aspirations of women evincing quite severe dislocations as a consequence. Many of these dislocations are revealed in shifts in the criminal behavior in which women engage. Significantly, the letter of criminal law has shifted to a lesser extent in response.

Associated with a relatively Westernized criminal code and rising expectations of a Western sort that make their mark upon criminal behavior is a more traditionally Middle Eastern way of responding to and handling crime and applying criminal law. This distinctiveness is particularly apparent when crimes are committed by women. Many types of crimes are viewed as private affairs when women are the offenders or victims, with family honor being of particular concern. Women are often, but not always, disadvantaged as a consequence.

Responses to at least certain crimes are changing, however. This is especially true regarding middle class prostitution, which garners minimal public sympathy. In the case of middle class prostitution, the crime no longer reveals the woman's family involvement as much as her desire to situate herself more favorably in the wider society.

In effect, the thrust of social change as evinced through attitudes and behavior on both the criminal and law enforcement sides is toward a more publicly oriented stance on the part of women. Recent calls for a return to the preeminence of Islamic law, by contrast, stress the more traditional role of women in the family context. The outcome of this conflict between opposing social visions and ideologies is yet to be determined.

NOTES

1. Unless otherwise noted, cases and interviews with law violators and all enforcement officers were carried out over the seven year period from 1979 to 1986.

2. The figures should be carefully interpreted. Since drug related crimes carry a relatively long prison sentence, there are more overlapping sentences than one would find in crimes with shorter sentences.

REFERENCES

Ahmad, Tal'at N. 1979. *Thirty Years Struggle Against Crime.* Cairo: *el-Nahda* (in Arabic).

al-Amrusi, Anwar. 1981. *The Revised Penal Code.* Cairo: *Dar el-Ma'aref* (in Arabic).

'Attiya, Mohamed R. 1983. *Sex Crimes in Egyptian Penal Code.* Cairo: *el-Nahda* (in Arabic).

'Ebeid, Raouf. 1974a. *Crimes Against Persons in Egyptian Criminal Law.* Cairo: *Dar el-fikr el-arabi* (in Arabic).

———. 1974b. *Causality in Egyptian Criminal Law.* Cairo: *Dar el-fikr el-arabi* (in Arabic).

el-Kilani, Nagib. 1980. *The Ailing Society*. Cairo: *el-Ma'aref* (in Arabic).

el-Magdub, Ahmad. 1976. *Women and Crime in Egypt*. Cairo: *el-Nahda el-arabia* (in Arabic).

el-Marsafawi, Hassan. 1981. *Principles of Criminal Procedures*. Cairo: *el-Ma'aref* (in Arabic).

———. 1983. *Crime and Punishment in Egypt*. Cairo: *Ma'aref* (in Arabic).

Farag, Khalid. 1977. *Legal Bases of Crime and Punishment*. Cairo: *Ma'aref* (in Arabic).

Ministry of Interior. 1957–1981. *Public Security Reports*. Cairo: Ministry of Interior Publication (in Arabic).

Ministry of Justice. 1933–1977. *Crime Statistics*. Cairo: Ministry of Justice Publication (in Arabic).

National Center for Social and Criminological Research. 1962a. *Prostitution in Cairo*. Cairo: NCSCR Monograph Series (in Arabic).

———. 1962b. *Female Prisons in Egypt*. Cairo: NCSCR Report (in Arabic).

———. 1973. *Homicide: A General Survey*. Cairo: NCSCR Publication (in Arabic).

Prison Administration. 1958–1982. *Prison Statistics*. Cairo: Ministry of Interior Publications (in Arabic).

Ramadan, A. 1979. *Egyptian Criminal Code*. Cairo: *el-Nahda* (in Arabic).

3

LITIGANT STRATEGIES IN AN ISLAMIC COURT IN JORDAN

Richard T. Antoun

The following analysis of the impact of the Islamic court on peasants in one subdistrict of Jordan pertains to the period 1959–1967 and provides a baseline for understanding social change in the time period after the 1973 oil-pricing revolution. Astonishing changes have occurred in the life of the subdistrict since that time: villages have been electrified and supplied with piped water, populations have doubled, roads have been paved and thousands of automobiles and truck ply them, and a major afforestation effort has taken place. Most significantly, thousands of sons of the subdistrict work and study outside of it in foreign countries, some earning incomes quadruple those that prevailed in the early 1960s. Even before this period of radical social and economic change, however, women's rights were being recognized in and out of the Islamic courts and women were moving toward a public role in social life. This paper attests to these facts. While the families discussed below still lived in close-knit villages in which kinship ties remained close, still regarded the village guest house (*madafa*) and not the court as the primary arena of conflict resolution, and still operated in an arena in which economic opportunities outside the subdistrict and outside the country were limited, women's major role and women's recognition is nonetheless reflected.

In *The Study of Man* (1936), anthropologist Ralph Linton called attention to the "necessity of prolonged association of family members to permit training and organization into an effective cooperating unit" and "to achieve satisfactory personality adjustment." He elaborates:

> Such prolonged association between individuals of opposite sex can be assured in either of two ways. A society may capitalize on sexual attraction between adults and do all it can to give permanence to mated relationships, or it may capitalize on the associations formed on an asexual basis during childhood, reinforcing them and continuing them into adult life. Such asexual associations are most readily established between individuals brought up in the same functional family unit, i.e., real or socially designated brothers

and sisters. In other words, the association of adults which is the necessary nucleus of any family as a functional unit may be based on either a conjugal or a consanguine relationship (159).[1]

And Linton continues a little later:

Although nearly all societies recognize both conjugal and consanguine groupings, most societies tend to put their emphasis on one or the other, making it the basis for the authentic functional family (162).[2]

Still a little later, he says:

Thus a society may base its family organization entirely on either the conjugal or the consanguine unit, or it may recognize both. If it does the latter, the possibilities of varying emphasis on one or the other of the two units and of the division and ascription of functions to each are almost unlimited (172).

This Jordanian case is one of the complex instances of dual involvement to which Linton alludes. Local custom recognizes the consanguine relations, evidenced in the parent-child tie, as fundamental. Islamic law recognizes the fundamental integrity of the conjugal family within a larger consanguine structure (Coulson and Hinchcliffe 1978; Layish 1975). And both structural alternatives, as well as the legal systems that provide them optimal support, are manipulated by litigants as they vie for courtroom success. This chapter assesses the relative mobilization of consanguine versus conjugal allegiances in marital strategizing as they occur among Jordanian peasants. It also examines the relative use of Islamic law versus customary law in dispute behavior and conflict resolution as they occur in the marital context.

CONSANGUINE VERSUS CONJUGAL TIES: IMPACTS UPON DISPUTE BEHAVIOR

Many disputes in the Jordanian peasant community of Kufr al-Ma dramatize the tension between husband-wife and parent-child allegiances as they occur in a variety of family contexts in the Arab-Muslim world. Of these disputes, those that reach the courts for settlement often draw upon and reflect these same allegiances, as litigants build their courtroom strategies. In fighting to achieve better relations in marriage or to sever conjugal ties, women particularly find that normative expectations as regards one or another kind of relationship can be stressed or muted as a pathway to courtroom success. Most often, however, women find that an emphasis upon their natal ties best serves their interests.

The powers that women gain through consanguine ties are various and multiple. Among peasants in Transjordan and Palestine the importance of consanguine ties (especially father-daughter and brother-sister ties) is most clearly revealed in the position of the woman who is *hardana* or *za'alana'*, that is, the wife who returns to her father's or brother's home in "a state of anger" after what she considers to be unbearable treatment by her husband. As Granqvist points out:

> [T]he father's home remains the deciding factor in her life, a woman in her husband's house is dependent on the esteem she enjoys and the support she can still count upon in her father's house. This is why a "cut-off" woman (*qati'a*) whose male relatives—her father, her brothers, and her father's brothers—are all dead . . . is so much to be pitied, because she has no one from her own family to set against her husband's family who continue to be strangers to her (1935: 144).

In many instances, by resorting to her father's house a woman assures herself of better treatment and perhaps even higher status in her husband's household. Moreover, even if she moves to another community where her father and brothers exert less influence, she remains a member of their prestige group. Her father and his brothers are primarily responsible for her and for any violation by her of the modesty code.

I stress the position of women in their conjugal and consanguine families because, as Lewis (1962) notes, the problem of marital stability has usually been approached from the viewpoint of men and the unity of the larger agnatic group. In Kufr al-Ma, Jordan, a Sunni Muslim village, the position of the man with respect to his larger consanguine family is fairly well defined. His loyalty lies with his father and brothers. Indeed, marriage may bind him more closely to them if their toil produces the marriage payment for his wife.

As a result, in the case of a dispute between his wife and mother, he should take his mother's part, as the village preacher is fond of pointing out in his Friday sermon. The wife, however, is expected to work under her mother-in-law's direction and bear children for her husband's family while at the same time being legally and sentimentally tied to her own consanguine family. Dependence on her father and brothers is increased by the knowledge that her husband can exercise his unilateral right of divorce (*talaq*), although such a course is difficult and infrequent among Jordanian peasants.

The importance of the consanguine family in Kufr al-Ma is difficult to overstress. The out-marrying woman is still counted as part of her father's prestige group: she may seek refuge in her father's house, and her father and brother will argue her case for her against her husband in court. Nor does she take her husband's name upon marriage, but rather continues to be referred to as "daughter of. . . . "

Consanguine control over women's lives is particularly demonstrated with regard to *mahr*: the marriage payment. In local village custom, *mahr* represents a transfer of rights over a woman between two consanguine families (not, however, two corporate lineages in this case). As a rule, *mahr* comes from the bridegroom's father or older brothers and not from the groom. (With the increasing employment of young men in the Jordanian army, this pattern is changing, they themselves more frequently making the marriage payment.) It is given to the bride's father and not to the girl. In Islamic law, on the other hand, *mahr* represents the woman's religiously sanctioned individual right.

As will become clear in the following court cases, the father exerts control over his daughter's marriage in customary law fashion, although Islamic legal prerogatives are stressed. Moreover, his intervention in the early stages of the marriage is particularly prominent if the installments of the *mahr* are delayed.

The conjugal unit of man and wife is not always submerged by a larger family structure, and the competition of consanguine pressures and conjugal pressures can in fact be highly variable. In all contexts, however, some kind of estrangement in the family occurs (Gluckman 1956).

ESTRANGEMENT IN THE FAMILY

It is important to understand the normative structure of interpersonal relations appropriate to the consanguine family and even to the conjugal family when it is embedded wholly or partially in a wider consanguine unit. At the most general level this structure of interpersonal relationships has been described by the phrase "estrangement in the family" (Gluckman 1956). Estrangement in the family assumes affection between some dyads (e.g., brother-sister, mother-child, father-child) and emotional distance between others (e.g., husband-wife). It also assumes that the closeness of some and the emotional distance of others are interrelated. Estrangement in the family has a number of latent functions, including the promotion of same-sex social relations and the promotion of cohesion within suprafamilial units (kindreds, clans, villages).

Estrangement between husband and wife is a distinctive feature of Muslim Middle Eastern—here rural Jordanian—family relations. Husband and wife rarely go on visits together. Whenever guests are present and on public occasions, commensality is separate for males and females, it usually occurring in different rooms. An ethical separation also exists between men and women, with local custom joining traditional Islamic commentaries in evaluating women's susceptibility to moral lapses as greater than men's. Finally, Islamic law adds a legal dimension to such estrangement in two critical matters. First, any property that the wife brings into the marriage or any income or property accruing to her after its inception remains her own and is not susceptible to a husband's claim during her lifetime. Second, the support of the household is the husband's responsibility; the wife is exempted entirely from this obligation.

Of course, conjugal estrangement can vary in intensity and at its extremes can comprehend legal, economic, ethical, commensal and erotic aspects of behavior. One extreme instance—completely atypical and yet indicative of the early potentialities of the pattern—is the historical case of Mecca in the nineteenth century. Urban middle-class spouses in Mecca developed the following pattern of estrangement:

> The husband and wife keep secret the amount of their respective wealth since she thinks he isn't spending enough if she knows his wealth and his avarice will increase if he knows hers. Thus Mekkan women bring the money or entrust it to friends rather than bringing it to the nuptial dwelling. . . . Women are brought up to sharpen their teeth in their struggle with men. Thus men believe and are supported by the law that beyond their bodily attractions women have only Satanic qualities. . . . So most married Mekkan couples share together neither joy nor sorrow, neither good nor bad, outside the bed (Hurgronje 1931: 192).

In Kufr al-Ma conjugal estrangement is by no means so pronounced. Nevertheless, it exists as an expected pattern of behavior. Without taking cognizance of it, the conflicts and the resolution of Islamic court cases cannot be understood.

FORMAL CLAIMS AND PROCEDURES VERSUS REAL GOALS AND ETHOS

Based on a sample of court records in the subdistrict center of Deir Abu Said, Jordan, I recorded the following types of cases together with their incidence (see Table 3.1).[3] The great majority of cases are from the court records of 1959–60 but a few are from the years 1965 and 1966. Almost all, if not all, for the year 1959 were considered. The types of cases recorded are typical of those heard in the subdistrict center in the periods covered. The terms used to describe the cases (e.g., maintenance of wife; conjugal obedience) are direct translations of the types of claims as written in the court records and, as will be seen, do not necessarily indicate the substantive nature of the case.

The largest single category of cases (63) involves a wife's demand for maintenance. The second largest involves the husband's demand for conjugal obedience (25). Another category of cases (11) deals with a demand for the termination of maintenance payments, either to the wife, father, daughter, or a minor. All other categories of cases pale in comparison. Furthermore, a very significant proportion of cases raised in the Islamic court is dropped before reaching the stage of court judgment: 40 percent of claims for conjugal obedience were dropped, while more than half of the 63 claims for maintenance by the wife were dropped.

Several conclusions may be drawn from a perusal of Table 3.1. First, the court is heavily involved in economic issues relating to subsistence in the household. Second, the Islamic court is absorbed in issues that concern the rights of women, mainly in their roles as wives but also in their roles as mothers and daughters. Third, the pursuit of a court claim is frequently only one in a set of in-court and out-of-court tactics pursued by family members, mainly husbands, wives, and their fathers, toward certain ends. From the litigant's point of view it is not an attempt to obtain Islamic justice in some abstract sense. Rather, each litigant, explicitly or implicitly pursues a strategy that may involve certain moves in the Islamic court, certain moves in the civil court, certain developments in

Table 3.1
Incidence and Type of Case in the Subdistrict Court of Al-Kura, Jordan, in 1959–60, 1965, and 1966

	Type of Case	Incidence	Disposition
1.	Maintenance of wife	63	38 dropped 22 approved 3 rejected
2.	Maintenance of father	9	
3.	Maintenance of mother	3	
4.	Maintenance of minor	2	
5.	Maintenance of relative (brother or sister)	2	
6.	Upbringing maintenance	2	
7.	Waiting-period (*'idda*) maintenance	1	
8.	Cutting off of wife's maintenance	6	
9.	Cutting off of father's maintenance	3	
10.	Cutting off of daughter's maintenance	1	
11.	Cutting off of minor's maintenance	1	
12.	Increase of minor's maintenance	2	
13.	Conjugal obedience	25	10 dropped 3 approved 8 rejected 4 unaccounted for

Table 3.1 (continued)

	Type of Case	Incidence	Disposition
14.	Claiming of prompt marriage payment (*mahr mu'ajjal*)	2	
15.	Request for judicial divorce (*tatliq*)	1	
16.	Request for judicial divorce due to contention and dispute	1	
17.	Request for confirmation of unilateral divorce (*talaq ba'in*)	3	
18.	Request for possession of a minor	2	
19.	Request for permission to marry and prohibition of opposition	1	
20.	Request for inheritance portion	2	
21.	Request for confirmation of puberty	1	
22.	Orphan's request for possession of inheritance portion	1	
23.	Request for the value of livestock in a bequest	1	
24.	Request for the investigation of an inheritance request	1	
	Total	136	

the framework of village custom, recourse to government officials (to a land registry officer, subdistrict officer, or police chief) or to tribal arbitrators (the Pasha). When the particular end has been achieved in any of the above arenas, the litigant drops his court case regardless of the satisfaction or nonsatisfaction of the narrower court claim. This partially accounts for the high percentage of court cases dropped before judgment.

Marital disputes take on a sequencing while thay are in the courtroom arena, with a diversity of conflicting rights being aired. The following is typical. As a first step, the wife seeks refuge in her father's house in a "state of anger" (*za'alana*) after some real or alleged mistreatment by her husband. Shortly thereafter, the wife raises a claim in the Islamic court for maintenance (*nafaqa*) from her husband. He raises a counterclaim in the court for conjugal obedience (*ta'a zawjiyya*). The wife then charges that her husband has not provided a proper Islamic home (*bayt shar'i*) such as to justify her return. Before an affirmative or negative decision can be made regarding the husband's claim, an investigation of the house by the judge or his agent (usually the implementation officer, *ma' mur al-ujra*) must take place. If the home is found not to be legal and proper, the wife continues to draw maintenance while continuing to live with her father. If, on the other hand, the court rules that the house is legal and proper, the wife claims that the marriage is one of contention and dispute (*shiqaq wa niza'*), that it is unsalvageable, and that only a judicial divorce (*tatliq* or *tafriq*) can resolve matters.

The judge then proceeds to arrange various out-of-court mechanisms for settlement. The first is nomination of a mediation committee, composed of members of both families, to seek reconciliation of the couple. If this committee fails, he nominates another committee, composed of notables of their own clans or notables outside the two families (perhaps including the Pasha). They seek reconciliation or, failing that, arrange for judicial separation and division of the marriage payment. If the committee arranges for reconciliation but the wife refuses to return to her husband's home, the judge declares the wife to be rebellious (*nashiza*) and the husband goes with a delegation of kinsmen to her father's house to bring her back. If she still refuses, the judge calls on the implementation officer to execute the judgment of the court. The implementation officer reconciles the couple outside of court, executes the judgment, or does not do so.

Other scenarios are possible, of course. The case can be referred for resolution to the elders in the village guest house by the parties themselves or by the judge, the court case then being dropped. Or the second mediation committee that is nominated by the judge can arrange for judicial separation and the division of the marriage payment, with the implementation officer being charged with executing its judgment. One of the wife's main tactics through all of these proceedings is to postpone the sessions for as long as possible in order to continue drawing maintenance payments. The husband, on the other hand, seeks to expedite the proceedings.

In these cases, the judge also faces dilemmas peculiar to his role. One involves accommodating Islamic law to local custom, which it sometimes diametrically opposes. For instance, the parties to a marriage often specify one marriage payment publicly and officially and another, lower one, privately according to local custom. The question arises as to which the judge should accept. The Islamic law schools differ in this matter, some opting for the former, some for the latter, and some for the "going rate." One solution to the dilemma is to draw on all four Sunni Muslim law schools for interpretations, selecting the most suitable, all the while taking into account religious law, secular law, and the judge's own social philosophy. Another tactic used by judges in handling often conflicting demands of religious law, civil law, and personal philosophy is the avoidance of decision making: the judge seeks to have the litigants reconcile their own disputes through mediation (Layish 1975).

The ethos of the subdistrict court, i.e., atmosphere and emotional tone of the court proceedings, reveal this commitment to reconciliation. Although the court's calendar is official and bureaucratic (from 9 A.M. to 2 P.M.) and does not accommodate itself to the agricultural year as do, for example, some Mexican municipal courts (Hunt and Hunt 1969) and although the official appeals procedure is strictly within the Islamic court system and is not interlocked with the local sociopolitical structure, nevertheless, there is considerable adaptation of court activity to peasants' needs.

Moreover, the behavior of litigants toward one another and toward the judge within the court reflects the familiarity of the village guest house, a customary arena for dispute resolution, as much as it does the bureaucratic decorum of the courtroom. Villagers come into a small courtroom which is nothing more than an ordinary room with a large desk for the judge, a chair to one side for his clerk, and chairs along the walls for litigants. Most witnesses and interested bystanders wait outside in the hall until called. A few friends of the court may be present, such as the marriage officer (*ma'dhun*) of the subdistrict, a village mayor (*mukhtar*), or various village preachers who may be present in town on that particular day if the case involves litigants from their own villages. The word "town" is here used with some hesitation. Although the court is in the subdistrict center which also contains the offices of the land registry officer, civil judge, subdistrict officer, and agricultural agent, the community is no more than 4,000 in population and, apart from the bureaucrats and shopkeepers who live in it, is populated mainly by peasants (see Antoun 1972).

Villagers come into the courtroom with a mixture of easy informality and deference, present their problems to the judge, ask his advice, and even lean on his desk. They make requests which, if not granted, they make again and again using such familiar village expressions of beseechment such as "out of your beneficence," "by your life," "by the life of the Prophet," and "you are the father of us all." Often the judge gets angry, particularly when, through habit, villagers talk out of turn, interrupting each other's testimony. Women draw their shawls up to their faces out of modesty and often their testimony cannot be understood.

At other times, they come right up to the judge's chair and plead with him.[4] Some parties try to drive bargains with the judge, asking, when they find the judge intractable, "What will please you? What do you want?" Other villagers walk in unannounced and without permission so that the judge must angrily direct the court usher (who doubles as clerk) to throw them out. A practical day-to-day adjustment of the ethos of the great Islamic court tradition to the little tradition of village custom takes place at these points. At other moments, however, the tension between the traditions, in the sense of their ethos as well as in the content of the law applied, results in conflict rather than real accommodation.

IMPACT OF THE ISLAMIC COURT ON THE PEASANT FAMILY

The descriptions of three sessions of the Islamic subdistrict court, as they were observed and recorded with respect to three separate claims brought by litigants, follow.

Case 1

Type of Case:	Conjugal obedience
Date:	January 30, 1966 (third session of three)
Plaintiff:	Husband from Rihaba village
Defendant:	Wife from Rihaba village

The father of the plaintiff, a pilgrim or *hajj*, said there was no obstacle to his son's housing the first wife in the old house and moving the new wife into the new one, but the second wife's father was not willing. The latter said that he had eight brothers and four sisters living near the old house.

Judge (to both fathers): "If you want reconciliation (*sulh*) we will have it now. If not now, we will postpone it until later."

Second wife's father: "My daughter's furnishings have been eaten."

Judge: "He [the husband] has waited seventeen years [apparently referring to the first wife's barrenness]."

Husband's father: "Let's postpone divorce."

The two fathers agreed to delegate four individuals to reconcile the couple.

Judge: "You do what you want."

Wife's father: "We both have agreed on [four names] and the religious leader of the village [as mediators]."

Husband's father: "We don't need to put her in the new house if she doesn't like it."

Judge: "The court likes reconciliation by any means."

Someone: "It is not a case of contention and dispute."

Judge: "It is better to postpone the case until the mediators investigate."

The case was then tried, since the parties to the dispute could not agree on reconciliation.

The judge asked the wife about the possibility of reconciliation.

Husband: "I'll put both in the same house."

Wife: "I'm willing to live in my old room."

Judge: "Religious law [*shari'a*] prohibits putting two wives in the same house."

Husband: "He won't put her outside [this house]."

Wife: "I'll stay with Beni Dumi [a clan of the village], with any clan [as a place of refuge]."

Judge: "Move your wife into a new house."

Husband: "No."

Wife: "My father's brother's son [husband's brother] threatened me; I won't live with them."

Judge (to the husband): "Why didn't you appear on the day of the investigation?"

Husband: "It was raining."

Judge (for the records): "The plaintiff didn't come because of the rain."

Judge: "What do you want now? An investigation of the house?"

Husband: "Yes"

Wife: "This is far [from what I will accept]."

Judge: "Why won't you accept it?"

Wife: "I won't live in the upper quarter I won't be secure [there]."

The judge ordered an investigation of the house.

Judge: "Would you like us to postpone the investigation?"

Husband and wife: "All right."

Judge (dictated to the clerk): "The investigation has been postponed so that the people of good may mediate."

Judge: "How long a postponement do you want?"

Reply: "Three to five days."

The judge postponed the session for two weeks at the suggestion of the husband's father who said that it will take that time to get the merchants from the nearest town together to fit out a proper Islamic legal home due to the rain.

Wife: "We want a mediation of good will."

Husband's father: "God is more knowing."

Judge: "If you become reconciled come any day and notify me; if not, come on the day of the session."

Case 2

Type of Case:	Maintenance of wife
Date:	August 22, 1966 (First session)
Plaintiff:	Wife from village of Kufr al-Ma
Defendant:	Husband from village of Kufr al-Ma

The wife charged that there was no proper legal house. The husband said that he had raised a case in the civil court because they took his child and wife by force. He said he wanted her back. He wanted conjugal obedience (*ta' a zawjiyya*).

Judge: "Do you have children?"

Wife: "Yes, one, three months old."

Judge: "You must stipulate a maintenance allowance [for your wife]."

Husband (refusing): "Everything is available; I want her."

Judge: "You must stipulate a maintenance allowance."

Husband: "I'll give her nothing; I am not angry [*za'alan*] at my wife."

The wife contradicted the husband's previous statements.

Judge: "Unless the court goes and investigates to confirm the existence of a proper Islamic home, you have no rights."

Husband: "How am I going to eat and drink? I send a delegation [*jaha*] every day [to her]."

The husband refused to stipulate a maintenance allowance.

Judge: Then three witnesses will come and stipulate one that is more than you wish."

The judge told the wife to go and find witnesses who would be able to stipulate a maintenance. He got very angry at the husband's refusal to do so. Finally, three witnesses, all from the subdistrict center, came forward. They stipulated a maintenance of four Jordanian dinars a month (approximately ten dollars), three for the mother and one for the child, and they testified that the defendant was capable of paying the sum.

The husband raised a case of conjugal obedience immediately after the maintenance sum had been imposed. The judge told him to prepare a proper Islamic home and the court would go the same day and inspect it. The husband told the judge that he had sent this author and others to get the wife back.

Case 3

Type of Case:	Conjugal obedience
Date:	January 15, 1966
Plaintiff:	Husband of Kharaj Village
Defendant:	Wife of Izmal village

The husband's father stated that it was the wife's father who would not let his daughter go back to her husband. Why? He wanted to keep his coffee house running with the maintenance money his daughter received.

Judge: "This cannot happen."

Bystander: "Yes, we have cases like that."

The husband's father stated that a proper Islamic home was ready and the neighbors of the couple were an old man of eighty and his wife of sixty-five.

The daughter-in-law still refused to return.

The report of the official investigation of the husband's house by the judge of the district court in Irbid on January 3, 1966 was read. The investigation found the home to be proper and legal in relation to the class (*tabaqa*) of the husband, who is poor.

Judge (to the wife): "You didn't attend the investigation?"

Wife: "I was sick."

The judge proceeded to read the names of the experts who had investigated the house and proceeded to describe it: "One room is five meters by five meters and is constructed of stone overlayed with adobe. On the north it has two windows in good condition. There are four other rooms in good condition. Musa Ali, the owner, and his wife live in them. There is an open area and a courtyard. There are two entrances to the house. The doors are common to the wife and the owners. The outhouse and the oven are the property of the husband."

The wife said she would not live in the house; she wanted to live by herself. The husband said the house is legal (*shar'i*) by fact of the investigation.

Wife: "I won't live in it. I want a house by myself. I want my own kitchen and my own courtyard." She said that the water, the oven, and the outhouse are held in common. The husband said he provided her with her own clothesline.

Wife: "Why is the other wife living in a house by herself."

Husband: "I cannot build new facilities for water, an oven, and outhouse."

Judge: "Why has there been no investigation of the other house?"

Judge (to the wife): "Why don't you go to see the room? Look at it to see if you like it?"

Wife: "I have been with my father for two months [in a state of anger] and he has been spending on me. I want two outfits and two cloaks."

Judge (to the husband): "Why don't you pay the two month's maintenance and go home with her?"

Wife's father: "The glass, once it is broken, it cannot be repaired [referring to the marriage]."

Judge: "The mayor has come as a delegation to you. I am ready to stipulate a maintenance for you."

Wife's father (of his daughter): "She has been insulted by her co-wife. If she wants to go home let her go [but at the same time he indicates he is unwilling for a reconciliation]."

Wife's father: "It is not safe for my daughter to sleep in the quarter."

All the while the wife carried her child in her lap and attempted to elicit sympathy through looks and gestures.

The judge rejected the husband's claim for conjugal obedience because the house provided was not a proper Islamic home. After the session the judge explained why he had ruled against the existence of a proper Islamic home. There cannot be a stranger moving around within the courtyard. Moreover, the stranger neighbor had a guest house. He must put up a barrier dividing the courtyard, put his wife in a separate courtyard. Then he can raise a new claim for conjugal obedience or seek reconciliation. "Reconciliation is best," he said. The judge said the husband could not house her in a tent since other villagers lived in houses. "Those who live in tents are nomads," he said. The judge said the old man was a "stranger" and was not covered by the incest taboo. Even if he had no guest house, he would have ruled similarly.

These cases dramatize a number of points about the working of the local Islamic court, the cultural and social-structural context in which it operates and the resources it provides for women. First, the sequence and tactics of court politics is such that, regardless of the type of case raised (obedience, maintenance), other issues and tactics, drawn from both customary and Islamic law, are explicitly mentioned as necessary arguing points. In Case 3, for example, the husband's claim was for conjugal obedience, but resolution of that claim could not take place without taking into account the wife's "state of anger," the wife's and co-wife's claims for maintenance, and the provision of a proper legal Islamic house.

Second, the cases reveal several power sources available to women litigants. One is the woman's father. In all three cases the wife was living in a "state of anger" in her father's house, and each father spoke for his daughter in court. The consanguine family structure maintains its continued importance. The sexual division of labor between spouses is also a resource available to married women. "How am I going to eat and drink?" asked one husband. Women bake bread and prepare meals; if a husband attempts to do so he becomes the laughing stock of the village. Thus the wife's "state of anger" combines social and economic sanctions in her struggle to achieve better conjugal treatment.

Third, the cases reflect the fundamental Islamic values of equality, modesty and honor, and reconciliation. In Case 3 the legal principle of equality between spouses in the contracting of marriage (*kafa'a*) is extended by the judge into the postmarriage situation. That principle entitles the wife to treatment equivalent to that which she was accustomed in her father's house as well as that accorded to women of the same status in the husband's community. Cases 2 and 3 dramatize the importance of modesty not only as a fundamental value underlying Islamic law but also as an issue in court politics. The focus is the husband's provision of a proper Islamic house (*bayt shar'i*). The wife must be lodged in a house and courtyard where her privacy and honor will be protected. This requires a separate enclosure with a high surrounding wall, separate toilet and kitchen facilities, and a separate house entrance. The courtyard must be inaccessible to strangers not covered by the incest taboo, to wit, to potential sexual aggressors.[5]

Finally, Cases 1 and 3 indicate the ideological priority that the court gives to reconciliation. In Case 1, the judge says, "The court likes reconciliation by any means." His last words to the spouses were these: "If you become reconciled, come back any day [to notify me]."

To what degree are the cultural resources that female litigants use Islamic ones? Several insights into this issue are provided through analysis of two other cases witnessed by the author in the subdistrict court of Al-Kura in 1960.

Case 4

A shy young peasant woman accompanied by her father and mother came to file a claim for maintenance against her husband, who was a soldier in the Jordanian army. For his part the husband had come to the court to file a claim for conjugal obedience against his wife. The husband and wife came from villages that were some seven miles distant. The wife had been living with her father for the past three months. The wife's father had come to his son-in-law's house and taken his daughter away to his own home. This occurred after the nuptial knot had been tied and the marriage consummated.

The father told the judge that his son-in-law still owed him sixty dinars (approximately $150) in marriage payment. The husband said he had paid twenty dinars of the sum to his wife and had agreed to pay five dinars each month to his father-in-law until the full payment had been made. The father refused to allow his daughter to return to her husband until the full sum was provided. The father told the judge that his daughter wanted a divorce and that he would return fifty dinars of the 300 dinar marriage payment to his son-in-law if he would agree. The father then said to his son-in-law in the presence of the judge: "Give me my money and take your wife. I want what is coming to me."

The judge's face showed surprise and displeasure. He shot a question at the father: "Do you intend to take this girl's marriage payment?" The father replied: "Yes, we all take it; that is the custom here." The judge became extremely angry and told the father that if he displayed any further impertinence toward the court, he would have him ejected. Then he asked the wife to speak freely and without fear as to whether she really wanted a divorce. The wife's father glared at her, and her mother kept poking her in the back, whispering: "Say yes." Upset beyond bounds by this attempted intimidation of a witness, the judge banged his iron paperweight on the desk several times and yelled for the usher. He came running in, and in response to the judge's demand he removed the wife's mother and father from the courtroom.

Then the wife told the judge that she did not want a divorce and wanted her husband. The husband said that he wanted his wife back but that he had found that the father would not permit them to live together, coming and taking her away from his home. On further questioning by the judge, the wife said that she withdrew all demands for maintenance, that her husband had a proper Islamic home available, and that she would willingly return to it. The judge then told them to go home and live as man and wife. They left the courtroom.

A few minutes later the couple returned. They told the judge that they were afraid the father would waylay them on the road and make trouble. The judge then called the police post and had the father placed under observation. Again the couple left the courtroom.

But five minutes later they returned. The husband asked the judge what they should do if the father came back to claim the unpaid *mahr*. The judge said that was between him and his wife. If she wished to give up her claim to it altogether that was all right; if she wished to give it to her father that also was all right. But, she must not be forced. The marriage payment was hers, not her father's. The couple left for the third time and did not return.

Case 5

In the summer of 1960, a young peasant woman came to the Islamic court in Al-Kura accompanied by her father, asking for a judicial divorce from her husband who, she said, ill-treated her and beat her. She said that she detested him. The woman was several months pregnant and was living in her father's house, having fled several times from the conjugal home. The wife and her husband were first patrilateral cousins. The wife, however, was twenty-seven years old while her husband was only twenty, and she scorned him openly in court. The husband was accompanied by his father, who told the judge that he was not opposed to a divorce if the *mahr* was returned. The *mahr* was 230 dinars (approximately $575) and included a house worth sixty dinars and three sacks of wheat worth twelve dinars, given to the wife's father. The wife herself was given fifteen dinars worth of olive oil and an additional fifteen dinars in cash. The wife's father claimed that the final 128 dinars were given to his daughter, but, on questioning, she denied this claim.

The wife told the judge that for five years she had fought to forestall marriage with her first cousin. Finally they had bewitched her and gotten her to agree to the marriage while she was deprived of her senses.

Her young husband, who was a shepherd, told the judge that he had a *bayt shar'i* prepared for her. His wife said she would not return to her husband even if he housed her in a castle.

The judge reminded the husband that marriage was not simply a matter of a legal home. He encouraged him to divorce his wife since she was pregnant, had several times run away from his home, and had, on the testimony of witnesses, even tried to hang herself on his account. The judge then asked the wife's father what he thought of her statement of detestation. The father replied: "If we let all the women have their own way, no one would be married." The husband then stated adamantly that he would never divorce her. The judge told the wife's father to return the *mahr* and mollify his nephew since the wife had resolved to reject her husband.

The husband said that certain (supernatural) agents were stirring in her brain. He said that she lived happily with him for eight months and then something happened. He said that she would be forced to stay with him whether she liked it or not.

The husband's father then said that, if she wished, he would house her in the subdistrict center where she could live like a townswoman.

The judge then ordered the husband and wife and both fathers to go out into the hall, along with the marriage officer of the district and the town preacher, and work out some compromise.

They returned a little later and the marriage officer said that he had proposed a solution, namely suspended divorce. The wife's father would return the first installment of the *mahr*—say, twenty-five dinars. The rest would be returned in installments until all had been forwarded, when the divorce would become final. This agreement would be recorded and signed by both parties. The wife would remain with her father until the birth of the child who would belong to the father.

The husband then said that he would not divorce her until his father gave him another wife. The marriage officer told him that the twenty-five dinar down payment would be used to pay the first installment of the *mahr* for his new wife.

The mayor of Tibne, the village of both spouses, who had been listening, then said that the wife had taken suck from the teat of her mother-in-law in order to interdict further sexual relations between her and her husband.

The wife's father refused to pay the first installment of the *mahr*, and the husband's father then told the judge that his son demanded conjugal obedience on the part of the wife. She had run away to her father's house several times and, he said, had even tried to poison her husband. The judge told the husband again that he ought to divorce his wife. The husband replied: "Never!" and fled from the courtroom.

The first three cases illustrate the continued importance of the consanguine family structure and conjugal estrangement in the family. In Case 4, the influence of the father upon his daughter's affairs, even after her marriage, is demonstrated. This influence is related to his claim upon the marriage payment, which he openly tells the judge is his customary right, although the Quran explicitly states that the marriage payment is the wife's:

> And give unto the women (whom ye marry), free gift of their marriage portions; but if they of their own accord remit unto you a part thereof; then you are welcome to absorb it (in your wealth) (Sura 4, Verse 4).

The Quran also says:

> Lawful unto you are all beyond those mentioned, so that you seek them with your wealth, not debauchery. And those whom ye seek content (by marrying them), give unto them their portions as a duty (Sura 4; Verse 24).

The religious judge, then, has the full weight of religious law behind his opinion that *mahr* is solely the wife's property. He is not only angry but appalled that any man would deny a right that the Quran itself grants.

From the point of view of the father, however, he was doing nothing wrong. So deeply rooted is the local belief that the *mahr* is the father's that the young husband and wife returned three times to seek the judge's assurance should the father return to demand it.

Up until now, the importance of the consanguine family has been stressed. But the conjugal unit of husband and wife is not always submerged by consanguine considerations. Hence in the fifth and last case, the wife not only defied her husband but also her paternal uncle. And their defiance assumed a number of forms. Several times she fled to her father's home. She attempted to poison her husband and, it was reported, to kill herself. She took suck from her mother-in-law in order to effect a sexual prohibition recognized by Islamic law (the spouses thereby become "brother" and "sister"), and she had recourse to an Islamic court to demand a judicial divorce. Islamic law thus can work to support the wife in her demand for divorce against the interests of both the conjugal and consanguine unit.

In addition, Islamic law reserves to the wife all property earned by her after the marriage. Moreover, the husband cannot expect to draw on his wife's resources to support the household. He is solely responsible for the support of his wife and children. Although certain Islamic norms support the wife's rights through the medium of the conjugal family, other norms support the wife's status independent of or even against her husband.

WOMEN AS LITIGANTS: CONSTRAINTS AND TACTICS

There can be no doubt by now that women can and do resort to the Islamic court for aid, claiming their rights in a variety of cases involving maintenance, *mahr*, inheritance, the judicial dissolution of marriage, confirmation of divorce, or possession of a minor. Important questions on which virtually no research has been undertaken are the following: To what degree are Islamic stipulations invoked? What are the constraints upon women's resort to the court? What tactics do they apply when they make their claims? In the subdistrict court of Al-Kura it is possible to find tentative answers to these questions.

A limitation upon women's use of Islamic law options is their at least partial ignorance of the law. In Case 4, neither husband nor wife was fully aware of the wife's Islamic right to *mahr*. This partial ignorance delayed the resolution of the case in their favor. The wife in Case 5, by contrast, was not only unusual in the force and ingenuity of her tactics, whether they were Islamicly based or not, but also in her knowledge of a somewhat obscure point of Islamic law—that a man and woman who suckle from the same breast are prohibited from marrying—which she used to gain her ends. Along similar lines, the preacher of Kufr al-Ma once traveled to another village in the subdistrict which had no preacher in order to give a guest sermon there. Before the sermon, most of the village elders gathered in the guest house, and a discussion ensued about various religious and legal matters. One man asked, "Tell me preacher, if my father died, could I marry his wife?" The preacher was shocked by the question since such a marriage is clearly proscribed by the Quran. Most of the villagers, however, did not know this. Indeed when the author arrived in Transjordan in 1959, only some four out of twenty villages in the subdistrict had a preacher, the primary culture broker of Islamic tradition for peasants. When this author returned in 1965 every village in the subdistrict had a preacher, and such ignorance on the part of both men and women likely became less of a constraint.

The modesty code is particularly important in retarding women's knowledge of the law. Local custom does not allow women to attend the Friday congregational sermon at the mosque. Thus the preacher often punctuates his sermon with the phrase, "Go tell your women," and they receive legal news secondhand. One preacher was so unhappy with the situation that he urged the village to buy a loudspeaker so that the sermon could be broadcast throughout the village for all to hear, as is the case in some urban mosques.

But even when women are aware of their Islamic rights, a real question arises as to whether they accept them as legitimate when they conflict with local custom or class interests. For instance, local custom looks askance at women appearing in crowded public places such as courts and markets. Often women are reluctant to appear there, are uncomfortable if they go, and have to be coaxed to speak. Some women, however, speak their piece in court in no uncertain terms, as Case 5 indicates. One predictor of such behavioral variation appears to be class. Hill (1979) indicates that Egyptian upper- and upper-middle class women rarely resort to the court to claim their rights. Such behavior conflicts with the cultural code of their class and also might jeopardize the family's property interests.

Middle Eastern men's and women's perceptions of reality differ, as Dwyer (1978) and Rosen (1978) have shown. Women's growing awareness of Islamic law, however, gives them new options and resources which one can ignore only at the risk of one's own loss of status and prestige and even possibly legal punishment in a society that is becoming more, not less, Islamic with every passing year. Therefore, although village men's view of the world stresses the impropriety of women's appearance in court, women have every legal right to appear there. It is likely that women's view of reality will more closely approximate the great tradition of Islam on this matter and contrast with that of their men whether in a conjugal or consanguine structure. It is also more likely that their view of the world will prevail in the future.

Women apply a variety of tactics, inside and outside the court in order to realize their goals, and these tactics derive from both the traditional Islamic and customary village framework. The resort to a "state of anger" is part of village custom. Similarly, remarriage is one of the traditional options open to a woman who wishes social status and economic security, and it is often to protect this option that women refrain from resorting to the Islamic court, since publicizing one's troubles impeaches one's reputation for modesty and jeopardizes remarriage. Again according to local custom, the status of the foresaken woman (*al-mahjura*), a woman whose husband has taken other and more preferred wives, is plainly invidious. Nevertheless, such a status is sometimes regarded by women as an asset, for it allows the wife to remain economically in the husband's household, receive maintenance, have a share in family property, enjoy immunity from family pressure to remarry, and remain socially independent of her husband's household (she usually lives with her eldest son). Finally, making life miserable for one's spouse, as demonstrated in Case 5, can be an effective traditional female resource.

Within the traditional Islamic framework, wives may press claims for *mahr*, maintenance, and child support. They can manipulate suspended repudiation (*talaq mu'allaq*), a divorce which the husband may threaten to carry out if his wife performs a designated forbidden act; the wife can deliberately commit the act, thereby instigating a court verdict of rebelliousness (*nushuz*) against herself and triggering divorce. If the condition that is designated as activating divorce is the woman's flight from her husband's home, refuge at her father's house will bring that desired result. Further, women can utilize delegated repudiation (*tawfid al-talaq*), by which the husband gives his wife the power to divorce herself in his name for any number of reasons (his desertion, inadequate and/or immodest housing, his moving to another locality, cursing her, beating her, inequality of wives, inadequate clothing, or taking another wife).

THE IMPLEMENTATION OFFICER AS CULTURAL BROKER

One constraint that demands special attention, not so much regarding women's (and men's) resort to the court as regarding the rapidity with which the court executes its judgment, is the role of the implementation officer (*ma'mur al-ujra*). The implementation officer is one of those key local-level culture brokers who accommodates the great Islamic religious tradition to the variety of local circumstance and custom. In the Islamic court in Al-Kura he is not the only court broker: the judge himself, the clerk-usher, the marriage officer, and the village preacher are also court brokers, the latter two being effective friends of the court. But the implementation officer's function of execution of the court's judgment makes his broker role both official and critical. Since the implementation officer is an official of the civil court he links the two hierarchies, civil and religious, just as the Pasha (referred to above) links local custom and tribal law to the work of the Islamic court, albeit in an unofficial manner.

The implementation officer takes his cue from the judge's decision, but he has considerable leeway in how, when, and even if he implements the judge's decision. After a judgment of conjugal obedience against a wife, for example, the husband is left to proceed with his own kinsmen to fetch his wife from her father's house; only with the failure of this mission might the implementation officer intervene. In the case of a ruling against the husband for maintenance, the usual procedure in Al Kura is to publish the verdict in the newspaper. Ten days after the newspaper proclamation, the plaintiff can request execution of the judgment by the implementation officer. If the husband continues to refuse to pay, the implementation officer can request the police to jail him. Conversely, maintenance payments can be terminated any time before divorce by mutual agreement of the spouses. But to terminate them officially, the implementation officer must be notified. Otherwise the wife can return to the court in the future and claim the accrued maintenance which may later be substantial. Finally, in order to terminate maintenance payments which, in the case of divorce, stop at the end of the waiting period (generally after the wife has had three menstruations), the wife must personally notify the implementation officer of the passing of her courses. Only after she has communicated this information does the judge proclaim the termination of maintenance.

In the spirit of both Islamic law and local custom, the implementation officer prolongs attempts at mediation and reconciliation even after the court's judgment. Sometimes he succeeds; either the wife agrees to reduced maintenance or drops the claim entirely.

In one case that came to this author's attention, the judge had ruled in favor of the wife in a claim for payment of *mahr* and against the husband in his claim for termination of maintenance payments. The implementation officer did not execute either judgment. He probably hoped that the local process of village mediation would resolve the two claims. In another case in which the judge ruled against the wife for conjugal obedience, the implementation officer also did not execute the judgment. In that case, the officer was a close kinsman of a co-villager whose son was about to marry into the wife's family. The case ended in conditional and later final divorce, a goal sought by the implementation officer's kinsmen. Indeed, I asked one implementation officer how many court judgments for maintenance he had executed. He said he could only recall one: the husband was jailed for twenty days.

Judges are quite aware that implementation officers do not always act with alacrity in enforcing court judgments. One told me that if the implementation officer "had been walking a straight path" the defendants would be jailed, and "people wouldn't make a fuss about paying twenty-five cents a day [in maintenance]."

The discrepancy between court judgment and execution is important in several ways. The judge is invariably a stranger in his district. Posted temporarily, he must rely on the cooperation and advice of the locals—lower-echelon officials and friends of the court as well as high-status notables in the district—to dispatch his work. Also, since the implementation officer is part of the civil rather than the religious court hierarchy, formal sanctions by the judge are precluded. Perhaps most importantly, the historic weight of Islamic law and its spirit is staunchly supportive of mediation, reconciliation, and preservation of marriage. To the degree that the implementation officer, other court officials, and friends of the court work toward this aim, they do not contravene the spirit of the law, although perhaps its letter, when they defer or even ignore executing judgments.

CONCLUSION

Islamic law and village custom are similarly and mutually reinforcing in many respects (e.g., the propensity for mediation and reconciliation). In other respects (e.g., as concerns marriage payment or *mahr*), Islamic law and village custom stand in contradiction. Inside the court, the application of the Islamic norm proceeds rather consistently. Outside the court, variant modes of accommodation take place. The ultimate role in such accommodation is played by the implementation officer, whose leeway in executing court judgments and whose own involvement in the local social structure make such accommodation possible.

One sphere in which contradictory priorities and norms must be adjusted concerns the distribution of rights and privileges between consanguine and conjugal families. Family structure in Kufr al-Ma is basically consanguine, but the impact of Islamic law and the Islamic court has been substantial and has reinforced conjugal rights (Case 4). I am not suggesting here that the Islamic rules protecting wives are being fully observed in Kufr al-Ma or any other village in Jordan. However, I can state that women have become more and more aware of their rights under Islamic law and can and in fact do have recourse to the courts to claim their rights. Moreover, a woman, who has the support of the Islamic court, especially if it is coupled with her own ingenuity, can assert her own rights against her husband (Case 5) or, alongside her husband, against the larger consanguine family. The Islamic court in Al-Kura is supporting the woman as wife in the first instance against the claims of the larger consanguine family; in the second instance it also supports her as an individual with religiously sanctioned rights against the claims of both conjugal and consanguine units.

The inclination of Islamic law toward the consanguine and the conjugal family is a critical factor in understanding Middle Eastern family relations and the structure of familial disputation. It is also a subject that is misunderstood by many Western scholars. Coulson and Hinchcliffe's view that Islamic law "continued to reflect the patriarchal and patrilineal nature of society" (1978: 38) seems to be generally accepted by Western scholars with the exception of a minority, such as Gibb and Watt. Layish's erudite analysis of Islamic courts in Israel also presumes that Islamic law reflects the viewpoint of the consanguine family in a society that has in fact become dominated by conjugal families. Enough evidence has already been presented here, however, to question this assumption. To cite one outstanding example, there is the great importance placed by Islamic law on the *bayt shari'i* in which the conjugal family structure is recognized in explicitly spatial, economic, and ethical terms.

To hold that Islamic law reflects the point of view of the consanguine family is as erroneous as to hold that it reflects the point of view of the conjugal family. The truth is somewhere between these two positions. That is, a consanguine family structure is recognized, but nested within it and equally recognized is the conjugal family structure. Evidence for this statement is found in the Islamic inheritance rules which recognize the principle of agnation—with the nearer agnate excluding the farther—but only after the allotted shares (*al-fara'id*) are extracted for the conjugal family. If there is any bias, it is in favor of conjugal relations. When the work of the Islamic court is considered with respect to this slightly off-balance normative structure, then, the balance of power can be swung firmly onto the conjugal side and even beyond it towards the rights of the individual married woman.

The relationship of individual Muslims to the workings of the Islamic court, then, is highly complex. A number of constraints exist, particularly upon women regarding the utilization of the court. Equally important within the court setting and in the context of the traditional framework of Islamic law, a number of options exist by which women not only can solidify their position in a conjugal family but also can claim their individual rights against male members of their consanguine and conjugal families. In forwarding such claims, they invoke both Islamic and customary procedures, principles, and norms.

NOTES

1. Two dyads are crucial for the operation of the consanguine family: the sibling tie and the parent-child tie. In the quotation above Linton has given more emphasis to the sibling tie. In the preceding analysis, because of the nature of the court cases discussed, more attention is given to the parent-child, specifically, the father-daughter, tie.

2. The family structures described by Linton refer—to use the terms of another anthropologist (Oliver 1958)—to the "normative" and "suppositional" aspects of behavior and not to the actual "historical" composition and incidence of family types. That is, the terms conjugal and consanguine family reflect how members of the society view their families either in terms of how they ought to be (the normative aspect) or how they are in fact believed to be (the suppositional aspect). As a number of anthropologists point out in an evermore sophisticated fashion, the actual historical incidence of family types is complex and relates to a family cycle of development (Fortes 1949; Goody 1958) oriented either toward ecological (Stenning 1958), inheritance and property (Goody 1962), economic (Smith 1972), or cultural (Spiro 1949) factors or some combination of the above.

3. Most of the data used in this essay were collected in the Sunni Muslim Arab village of Kufr al-Ma, Jordan and in the adjoining subdistrict center of Deir Abu Said in the years 1959, 1960, 1965, and 1966. In 1968 the village's population was approximately 2,000. Its livelihood derived from a combination of agricultural (dry cereal farming), unskilled and semi-skilled labor, petty trade, and military endeavors (police, national guard and army). For further details about the social structure of the village, see Antoun 1972.

4. Hill (1979) has suggested that in Egypt one of the reasons for the prohibition of women as court bystanders is their use of village idioms of apostrophe and beseechment which convert the atmosphere of the courtroom into something other than official decorum.

5. The requirement of the husband providing a *bayt shar'i* for his wife has a Quranic basis in the verse, "Lodge them where you are lodged, according to your means, and do not press them so as to straiten their circumstances" (Surah 65, Verse 6, Arberry,

285). The *bayt shar'i* differs according to the economic status of the spouses. In a small peasant village in Jordan, for instance, for small landholders the following household articles were stipulated as necessary for a *bayt shar'i*: two mattresses, one quilt, a pillow, a straw mat, flour, rice, onions, olive oil in season, cracked wheat, a teapot, teacups, a large washing pan (for laundry), a primus, a pound of salt, clarified butter, tea, sugar, a long over-dress (*thawb*) for the wife, an underdress and a neck wrap.

REFERENCES

Antoun, Richard. 1968. "On the Modesty of Women in Arab Muslim Villages: A Study in the Accommodation of Traditions." *American Anthropologist* 70: 671–97.

———. 1972. *Arab Village: A Social Structural Study of a Trans-Jordanian Peasant Community*. Bloomington: Indiana University Press.

Arberry, Arthur. 1955. *The Koran Interpreted*. New York: Macmillan.

Bailey, F. G. 1963. "Decisions by Consensus in Councils and Committees." In Michael Banton (ed.). *Political Systems and the Distribution of Power*. New York: Praeger.

Coulson, Noel, and Doreen Hinchcliffe. 1978. "Women and Law Reform in Contemporary Islam." In N. Keddie and L. Beck (eds.) *Women in the Muslim World*. Cambridge: Harvard University Press.

Dwyer, Daisy Hilse. 1978. *Images and Self-Images: Male and Female in Morocco*. New York: Columbia University Press.

Fortes, Meyer. 1949. "Time and Social Structure: An Ashanti Case Study." In Meyer Fortes (ed.). *Social Structure: Studies Presented to A. R. Radcliffe-Brown*. Oxford: Oxford University Press.

Gibb, Hamilton A. R. 1958. *Lectures on Islamic Institutions*. Harvard University (unpublished).

Gluckman, Max. 1956. *Custom and Conflict in Africa*. Oxford: Blackwell.

Goody, Jack. 1958. *The Development Cycle in Domestic Groups*. Cambridge: Cambridge University Press.

———. 1962. *Death, Property, and the Ancestors*. Stanford: Stanford University Press.

Granqvist, Hilma. 1935. *Marriage Conditions in a Palestinian Village*, part 2. Helsinki: Helsinfors.

Hill, Enid. 1979. *Mahkama: Studies in the Egyptian Legal System*. London: Ithaca Press.

Hunt, Eva, and Albert Hunt. 1969. "The Role of Courts in Rural Mexico." In Philip C. Bock. (ed.). *Peasants in the Modern World*. Albuquerque: University of New Mexico Press.

Hurgronje, C. Snouck. 1931. *Mekka in the Latter Part of the Nineteenth Century*. Leiden: E.J. Brill.

Layish, Aharon. 1975. *Women and Islamic Law in a Non-Muslim State*. Jerusalem: Israel Universities Press.

Levi-Strauss, Claude. 1945. "L'Analyse Structural en Linguistique et en Anthropologie." *Word* 1 (1): 63–78.

———. 1956a. "Language and the Analysis of Social Laws." *American Anthropologist* 53 (2): 155–63.

———. 1956b. "The Family." In Harry L. Shapiro (ed.). *Man, Culture, and Society*. Oxford: Oxford University Press.

Lewis, Ian. 1962. *Marriage and the Family in Northern Somaliland*. Kampala: East African Institute of Social Research.

Linton, Ralph. 1936. *The Study of Man*. New York: Appleton-Century.

Oliver, Douglas. 1958. "*An Ethnographer's Method for Formulating Descriptions of Social Structure*." American Anthropologist 60: 801–26.

Radcliffe-Brown, Alfred. 1956. *Structure and Function in Primitive Society*. Glencoe: The Free Press.

Redfield, Robert. 1956. *Peasant Society and Culture*. Chicago: University of Chicago Press.

Rosen, Lawrence. 1978. "The Negotiation of Reality: Male and Female Relations in Sefrou, Morocco." In N. Keddie and L. Beck (eds.). *Women in the Muslim World*. Cambridge: Harvard University Press.

Simmel, Georg. 1955. *Conflict*. Kurt H. Wolff, trans. Glencoe: The Free Press.

Singer, Milton. 1972. *When a Great Tradition Modernizes*. New York: Praeger.

Smith, Raymond. 1972. *The Negro Family in British Guiana*. London: Rutledge and Kegan Paul.

Spiro, Melford. 1949. *Venture in Utopia*. Cambridge: Harvard University Press.

Starr, June, and Barbara Yngvesson. 1975. "Scarcity and Disputing: Zeroing-In on Compromise Decisions." *American Ethnologist* 2: 553–66.

Stenning, Derrick. 1958. "Household Viability Among the Pastoral Fulani." In Goody, Jack (ed.) *The Development Cycle in Domestic Groups*. Cambridge: Cambridge University Press.

Watt, Montgomery. 1956. *Muhammad at Medina*. Oxford: Oxford University Press.

4

LITERACY AND THE LAW: DOCUMENTS AND DOCUMENT SPECIALISTS IN YEMEN

Brinkley Messick

Anthropological research on the implications of literacy in traditionally literate societies is still in its infancy. Robert Redfield first identifies literacy as a research problem in 1930 in a chapter entitled "Literature and Literacy" (1930: 170–93). Although dealing mostly with oral tradition, he calls attention to a new range of social phenomena to be encountered in so-called complex societies. Redfield's suggested approach is to focus on "the uses to which the knowledge of reading and writing is put" (1930:171). This line of inquiry remained dormant until the appearance of Jack Goody's *Literacy in Traditional Societies*. Goody maintains, and the contributors to his volume demonstrate, that the social organization of literacy takes many traditional forms. "Writing," Goody states, "is not a monolithic entity, an undifferentiated skill: its potentialities depend on the kind of system that obtains in any particular society" (1969:3; cf. Messick 1983a).

Following Redfield and Goody, my analysis of legal document usage in the Middle East is sociological.[1] I am not concerned here with either the historical or philological value of documents, but rather their use as social tools that figure in human undertakings. I shall indicate how documentary practices in Ibb, a highland Yemeni town of 20,000, are related to social life and the functioning of legal institutions. In order to study the production and use of documents, ethnographic method must be combined with the principles of Islamic legal theory. Documents are one of the means by which abstract legal norms become concrete; they are a meeting point for the law and its social uses.

Although legal documents were integral to the conduct of affairs in the Middle East for more than a millenium prior to Islam (Moscati 1957: 84, 87), Islamic laws of evidence did not recognize them. Despite an apparent endorsement in a Quranic verse ("Cow" Sura, Verse 282) and continued general use of documents, early Muslim jurists denied the validity of written proof. The only acceptable evidence, in theory, was oral: testimony, confession, and oath. The resulting "ambiguous status" (Wakin 1972: 4) of documents in formal legal procedure illustrates the "perpetual problem" (Schacht 1964: 209) of Islamic law: the divergence of theory and practice.

Subsequent generations of Muslim jurists expended considerable effort to make theory and practice converge. North African scholars of the Maliki legal school applied circuitous reasoning to give documentary usage a basis in legal theory. The outcome was a "triumph" (Tyan 1959: 66) of written instruments as legally acceptable proof. In other areas of the Middle East, the triumph remained less complete, and scholars sought to bridge the gap between theory and practice by authoring carefully detailed formularies, complete with model document texts, as guides for notaries and others who prepare legal documents (Wakin 1972).

It is due in part to the problematic status of documents in Islamic legal theory that an analysis of documentary practice offers an instructive entree into the character of traditional legal procedure. Highland Yemen provides a suitable setting for the task. In nearly all the countries of the Middle East and North Africa, ambiguity about the acceptability of documents has been replaced by new conceptions of documentation. In Yemen, however, older, indigenous ideas about legal documents remain viable. Highland Yemen (the current Yemen Arab Republic) had no period of colonial rule by a Western power, unlike its neighbor to the south, the People's Democratic Republic of Yemen, which was under British administration from 1839 to 1967. Only following the Revolution of 1962 and a civil war which embroiled the country until 1970 have Yemenis contemplated augmenting *shari'a* law and the exclusive *shari'a* court system with Western-inspired legislation and commercial courts. Indeed, according to the Yemeni Constitution of 1971, *shari'a* still is "the source of all laws" (Article 3).[2]

Documentary practice in Ibb harkens back to an earlier scale and style of society, one in which the first extension of the written medium was the telegraph, introduced by the Ottomans. Modern Yemen now knows radios, telephones, telex, and television, and daily newspapers reach provincial towns such as Ibb by bus. Wet-process copiers, run by gasoline engines, have taken over some of the work of handcopyists. Literacy in Ibb has a lengthy heritage: a local man wrote a history of the Ibb region in the fifteenth century, while two of the contemporary group of published Yemeni historians have been Ibb residents. For centuries, the town has served as a governmental, commercial, and landlord center for an agrarian hinterland (Messick 1978).

DOCUMENT HOLDING IN IBB

In the United States documents are recorded in county courthouses and the originals are protected in bank safe deposit boxes. Yemenis like the idea of safe deposit boxes, but banks only appeared in Ibb in the 1960s, and their functions are limited to handling international remittances from overseas workers and issuing letters of credit to merchants for importation. People are still very reluctant to deposit their money, much less their documents, in the banks. Both are kept at home. Bunches of long and narrow rolled documents and shorter folded ones are bound together with a string, wrapped in cloth, and locked in chests.

For the most part, documents remain stored; it is only on rare occasions that they must be brought out for examination. In times of political unrest, people immediately take steps to protect their documents. An individual in personal danger will give his documents to a neighbor or friend. If there is a threat of general plunder—realized, for example, in 1948—many townspeople send their documents out to villages for safekeeping.

All types of legal instruments in Ibb are known by the generic term *mu'amala* (pl. *mu'amalat*).[3] Each type also has a specific name: a sale document is a *basira*, for example, and an individual's inheritance document is called a *farz*. In local usage *mu'amala* refers both to the legal undertaking itself—the transaction or disposition—and to the written document in which the undertaking is set down. In classical legal usage the term *mu'amalat* has a related set of meanings. Schacht defines *mu'amalat* as "pecuniary transactions" (1964:145). In a standard manual of Yemeni jurisprudence, *Kitab al-Azhar*, the subject matter is broken down into two general sections, entitled *'ibadat* (ritual obligations) and *mu'amalat*. The latter section is subdivided into chapters on sale, rent, marriage, loan, gift, foundations, and so forth—the categories of transactions and dispositions.

Two other varieties of documents which are found with a person's *mu'amalat* should be mentioned. Legal opinions (*fatwa*, pl. *fatawa*) are prepared upon a petitioner's request by a legal official called the *mufti* (Messick 1986). Legal judgments (*hukm*, pl. *ahkam*) are issued by a court judge or *hakim*. Opinions are not binding, while judgments are. Such opinions and judgments are kept with property documents to which they refer.

In Ibb, the use of all these types of documents is part of a wider dependence on writing to accomplish public and private acts. The everyday conduct of government business is handled by means of notes passed before an official, governor, or head of state. Guards carry notes upstairs to the governor's quarters from petitioners halted on the ground floor of the government building. At the judge's house, a young grandson takes messages up to the private afternoon sitting room of the Ibb judge. The same sort of reliance on written messages is also characteristic of private interaction. It may be expected, for example, that marriages are formalized in written contracts, but it is surprising that most of the informal preliminary contacts between townsmen arranging a marriage are written too.

Most legal documents, that is, the narrow category of *mu'amalat*, circulate less than the more transitory proposals, petitions, and other messages. *Mu'amalat* only change hands under such conditions as a transfer of ownership or if they must be brought forward in a dispute. A central issue is, therefore, who has control of them. The complexity of the issue is illustrated by examples from documentary practice in Ibb.

Marriage in Ibb gives rise to crisscrossing inheritance and foundation-share claims which frequently are the subject of disputes. On the level of documents, this is expressed in a precautionary practice whereby husbands and wives keep their personal documents separate. In theory, there is no mingling of assets between husband and wives, although if their relationship is strong, and especially if there are children, the household finances are usually handled jointly. Nevertheless, a woman will often keep her documents at her father's house, especially if she is in conflict with her husband. If a wife's documents are kept at her husband's house, they are stored separately in her own locked trunk.

Another standard source of disputes pits an oldest brother against his siblings. Younger brothers and sisters must act as respectfully toward their older brother as they would to their father. When the father dies, it is said that the oldest son takes the father's place. Traditionally, fathers tried to favor the oldest son with special benefits from the estate.

Documents typically are a part of the oldest brother's exercise of family power. At the death of the father, it is this brother who takes control of the estate documentation. At best, he oversees the estate and allows the other heirs revenue from their rightful estate shares. Frequently, he will keep his siblings' inheritance documents in his own hands. This might not be serious except for the fact that disputes among siblings over inheritance matters are among the most common in Ibb, and access to the relevant documentation is essential.

People fear having their documents taken away from them when they must be shown to powerful individuals. An extreme example of such fears concerns a peasant who tried to assert an ownership claim to a piece of property, in conflict with a powerful local shaykh. In a meeting between the two, the peasant brought out the document in question as proof of his ownership. The shaykh extinguished the peasant's right in an unusual manner: he ate the document.

As a precaution against such aggression, intermediaries are used. These are people to whom documents are revealed in security or who carry copies of documents to show an official or adversary. In this connection, it may be noted that one of the most common ploys in disputes is to say that someone "has documents" supporting his contention. It is understood that if the latter do in fact exist, documents may not be brought into play until the final moment. The possibilities for bluffing are similar to a card game. Individuals cannot be forced to produce documents, and the withholding of documentary evidence is a frequently used and effective disputing stratagem. In court proceedings, a claimant will either present the documents that he holds or bring witnesses to the effect that the defendant has the relevant documents. Sometimes a claim will be initiated on the basis of supporting documents that the claimant purportedly has and will later supply. If the proceedings continue and it turns out that the claimant does not have these documents, the judge may impose a jail sentence or fine.

If personal documents are not in the individual's possession and not with an older brother or father, then one other person may be expected to have them: the local judge. If a judge holds a legal instrument for very long, it may never be returned. Several people told me that they lost the documentation for one property or another when an old judge died.

In an active dispute, individuals who have initiated court proceedings frequently must bring their documents to the judge for examination. When asked to return such documents after the settlement, the judge will be expected to require payment of a small sum. In former times, this payment may have been an unsolicited "gift," not viewed as an abuse, but times are changing. Payments seem to have grown in scale at the same time that they have become identified in the public mind as "corrupt." Judges once viewed as dignified and honorable are thus now often thought to be unprincipled. To protect the original and to avoid giving the judge money to get a document back, some men take advantage of new technological developments and make photocopies to give the judge.

To summarize some of these issues of document control, I will quote from a taped interview with a man discussing a dispute. He owned a vacant lot that a neighbor once tried unsuccessfully to buy. Frustrated, the neighbor went behind my informant's back to the Ibb governor and suggested that a proposed new treasury office be built on the lot in question, with the neighbor as contractor. The neighbor told the governor, who was new to Ibb, that the lot was unowned. This came to my informant's attention, and a dispute ensued:

> At the time I didn't have the ownership documents for the property since they were in the hands of my older brother, who had died. I went to his house and asked his wife if I could look through some papers, to find the documents. She gave me a few papers, and I found the documents for the lot. I went to the *mufti's* house to present the documents to him. I asked him to go up to see the governor, which he agreed to do. He went, but the governor was preoccupied, and he was unable to bring the matter up. In the meantime, friends of mine made a bond to be offered the governor whereby I was to be asked to show what papers I had in my hand. On my side was Qasim al-'Ansi. I was often a guest in his house, and he was one of the governor's secretaries. I took my documents to him, and I told him the governor wanted to see them, but that I was afraid he would take them from me. I wanted al-'Ansi to take copies up to the governor's office, and he said he would. He told the governor, "This man is correct in his ownership claim, he and his grandfather and the generations before."

THE EXCHANGE OF DOCUMENTS

Documents do change hands at transaction times. When a parcel of land is sold and has been the subject of previous sales, at least one old sale contract is extant. This ought to be given to the new owner at the time of the new sale. On one occasion, I was shown a series of such contracts relating to a land plot going back as far as three hundred years, all in the possession of the contemporary owner. By contrast, when a sale involves inherited property, the relevant document is a person's inheritance instrument, the *farz*. In such cases, a sale contract is written for the current sale and kept by the buyer, but a notation is also written adjacent to the entry for that property on the seller's *farz*: "The contents of this document [section] are transferred to the buyer X according to the *basira* in his hand. Written by Y [date]". The *farz* itself, listing other inherited properties still owned, stays with the seller.

Other documents that must change hands at transactions are those resulting from a dispute. If a property was the object of a past legal contest, then the relevant settlement papers also should be provided the new owner. One man in Ibb, for example, purchased both halves of a land plot that had been divided as a result of a dispute, and, as a consequence, he had two *hukms*, copies of the same settlement decision once held by each party to the old conflict.

In a complex legal-economic undertaking, each of the component transactions becomes the subject of a separate document (cf. Wakin 1972:11). In a land sale I observed, the preparation of the final *basira* was preceded by that of two earlier instruments. Since the buyer did not have the full purchase price on hand, the first of the two prior documents was a fictitious "receipt" of the full amount of the sale, while the second embodied a "loan" equivalent to the sum that actually remained to be paid. This maneuver on paper was necessitated by a desire to keep the final contract "clean," that is, unencumbered.

It is not always the case that the full set of transaction terms are recorded in document form. In some categories of undertaking, the financial arrangement is not specified. An example is the *tanazul*, whereby an individual "steps down" as supervisor of a trust (*waqf*). The associated document makes no mention of the money paid to the retiring individual by the new supervisor. Similarly, marriage documents only mention the sum known as *mahr*, which, in Ibb, is not actually paid to the wife until divorce or at the husband's death. Two other payments to the bride's family are far larger, but are not noted in the documents.

DOCUMENT SPECIALISTS IN SOCIAL CONTEXT

A group of men specializing in the preparation of private legal documents exists in Ibb. Any townsman can list their names. Document specialists work in the private sector, mostly in matters related to rights and obligations in land, and are central to the conduct of private business. Their social identity is critical to an understanding of the place of legal documents in Ibb society.

The most common verbal formula for a document specialist is "writer of *mu'amalat*"; another is the simple expression, "He writes for people." The term *katib*, meaning "writer" or "scribe," is a broader term that refers to several categories of professional writers in Ibb, including the document specialists. The document writers should not be confused with the hand copyists, also known as *katibs*. As in many countries of the Middle East, Yemeni copyists set up their boxtop desks outside government buildings. These copyists are capable of writing simple petitions and making duplicates of letters and messages. They are not qualified, however, nor would anyone approach them, to write or interpret a legal instrument.

Document specialists engage in a variety of collateral tasks. Some of the technical skills of private document writing overlap with traditional bureaucratic skills, and many of the town's document writers have held government positions. Especially for marriages, the document writer is often a man of religious knowledge who works as a mosque employee or as a Quranic instructor for preschool-aged children. Teachers in Ibb's former institution of advanced Islamic education received bed and board for teaching mornings in the main mosque; they earned cash income by writing *mu'amalat* in the afternoons.

As a sideline to their work of writing contracts, document specialists in Ibb play an important part in dispute resolution. In this highly contentious society, settlements commonly take the form of transactions, each of which must be written up in document form. At one dispute resolution I observed, four documents were written and witnessed, each dealing with one strand of contention: a divorce, an old inheritance claim, physical injury, and an overall money settlement. In such contexts documents are settlement tools. As opponents are brought together, a document writer, acting as a mediator, will prepare a succession of written settlement formulations, ever more closely approximating the finally agreeable terms. Court judges and arbitrators are alternatively available in Ibb, but document writers working as mediators are equally common settlement agents.

In a study of law in one of the former sultanates of South Yemen, Maktari found that document writing was performed by the *wakil*, or legal representative (1971:96). In Ibb these are two distinct occupational identities. In theory, Ibb *wakils* are as well educated as the document writers. They should be, for it is they who formulate written claims. But *wakils* in Ibb tend to be better known as specialists in the public spoken word. Document writers are specialists in the written word, and only secondarily adept at private oral persuasion. Professional skills identified in the West with the work of a lawyer are in Ibb subdivided into two specializations. Because *wakils* are thought to prey on naive disputants, they ranked distinctly lower than document specialists in the public's estimation.

Document specialists are among the traditionally educated elite in Ibb society. In the old educational system, advanced instruction meant study of *shari'a* (religious law), so that learned men emerged with the necessary conceptual tools for document writing. Educated men who do not consider document writing a profession may write one from time to time, typically upon request from a family member, neighbor, or friend.

Educational change in Yemen has been abrupt since 1962, and formerly rigid status barriers are dissolving. More universal access and a secular curriculum have replaced a pyramidal system of instruction. The religiously trained *'ulama* were viewed as closer to a full realization of the Muslim ideal and in line for leading positions in the town society. Education and correct occupation are linked with social honor, and document writing is a high status, honorable profession, unlike the work of butchers, greengrocers, and street cleaners.

There are several general qualifications for becoming a document writer in Ibb, although these are nowhere codified. An individual should have an excellent script, knowledge of the *shari'a*, and a record of honorable conduct (*'adala*). No specialized training in document preparation existed at the old mosque school, but most of the necessary legal formulations were acquired there.

Successful document specialists find satisfaction in involving themselves in the affairs of others. Such behavior is highly valued in Ibb so long as it is connected with a primary interest in facilitating undertakings and achieving peaceful ends. *Wakils* generally fail this test, but document writers must be above reproach. Approved male behavior in Ibb dictates that a man circulate in the town streets every morning. Only feeble old men are justified in staying at home; retiring individuals who withdraw themselves from public scrutiny are viewed with suspicion. Document writers epitomize this outgoing male standard.

Document specialists become privy to the secrets of their clients' legal acts. They have extensive information about the daily flow of property transactions. That this information is sensitive is illustrated by the appeal of a local poster boosting education: "Become educated and protect your secrets." Document specialists also may be entrusted with a client's personal documents and often keep money on deposit until a transaction is consummated (cf. Schacht 1948:521).

Ahmad al-Basir, who died in 1978 at about ninety, was the last representative of an earlier generation of document specialists in Ibb. He was a scholar in the classic mold. His intellectual interests extended well beyond the law to history and poetry. He always wore the attire of the traditional educated elite: an *'imama* head cover and a long and billowy white gown over a white undergarment. In an embroidered dagger belt he carried the appropriate slant-style dagger. His close cropped beard, dyed with henna, was an additional mark of his status. Biographical dictionary entries trace his ancestry to Sa'ada in the northernmost highlands; his Ibb region ancestors were judges and teachers.

One part of al-Basir's long career was spent as a document writer. He began as a mosque schoolteacher and later held several high administrative positions in local government. At the height of his work as a document specialist, the *diwan* of his house was said to be filled every day with people seeking his professional assistance. Unlike all of the contemporary document specialists, this was for many years his exclusive occupation.

In present day Ibb there are numerous occasional writers of documents, but ten are identified as professionals. In this group are two *faqihs*, two part-time merchants, and a court scribe—all of whom handle small volumes of relatively unimportant documents. Four other men account for the weightiest and the majority of the documents produced in the town. One is the *mufti* of Ibb Province. Two hold positions under the full-judge level in the local judiciary, but neither spends more than an hour or two per day in his official capacity. Like many men in the modern town, they have a government position basically for the sake of the monthly salary. The last of the four principal document writers seems to indicate a new direction for the profession. He lacks the scholarly depth and interests of the others; yet he is technically proficient. Out of a shop in the marketplace, he operates what is virtually a real estate business, dealing with all manner of transactions and disputes related to land. With the advance of commercialization in Yemen, the volume and value of land sales have increased dramatically, and this specialist has been in the midst of the action in Ibb.

Transactions, especially those involving land, generate income for witnesses, intermediaries, and document writers. Document writers receive a fee which is paid by the buyer (see Wakin 1972:41, n2). The fee is nominal for minor instruments such as marriage contracts or leases; some are even written for free by nonprofessionals. But land sales, inheritance matters, and dispute settlements may bring the writer more than a government functionary earns in a month for no more than an hour's work.

A document specialist's high status underlines the pattern of payment. Tyan's discussion of payments to historical Middle Eastern notaries applies to the present-day case in Ibb. "Due to the dignity of the profession, notaries avoid, 'out of modesty,' speaking of money at the time of the performance of one of their official acts, which could give rise to bargaining of the sort that occurs in low status professions and crafts" (1959:29, my translation). A reluctance to appear motivated by a base concern for income fits with a traditional aura of noble bearing actively projected by the educated elite of Ibb. In any case, a document specialist will accept what a client pays and would seek more only after the fact and through an intermediary. In fact, what is paid is not determined by a client's whim, but in accord with what is considered customary. The sum depends on the overall value of the transaction and on whether or not the document writer provided any services beyond the preparation of the document, such as persuading the two sides to come together at the last moment or assisting the parties in overcoming obstacles.

To these legal-economic events, the document specialist brings not only the requisite legal expertise but also and more importantly in Ibb, his personal honor and reputation. These are established and maintained before the community and substantiated in the course of daily interactions. As is true for members of the judiciary, appropriate decorum is essential. Such men cannot indulge in frivolity, must be of stern comportment, and must wear appropriate attire. If a writer's reputation is brought into question, if any doubt arises about his integrity, then his document-writing business will fall off abruptly to nil. In one case in Ibb, word spread concerning the bad conduct of one local specialist, and his career came to an end.

Honor and reputation are closely connected to qualifications for legal witnessing, and witnessing is the basis of a document's legality. In Ibb, the document writer is considered the primary witness for the legal undertaking he places in writing. He must hear the legally binding statements from the contracting parties, such as the offer and acceptance uttered by seller and buyer in a land sale. He puts these statements in writing along with the terms of the contract, and then he must sign his name. Until about thirty years ago, a seal containing the writer's name and a date were also necessary. Documents are not signed by the principals, as their signatures have no legal weight (Wakin 1972:51, n1). For contracts, two witnesses are the formal requirement of the law. An unwitnessed document, locally known as a secret (*sirri*) document, has no value. For relatively insignificant instruments, any two males who happen to be available will suffice as witnesses, but in important matters, many extra, socially prominent witnesses may be gathered to sign their names. The bottoms of such documents read like a *Who's Who* in the town in a given era.

In Islamic law *'adala* is required of a witness. This refers to upright moral character and is a quality which may be assessed by a judge. In many historical communities of the Middle East, there was an institution of professional witnesses (Tyan 1959:12). These were men who had received prior certification as acceptable witnesses from a judge. Before this institution emerged, according to Tyan, contracts were unduly fragile and vulnerable, since the all-important witnesses could simply be rejected by a judge.

Ibb has not known the institution of certified witnesses, perhaps due to its small size. Ibb is more of a face-to-face society. The townspeople are not all intimate associates by any means, but in an outward, public sense they know each other. In such a community, *'adala* refers not so much to abstract moral qualities as to an individual's location in the social order and his record of public behavior.

If a dispute over a contract occurs, the writer is the first line of defense for the documentation. Documents do figure in legal proceedings, but it is the writer, even though he does not appear, who must hold up in court. His personal honor and reputation are weighed in an evaluation of any document he has written and signed. Documents seem to stand alone as pieces of evidence, only because of the judge's intimate acquaintance with the local men who produce them. Handwriting alone is often sufficient for an Ibb judge to know who wrote a document.

THE NECESSITY OF DOCUMENTS

The widespread use of written legal documents in Yemen may be accepted as fact, but an important question remains. What is the legal or practical necessity of such documents? As opposed to American law in which a document "gives formal expression to a legal act or agreement, for the purpose of creating, securing, modifying, or terminating a right" (Black 1968: 941), Islamic legal instruments "represent only an after-the-fact record of a transaction." According to theory, such documents "are not constitutive instruments, for the legal obligations exist whether or not they are spelled out in the documents" (Wakin 1972:30). As Schacht has noted, "there are no legal acts which must be embodied in a document" (1964:193). Nevertheless, documents commonly accompany transactions and are used as proof and as settlement tools in formal and informal legal proceedings. In order to determine whether or not a legal right will stand in the absence of a supporting document, it is necessary to look beyond the immediate legal level alone; no blanket statement about the efficacy of written documents can be made.

Documents are one mode of support for the rights or obligations established in legal undertakings. In the case of the peasant whose document was eaten, the document was clearly important. In such situations, the last grasp on a right may be eliminated by the destruction or loss of control of relevant documentation. Documents can win legal contests, and disputants in Ibb frequently build legal strategies around written evidence. In one lengthy, extended-family dispute over a family foundation (*waqf*), a man was able to single-handedly fend off the repeated legal attacks of the rest of his family due to his possession of one clear-cut text. Through fifteen years of litigation, judgments repeatedly returned to the original sound document as the basis for findings. But in a court case I followed, secure documentation did not carry the day. Despite his presentation of extensive and sound supporting documents, a man widely perceived in the community as a scoundrel was unable to get a firm ruling in his favor.

There are instances of transactions without documentation. Land sales involving townsmen are always placed in writing, but sales between members of the same rural village may not be. The entire burden of support for the undertaking rests directly upon witnesses, whose witnessing act is not reinforced by their signatures. Such documentless land transactions are rare, occurring, if at all, in rural villages, but they emphasize the fact that the ultimate legal security for any undertaking rests with witnesses.

Why do villagers sometimes omit documents? It is not that writers are unavailable. I would argue that adequate security for such undertakings exists in the form of the personal bonds of a small community, rendering any further guarantee superfluous. I knew a man who moved to Ibb from a village. He told me that in lending considerable sums to a person from his home village no document was required, or, at most, an extremely simple I.O.U. of one line would suffice. By contrast, he said, a loan of even a small amount to a townsman would require a full-fledged written instrument.

One sector of legal-economic activity in the town is regularly undocumented: commerce. Petty retail sales take place, of course, without any documents, but the same is true of wholesale transactions between members of Ibb's merchant community. While more and more Ibb merchants are keeping regular written records and receipts have long been known, nothing equivalent to written land sale contracts exists in wholesale commercial sales. Trust alone underpins even high value transactions among established trading partners. Such trust is built up in repeated successful dealings. Land sales or inheritance divisions lack the repetitive character, not to mention the trust, that makes documents dispensible among merchants.

It is possible to sell a property while lacking the appropriate documentation, if the seller's ownership right is publicly accepted. In its history, Ibb has been plundered many times, and personal documents were often lost or destroyed (Zabara 1359 A.H.:875–77, where the destruction of *mu'amalat* in Ibb in 1708 is specifically mentioned). When such disasters befell the town, members of the community gathered afterward at the judge's house to remake documents.

People bore witness to each other's rights of ownership. Many such rights are generally known (*ma'ruf*, *mashhur*). And, as has been noted, some people do not have control of their own documents since they are held by the judge, the person's father, or an older brother.

Not all documents produced in Ibb are written by specialists or even by men qualified to prepare a correct instrument. As a result, actual documents range the entire legal gamut from unassailable to slipshod. Examples of air-tight legal instruments have been provided by scholars throughout the centuries in so-called *shurut* works, dealing with the science of documents. The documents offered as samples were designed to sidestep the subtle differences between the several Islamic legal schools. Paragons of legal precision, they rely for endurance exclusively on their own internal formulation. Suitable for all times and places, they are neither grounded in nor constructed for any particular social-historical context.

Documentary practice in Ibb, however, is intimately tied to local social dictates. The legal quality of a document is often a function of the social relationship between the contracting individuals. The soundest documents, produced by the foremost document specialists, tend to be associated with undertakings in which the human relationship is relatively insecure. By contrast, weak documents, often authored by nonspecialists or even rank amateurs, are typical of dealings between friends or close associates. In transactions between certain categories of relatives, the documentation is often less than complete. In one example I encountered, a land sale for 100,000 riyals ($22,222) was written on a flimsy scrap of school notebook paper. A document specialist who examined the document found it to be lacking (*naqis*) and remarked that the absence of attention to legal formality seemed to indicate that the parties were close friends. They were, in fact, distant cousins in an extended family, men who considered their personal relationship the primary level of support for their transaction.

Relatives are apt to be untrusting, however, if they are joint heirs or common beneficiaries of foundation revenue. Trusting behavior between brothers, for example, is as highly valued as it is rare. In their legal-economic affairs, brothers relate to one another with the formalities and legal trappings of total strangers, so that full and strict documentation is more likely within a nuclear family than between distant patrilineal cousins or friends. In undertakings with actual strangers or individuals with bad local reputations, the soundest documents are sought.

REINFORCING LEGAL DOCUMENTS

Aside from documents, several legal mechanisms are available to buttress a given transaction, such as formal guarantee (*daman*), bond (*kafala*), pawn (*rahn*), and earnest money (*'urbun*). Documents may also be strenghthened in external ways, that is, above and beyond the internal construction of the text itself. I have already mentioned that additional witnesses may be used. The names of socially prominent people may also appear as witnesses to an undertaking, giving great support to the undertaking's longevity. In addition, it is possible to seek a countersignature from a local legal official, the local governor, or even the head of state. Such authentications (known by the terms *tasdiq* and *i'timad*) are always located in a large space at the top of the document paper. A consequential signature and the date are typically preceded by a simple, one-line affirmation "of what is written below." When a document reinforced in this manner is presented at some later time for examination, attention gravitates to the significant space above the text. It is also in this top space that official transfers are noted, giving the reader information about the history of the document. With the passage of time and changes in local officialdom, document holders sometimes reinforce their instruments with further signatures of new incumbents.

While personal seals have fallen into disuse in recent years, the official seal is still extremely important. The ultimate seal is that of the head of state. In a visit to Yemen in 1933, Carleton Coon observed the application of the Imamic seal: "A secretary handed him [Imam Yahya] a document for approval; he poured some pink powder from a box lying with his writing materials and affixed his seal to it. The secretary blew the loose powder away, and the document was ready" (1958:291). Long afterward, the distinctive trace of the powder remains on the document paper with the Imamic seal to indicate the lofty source. Imams had their seals placed on dispute settlements that they engineered and on transactions they wished or were asked to affirm. In Republican usage, every official administrative letter and a good many private documents bear a governmental seal, placed over an official signature. According to a prominent Ibb *wakil*, the availability of a document bearing an official seal—that of any state, Ottoman, Imamic, or Republican—should help win a court case.

To *qayyid* a document means that a copy of the text will be written into a court register between records of judicial decisions. An entry number (volume and page) is placed in the corner of the original, and a small registration fee is paid. In the Ottoman period (1872-1918), such registration was required. Inheritance documents and land sale contracts from that era bear Ottoman revenue stamps as evidence of the collection of a recording fee (*rasmiyya*). Under the Imams, this practice was discontinued, but it has been reinstituted, in theory, by the Republicans.

Such registration is nowhere required in Islamic law. Tyan has correctly observed: "An essential characteristic of the Muslim notarial system is that it involves neither an authentication furnished by the intervention of public authority, nor the publication of juridic acts" (1959:13). An Ibb scholar concurred: "Why should we register documents? We have a system based on custom (*'urf*) and legal knowledge (*'ilm*) that has lasted for 1,400 years." In his view, nothing of a legal nature was added to a document by registration and, he maintained, no one would ever require that a document be registered in order to accept it as valid.

As in the case of additional witnesses and weighty countersignatures, court registration exists as an option. One local landowner told me he would only have an instrument registered if he did not know the other party to a contract. Documents may be submitted for registration if they are extremely important or if the undertaking appears otherwise unstable. Yemenis generally place a higher value, however, on keeping their affairs secret.

Among the men who handle documents frequently, whether they be members of the judiciary, bureaucrats, document specialists, or wealthy private individuals, there is an extremely high level of sensitivity to the most subtle imperfections ("internal" or "external") in a text. In our own legal system, this aspect of documents is the province of a distinct subprofession, the "questioned-documents examiner," to whom a lawyer may appeal for expert testimony. It is impossible to say how much forgery occurs in Ibb, but it is certainly well known. Once I was handed what was described as a 300-year-old document. As I was on my way to visit a local scholar, I showed it to him. We were reading it through when my friend suddenly held the paper up to the light. This revealed two things to him. First, the paper was yellowed on one side only, suggesting that it may have been aged in a smoker. More significant, however, was the watermark, indicating a brand of heavy document paper, that had not come to Yemen from Istanbul until 1922. Other features of what turned out to be an incompetent forgery were adduced: there was no government seal (not strictly required), no writer's signature, the ink was "new" upon the paper, and the script style was both relatively modern, and several lines appeared to be in a different hand.

Another mode of falsification in Ibb is the reuse of seals. I was shown an especially crude example in which a cut-out old seal had been pasted on a new instrument. Antedating and postdating are a far more subtle and widespread abuse. In general, if a judge finds a document to be blotted (*matmus*), altered (*mughayr*), or otherwise determines that it is forged (*muzawwar*), he will not rely on it.

CONCLUSION

As has been demonstrated in numerous studies of legal systems around the world, "legal processes are social processes" (Collier 1975:121). Legal action does not occur in an isolated legal sphere but can only be understood in relation to the wider organization of social-cultural life. The same is true of documentary practice, which has been examined here as a legal institution with social roots and social implications.

In Yemen, documents represent and are used to guarantee rights and obligations in land and other resources. They are considered essential both in routine transactions and in disputes. Moreover, Yemenis have elaborated an extensive and sophisticated body of knowledge concerning their legal documents. Document specialists are key figures in the legal-economic life of Ibb. Their skills and capacities range beyond the handling of transaction documentation to work as mediators in disputes. Their social identity combines high educational achievement with social honor and a secure public reputation. They are, however, members of a disappearing traditional elite.

Witnessing is the linchpin institution in Yemeni legal processes, including documentary practice. The legal value of documents is built upon the honor and reputation of witnesses, first among these being the document writer himself. Witnessing depends on the witness's place in the social order and upon a reputation established in the course of daily life.

Hence it is difficult to draw firm conclusions about document legality based on the textual features of a document alone. The character of witnesses and the relationship between the contracting parties usually have a greater impact on eventual outcomes. An undertaking buttressed by an airtight document may fail for other reasons, while one supported by a seriously flawed instrument may remain untroubled over time. What Wakin referred to as the "ambiguous status" of documents in the Muslim world seems as true of Yemeni practice as it was of classical theory.

Yemenis do not consider their use of documents problematic, but from the point of view of analysis, the precise legal status of documents is difficult to pin down. In the sense that both are structured in terms of witnessing, there is no great divergence of theory and practice. And yet the structure of documentary practice gives evidence of the conflict between written and oral modes of proof, which is part of an oral/written tension that is characteristic of Islamic literate culture in general.

NOTES

1. Research in the Yemen Arab Republic from September 1974 to March 1976 and from January to June 1980 was supported by a predoctoral fellowship and a postdoctoral grant from the Joint Committee on the Near and Middle East of the Social Science Research Council and the American Council of Learned Societies.

2. Customary law is extremely important, however, in both rural and urban settings. See Chelhod (1975) and Messick (1983b).

3. Other terms frequently used are: *wathiqa*, pl. *watha'iq*; *hujja*, pl. *hujaj*; *waraqa*, pl. *awraq*.

REFERENCES

Black, Henry Campbell. 1968. *Black's Law Dictionary*, 4th ed. St. Paul, Minn.: West Publishing.

Cheldhod, Joseph. 1975. "La Societé Yemenite et le Droit," *L'Homme* 15(2): 67-86.

Collier, Jane. 1975. "Legal Processes." *Annual Review of Anthropology* 4: 121-44.

Coon, Carlton. 1958. *Caravan.* New York: Holt, Rinehart and Winston.

Goody, Jack P. (ed). 1968. *Literacy in Traditional Societies.* Cambridge: Cambridge University Press.

Maktari, A. M. A. 1971. *Water Rights and Irrigation Practices in Lahj.* Cambridge: Cambridge University Press.

Messick, Brinkley. 1978. *Transactions in Ibb: Economy and Society in a Yemeni Highland Town*. Ph.D. diss. Princeton University.

———. 1983(a). "Legal Documents and the Concept of 'Restricted Literacy,'" *International Journal of the Sociology of Language* 42: 41-52.

———. 1983(b). "Prosecution in Yemen: The Introduction of the Niyaba." *International Journal of Middle East Studies* 15: 507-18.

———. 1986. "The Mufti, the Text, and the World: Legal Interpretation in Yemen," *Man* 21:102–19.

Moscati, Sabatino. 1957. *Ancient Semitic Civilizations*. New York: G. P. Putnam's Sons.

al-Murtada, Ahmad b. Yahya. n.d., *Kitab al-azhar fi fiqh al-a'imma al-athar*. n.p.

Redfield, Robert. 1930. *Tepotzlan*. Chicago: University of Chicago Press.

Schacht, Joseph. 1964. *An Introduction to Islamic Law*. Oxford: Clarendon Press.

———. 1948. "Review of Emile Tyan, *Le Notariat*", *Orientalia* n.s. 17: 519-22.

Tyan, Emile. 1959. *Le Notariat*. 2nd ed. Harrisa, Lebanon: St. Paul.

Wakin, Jeannette. 1972. *The Function of Documents in Islamic Law*. Albany: State University of New York Press.

Zabara, Muhammad. 1359 A.H. *Nashr al-'arf*. vol. 2. Cairo: Matba'at as-Sa'ada.

5

ISLAM AND THE STRUGGLE OVER STATE LAW IN TURKEY

June Starr

The secular world watches intently as a growing number of Middle Eastern countries, such as Iran and Libya, affirm the superiority of Islamic nationhood. The currents of Islamic resurgence have swept through largely pacified Islamic populations in the Soviet Union, creating new unrest (Austin 1980:14). Among Muslim minorities in India and majorities in Pakistan, Islamic rhetoric is increasing. Certain Islamic scholars say the tide of secularism and Western "superiority" in the Islamic world has turned. Western domination, which began in the sixteenth century or even earlier, is receding from its highest mark (Tyabji 1979:6–7). With Islamic nationhood firmly entrenched in Iran (*New York Times* Oct. 1985), Turkey figures prominently in debates about the ability of neighboring "secular" Middle Eastern nations to hold the bulwark against Islamic resurgence.

The struggle for a secular state in Turkey neither began nor ended in 1926 when, under Ataturk's rule, European Civil and Criminal Codes were introduced. Yet 1926 does mark a radical departure from the earlier inroads that European law had made in the Ottoman Empire. In 1926, for the first time in history, Islam was clearly separated from the secular law of the nation and confined to its religious sphere only.

Thirty years after this remarkable occurrence, however, an International conference held in Istanbul to evaluate the "Reception of Foreign Law in Turkey" contained only one paper which discussed the secularization of Turkish law. Disestablishment of Islamic law did not seem a hot topic in 1955, perhaps because many of the assembled scholars agreed with H. N. Kubali's assertion that "the adoption of the Swiss Civil Code in 1926 represents by no means so abrupt a transition from one legal system to another as is generally supposed; it is not really revolutionary. Considered as one of a series of receptions effected in different branches of the law, it is the last stage in an evolution which, whilst admittedly slow and belated, has gone on steadily, without interruption, for the last one hundred and fifty years" (1957:66).

After summarizing the major events in Turkey's march toward secularism, this chapter presents findings from sixteen months' empirical research in rural southwestern Turkey (1966–1968) to suggest the extent to which national secular law is followed in a comparatively remote and rural area. Law is discussed as a system of ideology, behavior, and institutions. I argue that the village-level legal system and the state system provide processes, types of decisions, and outcomes different from each other. Different types of litigants (rich/poor, female/male) gravitate toward the system which gives them greater advantage and leverage and not because one system has religious components while the other is secular, or because one system is the villagers' folk system while the other is state-oriented and state-managed. In effect, the local-level system has not been destroyed by the expanding nation-state but continues to flourish (perhaps with less potency because disputants now have multiple options for pursuing grievances) within its domain as an informal system of social control. At the same time I argue that the national legal system provides more universal standards of behavior, a regularized process[1] for hearing disputes and arriving at decisions, and some relief from local interests which may have an Islamic association.

THE DISESTABLISHMENT OF ISLAM

The process of disestablishing Islamic law and of establishing a nonreligious state began in 1839 under the reformist Tanzimat government. The millet system had defined the right of minorities—Christians and Jews, for example, to adhere to their own family laws. Equal rights were given to minorities under the Royal Edict of 1839 because of heavy pressure from European powers (Feroze 1962:131). This right needed to be reaffirmed repeatedly during the nineteenth century (Davison 1963:3–4, 42–44). The revised Penal Code of 1940 (*Ceza Kanunnamesi*), for example, carefully restated the equality of all Ottoman subjects, although it remained essentially within *Seriat* jurisprudence (Lewis 1966: 108–9). In the same year "mixed tribunals" of Muslims and non-Muslims to hear commercial cases involving foreigners were established in the newly created Ministry of Justice (Findley 1986: 7). Mixed police courts soon followed (Davison 1963:44). The admissibility of Christian testimony against Muslims represented another breakthrough, and by 1850 a new commercial code largely based on the French one was adopted (Davison 1963:3–4).

No opposition to the development of secular courts was as strong as that of the Islamic clergy or *ulema*. They were not prepared to embrace equality of Muslims, Christians, and Jews; nor did secularization appeal to them (Davison 1963:4–9, 42–43). A government report in 1846 recommended that a secular school system be created to parallel the only existing educational system of Islamic schools in Turkey.

The reformist Edict of 1856 expressed ideas of change and secularization more forcefully than the early attempts at reform by the Tanzimats in 1839. For example, this new document mentioned neither the exalted Ottoman past nor the holy Quran. In concise language it stipulated reforms. Muslims and non-Muslims were to be called to military service. Apostasy from Islam was no longer to be punished by death. Banks would be established. European capital and skilled professionals would be allowed to enter the Empire. Tax farming would be abolished. Codifications of criminal and commercial law would be undertaken. The prison system would be reformed. Mixed tribunals would be instituted for lawsuits between Muslims and non-Muslims (Davison 1963:44, 54–55).

The Constitution of 1876 moved further to accept Western principles of representation in government (Ibid.:363–67). A Criminal Code had been adopted, and it outlawed punishments, such as lapidation for lying, and severing of the right hand for thieving. But it was not until 1920, when the Caliph and Seyh-ul Islam capitulated to the Ottoman enemies who were already occupying the Turkish homeland, that "Turkish secularism for the first time became a serious political force" (Lewis 1966:396). Until then, the religious hierarchy had remained strong, despite all the changes advocated by the Ottomanists, the Young Turks, the liberals, and the nationalists (Lewis 1966:397). Lewis suggests:

> The religious basis of the state had been reaffirmed by the assertion, in the late nineteenth and early twentieth centuries, of an Ottoman Caliphate; the religious loyalty of the people had been sharpened and intensified by the long series of foreign and civil wars, all of them against Christian adversaries. The first World War, with its German-made *jihad* and its British-made revolt in Arabia, blurred the simple lines of religious identity and conflict, but the Kemalist struggle to defend Anatolia against the ancient and familiar Greek Christian enemy brought a new intensity of religious identification and loyalty.
>
> The defection of the Caliph and the Seyh-ül-Islâm in the midst of the struggle were bitter blows. . . (p. 397).

The intense hostility of the religious leaders in Istanbul and terrorists' actions of the Caliphate's army against Ataturk's nationalist army made reconciliation impossible, but Ataturk still attempted a compromise with the Islamic factions. He retained the Caliphate even after he had abolished the Sultanate. This compromise lasted until 1924, when coexistence was no longer possible. Ataturk then made a series of sweeping changes which repealed the Holy Law, known as *Seriat*, thus disestablishing Islam (Lewis 1966:398).

All of the earlier legal reforms, however extensive they seemed, had not affected the *shari'a* or Islamic law which governed family life. The laws of marriage, divorce, inheritance, and custody of children for Muslim adherents continued as before. In 1876, the *Seriat* had been codified in the *Mecelle* and proclaimed the law to be followed throughout the Ottoman Empire. Although the *Mecelle* and later the new Ottoman Family Law of 1917 marked certain advances in the rights of women in Ottoman domains, neither broke free of the conceptual rules of Islamic family law. This was not to happen until 1926, when the revolutionary government of Ataturk set aside a millenium of Islamic family law by adapting the Swiss Code to replace the *Seriat*. Secular criminal codes had been introduced in the 19th century, as mentioned earlier.

That so fundamental a change in family law could be initiated within record time—a mere six months—seems extraordinary. But, the twenty-six-member drafting committee all had studied law at Lausanne, Switzerland, and for them it was comparatively easy to adopt the family code they knew, the Swiss Civil Code (Ostrorog 1927). The Swiss Code, modeled after the German Code, has been called the most legalistic and rule-based code in western Europe by the late eminent Harvard Law professor, Lon Fuller.

Thus, a secular Civil Code was introduced into Turkey with little fanfare and with slight modification to fit Turkish needs: for example, the age that males and females could marry was lowered, and rules to limit excessive exchange of gifts between the families of the bride and groom were incorporated. The religious courts, using *Seriat* law, had been closed and dismantled in 1924. New secular courts were created to use the new Civil Code and these would be supervised by the Ministry of Justice.

In addition to legal reform, Ataturk acted swiftly to introduce other new, secular structures that would destroy the power of the ruling Islamic clergy, the *ulema*: for example, the Caliphate was abolished in 1924 and this undermined the entire religious, heirarchical organization within Turkish society (Lewis 1966:260). In 1925 Ataturk also acted against the dervishes and religious orders which held considerable power in the countryside. In a series of decrees, he confirmed laws passed by the Assembly which dissolved and banned the Islamic brotherhoods, impounded their assets, closed their convents and sanctuaries, and prohibited prayer meeting and ceremonies (Lewis 1966:405). The mosques and sanctuaries of the famous whirling dervishes of Mevlana were made a national museum in Konya, and the dervishes were not legally allowed public performances again until 1964.

The *Seyh-ül Islâm* had been abolished in 1924 and the work of his department was divided between two secular ministries: a Directorate of Pious Foundations and the Ministry of Religious Affairs (its presiding officer to be nominated by his direct Supervisor, the Prime Minister) (Lewis 1966:407). All work of this Ministry—the administration of mosques, the appointment and dismissal of *Imams*, *muezzins*, and *muftis*—are now firmly under secular control.

Lands previously held in Islamic trust (*evkafs*), and all other Islamic buildings, including lodges, brotherhoods, and mosques were placed under the jurisdiction of the fledgling, secular Directorate of Pious Foundations (ibid.). In 1931 this office took over the task of paying the salaries of all *Imams* and *muftis*, thus reducing further the authority of the Religious Affairs bureau.

Religious education by the laws of 1924 had been taken from the control of the *ulema*. The religious schools, the *medreses*, were closed, as were the old theological seminaries (ibid.). Training for minor religious personnel was placed under the jurisdiction of the Ministry of Education. Advanced religious training was at the former Suleymaniye *medrese*, which had been reconstituted as a Faculty of Divinity and made part of the University of Istanbul. The University of Istanbul fell under the jurisdiction of the secular Minister of Education. Thus, the power of the *ulema* was drastically curtailed, for they were no longer in charge of education, pious foundations, or the law.

Civil society was introduced to the social and cultural symbols of secularism, as marriage, the calendar, the alphabet, and dress were reformed. The male fez and the female veil were prohibited. By 1928, the word "Islam" had been removed from the Turkish Constitution, as were all the references to an Islamic state (Lewis 1966:398).

The provincial administrative system previously had been reorganized along French models. *Gendarmerie* (who were military soldiers) were stationed for two-year periods in the countryside to keep the peace, while urban police were used in district capitals, towns, and cities. Soldiers and police were stationed in areas where they had no ties of kin or neighborhood. Moreover, the Village Law of 1924 (*Koy Kanunu*) gave Turkish villages a new legal identity and created administrative, social, and health standards for villages to meet in areas, such as clean drinking water and a wall between human and animal quarters.

In sum, the movement towards a secular society and secular state took place at the expense of the *ulema* and other conservatives who used "the shield of religion to try to continue their hold over Turkish society" (Kili 1969:107). Although there were rebellions and challenges to the new secular Republic, they were quickly put down, because Ataturk and his coterie had the backing of the Turkish military, the civil servants, the intellectuals and young people generally (ibid.).

ORGANIZATIONAL STRUCTURE OF THE SECULAR COURTS AND SUPPORTING INSTITUTIONS

Drafted by the Constituent Assembly of the Turkish Republic in 1924, the Constitution established Turkey as a federal system of government with the Prime Minister as a head of state. Beneath this office was a council of twenty ministries, one of which was the Ministry of Justice. The Ministry of Justice is in charge of the court system, while police and gendarmerie are under the control of the Ministry of the Interior.

The Village Law of 1924 required that each village elect by adult franchise every four years a council of elders and a village head. The council and head were empowered to hear local disputes and to impose fines (the equivalent to $5.00 in 1967), and they worked with varying effectiveness.[2] Above the village was a subdistrict officer who was an appointee of the central government and generally a local man. District and state directors are career civil servants who have obtained university degrees and who are appointed from within a civil service hierarchy. Judges and public prosecutors were also career civil servants who had obtained law degrees from a Turkish Law Faculty (two in 1967, six after 1983). Upon graduation a student chooses between a career as an attorney or a career in the Justice hierarchy. A lottery is held to determine who apprentices as judge and who becomes a prosecutor. During a career it is possible to move from the position of prosecutor to that of judge, the usual direction of change.

By the 1960's to become a police captain or a police chief, a man had to have graduated from a six months' course at Turkey's only police academy. Police were accorded lower status and pay than judges, prosecutors, district administrators, and captains of the gendarmes—in part because they had received less education.

CHOICE OF A DISPUTE HEARING AGENCY

A villager who chose to pursue a claim had a variety of options; each one provided a different consequence. In the village, a person might have chosen to invoke the informal social control system, embedded in village cultural practices. If the claimant sought extra help, he might have activated his social networks outside the village, or he/she could use hierarchically ordered agencies of the modern Turkish state. State institutions included the village headman, the village council, the subdistrict director, or the district courts (the lowest level of the national court system). If a complaint involved an alleged criminal offense, he/she could have reported it to the village headman, to the gendarme, or to the urban police located in the Town of Bodrum. Each state agency, such as the Harbor Authority, Post Office, or Tourism Bureau, also heard complaints that fell within their jurisdiction or pertained to their own personnel. Within the totality of these options, distinct patterns of use emerge.

CRITICISMS OF THE NEW SYSTEM

As a graduate student I had read with interest the remarks of legal scholars and social scientists who had assembled at a conference, "The Reception of Foreign Law in Turkey", in Istanbul in 1955 (1957:7–81). Because so much of my subsequent field research in southwestern Turkey (1966–1968) was designed to test the assertions of the alleged "failures" of the new law codes to meet the requirements of social life, I summarize the "failures" the scholars reported before presenting my own findings and conclusions.

First, researchers said that the new civil and criminal codes did not fill gaps in the village legal system, but instead, by undermining existing Islamic customs and practices, the new secular law had introduced moral laxity and confusion into the villages. Village women were not waiting the traditional Islamic three months of *'idda* after widowhood or divorce to remarry. When the researcher pointed this out, villagers answered, "And who will feed the children and bake bread while we wait three months?" (Stirling 1957:30).

Researchers suggested that many provisions of the new codes also were not being followed. Women and men were marrying without going through a state-recognized civil marriage ceremony and they were remarrying without a "legal" divorce. Thus some couples were living in adulterous or bigamous relationships, according to Turkish law. This occurred because in the eyes of villagers the celebration of a village wedding (rather than registering a marriage in the district office) legitimated a marriage (Stirling 1965:209). Also, several fathers, who had given a widowed or divorced daughter in marriage to a husband in another village for reduced bride price, remarried her to a third man for an additional bride price during one of her visits home (Stirling 1957:31). Thus, researchers claimed the new Civil Code "left the village informal system totally unsupported, with no means of plugging the gaps at its weak points. Hence the system which the new laws were intended to abolish continued, but in less orderly form" (Stirling 1957:31–32).

Interpretation of 1950 statistics supported the claim that villagers were not registering their marriages with the state.

> According to the latest annual of statistics, the number of civil marriages performed each year in Turkey does not exceed 70,000. It is evident that these marriages, performed as they are in accordance with the provisions of the Civil Code, do not constitute the sum total of the marriages contracted in Turkey. In countries such as Rumania and Yugoslavia, which have about the same population as Turkey, the annual number of marriages is between 150,000 and 180,000. On the other hand, the census taken every five years in Turkey shows that the population increased by 9 percent during the same period. This, however, is a percentage to be found in countries with a large number of marriages. This fact alone proves that there are many couples living as man and wife who were never united as prescribed by the Civil Code. Naturally, children born out of these unions are illegitimate. (Timur 1957:34–35)

Assertions about "irregular unions" are substantiated by the fact that the Turkish National Assembly enacted laws legitimizing children of such unions in 1932, 1933, 1945, 1950, 1956, and 1965, 1974, and 1981. Yet, at least half the marriages were registered in the 1950s. At that time, a serviceman's paycheck and benefits earned in the Korean War turned out to be a great inducement to registering marriages with the correct state agency.

Another failure has been described with regard to the Land Distribution Commission's work in a wheat-farming village, founded in 1905. Striking a critical note, the researcher stated:

> [A]ll married men were eligible so long as they had not sold any land before, lived in the village permanently and would cultivate the land themselves. This meant that the married sons of wealthy households qualified as landless during the lifetime of the household head, since he is the only holder of land rights. Meanwhile, those villagers who had to sell some of their land through necessity could not benefit from the distribution. . . . If we add to the above the fact that the government-owned land which was the subject of distribution by the Commission was already occupied and cultivated by some of the villagers even though they had no legal rights over it, we can easily see that the distribution process generated more problems than it solved. (Kandiyoti 1975:209–10)

This critique of the work of the Land Distribution Agency seems too harsh. The Commission left only four totally landless households in the village; 29 percent of all villagers had been totally landless before. Whenever a government agency intervenes in traditional agrarian relations, it empowers some groups at the expense of others (see Starr:n.d.a.).

A final criticism concerned the authority system in the village. The newly created office of village *muhtar* (headman) was endowed with considerable power. Researchers have claimed that the headman was likely to use this power to his own advantage, making many of his neighbors dependent upon him and crippling his enemies. "Few men want to be *muhtar*, and those who do may want the office for the wrong reasons" (Stirling 1953:42). Stirling had stated that the formal authority structure linking village to district town was divorced from the traditional Turkish ranking hierarchy, with the effect of reducing effective leadership in the village:

> There is no one who can initiate corporate action, no one who can resist effectively anti-social activities, such as ploughing up common pasture land, no one who has the necessary power and prestige to settle disputes within the village, or to enforce traditional customs. The *muhtar* cannot rule the village because he has no prestige; the village elders, who have wealth and religious and moral standing cannot rule the village because they have no political power and no backing from the government. The result tends to be a stalemate. All that happens happens by direct orders from above, which often fail to win any spontaneous support from the village. (1953:42)

Written in a functionalist framework, Stirling's evocative description of village politics in 1949–1950 suggests notions of harmonious communities where individuals spontaneously followed norms of conduct that had evolved from years of village-wide interaction.

However, conflict models of village social life suggest other interpretations. For example, a conflict model implies that power adheres in all relationships, and therefore it does not seem strange that some members of a community would put their own interests first. In the two villages studied by Stirling in 1949–50, a land "grab" seemed in process, as some villagers acted on advantages that could be gained from new definitions of private property under the Turkish Civil Code. Also, Stirling's description implies that two "foci" of power existed in the village: state authorized leadership and traditional leadership based on wealth, religious and moral prestige. A village *muhtar* achieved his status through village-wide elections; the village elders through the prestige system. The most powerful and prestigious males in Stirling's villages perhaps saw little advantage in spending time in meetings with officials and in negotiating settlements with other villagers. The opposition between two sources of power produced a stalemate, not a vacuum.

But, by 1962 the situation seemed changed in much of rural Turkey, according to a large scale study undertaken by Frey and Roos (1967:1–12). Turkish members of their team conducted interviews with over 6,400 villagers in large and small villages encompassing much of the country. They report that three-quarters of the villagers reported the headman as the most "influential" villager, that the more isolated the village, the more influential the headman, and that most headmen tended to be older, more literate, and more affluent than their fellow villagers. Not only does this evidence contradict Stirling's, but it suggests that Stirling's critique of the effects of the new Code may have been limited. Stirling has described for us villages not with "gaping tears" in the social fabric, but more likely experiencing the normal processes of social change that occurred as isolated villages were incorporated into nation-state administrative and legal systems.

ASSESSMENTS AND FINDINGS FROM A REGIONAL STUDY OF SOCIAL CONTROL

A survey, conducted earlier than my research, found that the headman was politically significant in some villages, and less so in others (Scott 1968). In the village I studied in the mid–1960s (Starr 1978a), the *muhtar* was indeed a critical link in the rural administrative system, carrying information between the district capital in Bodrum and the village, and when administrators visited the village, he made sure they were suitably entertained. He was one of the wealthier and more important village men, and was linked by kinship and friendship to one of the two village faction leaders (Starr 1978a:104). Although the Village Law of 1924 empowered the village headman (*muhtar*) and his elected council members with dispute settling powers, in this village he did not hear disputes, because villagers chose not to bring their grievances to him or his council. But, moral laxity and chaos in no sense prevailed. Villagers had a number of ways of exercising social control, including gossip, slander, vengeance and ostracism. They also had informal mechanisms for expressing and resolving conflict, the most prevalent method being self-help. When parties were of different statuses or violence was feared, an intermediary would be brought into the process. Of one hundred and four episodes of "conflict behavior" collected in the village, fully sixty-six were handled within the village, while thirty-eight were taken outside (see Tables 5.1 and 5.2).[3]

Since the disputes handled within the village included theft, adultery, rape, slander, insult, and debt, it is evident that the village had a functioning social control system. The village system was based on negotiation and mediation among household heads, among patrons for their clients, and the ever present threat of invoking official state sanctions by calling in the gendarmerie. This system constituted a semi-autonomous, normative folk law field of action that followed neither long term customary rules nor the norms of the "received" and "reconstituted" law of the nation. For the most part, this village law system supported ongoing, multiplex social relations, thus upholding the prevailing cultural system of male control of females, landowners over tenant farmers, and the older generation over the younger one. When an individual wished to escape the inherent inequality of these values, he/she pressed claims outside the village.

I found that the District Courts in Bodrum provided some relief from village inequities, especially for women against men (Starr 1978a; see also Starr 1984,

Table 5.1
Disputants Interacting with Remedy Procedures

	1	2	3	4	5	Totals
Within Village						
Agency						
1. Muhtar						0
2. Council*					1	1
3. Imam						0
4. Gendarme		1	2	2		5
5. Outside mediator, in village			1			1
6. Representative		3	2			5
7. Messenger		1	1			2
8. Healer		1				1
Self-Help						
9. Public Confrontation	2	7	3	2		14
10. Private Confrontation		11	7			18
11. Gossip		8	2			10
12. No Action		3		1		4
13. Avoidance		1	1			2
14. Breaking Contract		2				2
15. Refuse Help		1				1
Totals	2	39	19	5	1	66
Outside Village						
Agency						
16. Turkish Prime Minister**	1					1
17. Director of Bodrum		3				3
18. Court	3	4	4	6		17
19. Subdistrict Gendarmes			1			1
20. Harbor Authority, Bodrum			1			1
21. Appellate Courts, Ankara			4			4
22. Visit to Appellate Court, Ankara		1				1
23. Gendarmes Commander, Mugla		1				1
24. Police, Bodrum		2			1	3
25. Director of Province, Mugla		1				1
26. Gendarmes Commander, Bodrum		2				2
27. Gendarmes Commander, Izmir				1		1
28. Police, Izmir				1		1
29. High Criminal Court, Mugla		1				1
Totals	4	15	10	8	1	38

Sources: 1. Witnessed by anthropologist; 2. Happening during fieldwork; 3. Told by a principle from past; 4. Informant concerning distant past, 3 or more years; 5. Informant concerning recent past, 1–3 years ago.

*Reportedly happened 15 years ago. Told by only one informant, unable to substantiate.

**Letter to Turkish Prime Minister.

Table 5.2
Legal Level of Remedy Procedures Invoked

		Within Village		
Two-Party Negotiations			51	
Third Parties				
Messenger			2	
Healer			1	
Council			1	
Gendarmes			5	
Representatives			5	
Mediator			1	Total 66
		Outside Village		
Third Parties				
Subdistrict			1	
Gendarmes*	1			
District (Bodrum)			26	
Officials		5		
District Director	3			
Gendarmes Commander	2			
Law Enforcement Agencies		4		
Police	3			
Harbor Authority	1			
Court		17		
Province (Mugla)			3	
Officials		2		
Province Director	1			
Gendarmes Commander*	1			
Law Enforcement Agencies		0		
Court (High Criminal)		1		
Capital (Ankara)			6	
Officials		2		
Prime Minister of Turkey	1			
Appellate Court Officials	1			
Law Enforcement Agencies		0		
Appellate Courts		4		
Largest nearest city (Izmir)			2	
Law Enforcement Agencies				
Police	1			
Gendarmes	1			

*Here we follow a village distinction between going to the gendarmerie station to report an incident and going to a gendarme commander or writing him a letter to report an incident. In the former case, villagers are interacting with an agency; in the latter, with a Turkish official.

1985a, 1985b, and 1989). In addition, the district courts promoted what can broadly be called the norms of capitalism. Since village land had become a commodity sold on the market, arguments over land and houses, as well as many routine divisions of property at the death of a patriarch, found their way to court.

Pertinent to the debate about the acceptance of the new Turkish legal system are findings from an intermittent seventeen-year record of the dockets of the Bodrum Law Courts. Cases were collected at all four courts: High and Lower Civil Courts, Middle and Lower Criminal Courts. Located in the town of Bodrum, the court served a jurisdiction of 30,000 town dwellers and villagers. The thirty villages varied in size from 193 to 2,000 people, while Bodrum town had a population of 5,200 people in 1967.

The courts did not take all cases which were brought there. Some were rejected because the initial paperwork was incorrect and needed to be redone; others because there were no witnesses; still others because the problem was not sufficiently developed to be considered a "legal" problem. It did not contain an issue which could be classified as falling under a codified or statutory rule. Still others, by far the majority, were rejected because the problem needed first to be brought to the attention of the agency where the "alleged" offending individual worked. Complaints against police, gendarmerie, and bureaucrats fall into this category. Only after a decision was reached there, could an issue be introduced at court (Starr 1978: 112–13).

In criminal cases, the case might be terminated at either the gendarmes' station or police headquarters. If the case continued, the next stage was the Public Prosecutor's Office, where a decision was made as to sufficient evidence for prosecution. Cross-complaints were also introduced here, and judges tried to hear such cases together. Also, sixty-six cases concerning private land claims against the government Forestry Department were being held in abeyance until a special judge could come to Bodrum to hear these cases as a group.

Finding 1. Pool and I (Starr and Pool 1974) found that between 1950 and 1967 the courts showed "no substantial and consistent changes in the volume of cases," and that the use of the courts by gendarmerie, police, government agencies, and private citizens was stable rather than growing during those decades. Thus a shift in favor of the formal institutions of an avowedly secular government was not in evidence from the raw court data.

Finding 2. Second-order trends confirmed previous impressions of a shift in prosecutions in relation to a shift in political party power.

Finding 3. Certain prosecutions—such as failure to send children to school and decisions favoring debtors over creditors—changed with the political party in power but contrary to our expectations, the frequency of prosecution in general was not responsive to changes in the political party (Starr and Pool 1974:542).

We were especially interested in "sensitive cases"—those that the Turkish national government would take an interest in—because they challenged the existing social order that the government was promoting. The most sensitive cases of all, those involving political subversion or violation of laws against religious indoctrination, were tried in secret and thus did not appear in the docket.

PENETRATION ACROSS SPACE

How far into the countryside did the government judicial system have an impact? Our hypothesis that the volume of cases handled in court would vary directly with the nearness, ease, and accessibility to the court was not confirmed. Ease of access was defined as equivalent to road quality and access to public transportation (Starr and Pool 1974: 566). There was next to no association between distance from the town of Bodrum and the number of cases per capita from a village. (This was based on an aggregate number of cases from villages for which we had complete docket records, based on the village of the principal defendant. I did not have information as to the place where the dispute took place; often in criminal cases little information concerning the complaining party was available). Both very central and very remote villages were represented among those with unusually high, unusually low and about average per capita case volumes. Indeed, the village with the lowest per capita case volume was the second closest village to the town of Bodrum. Thus court data gave no support to the idea that remote villages are less touched by and less responsive to the state's judicial alternatives.

Modifying the nearness-to-the-court hypothesis to take into account the presence of gendarmes' stations did not rescue it either. In fact, villages within two kilometers of a gendarmes' station had a lower combined case volume (.0084), while villages more remote had a higher one (.133)—just the opposite of the hypothesis. We concluded that the presence of the gendarmes' station kept some disputes from going to court. The intensive data, collected in one village, on this point are inconclusive: gendarmerie both made arrests (and thus initiated cases) and also refused to do the paperwork (thus discouraging certain "criminal" complaints), especially when familiar with the circumstances of the parties involved (Starr 1978a:208, 267).

Villages' aggregated per capita caseloads varied wildly, ranging from .15 to .02. Yet village size was found to be practically unrelated to per capita case volume.

Even the town of Bodrum did not have a substantially different case volume from the villages in its district. The village with the heaviest case volume (.15) was less than Bodrum town's (.17 per capita). But Bodrum ought to have the largest relative number of cases, as here defined, because in any lawsuit where a government agency was sued, the place was listed as Bodrum town, since its headquarters was located there. When adjustments were made for this distortion, Bodrum's case volume looked similar to the surrounding villages. Subtracting all cases in which a principal defendant was an agency gave Bodrum a case volume slightly lower than the aggregated case volume for all villages: .099 as opposed to .118.

Bodrum's volume of cases involving physical violence was equal to the average volume of such cases originating in the villages in the district. The volume of physical violence cases aggregated for all villages near gendarmes' stations is scarcely higher than that of the town: .017 as compared to .014. Villages not close to gendarmes' stations has an aggregate number of .016. Thus explanations in terms of center-periphery gradients do not suffice. Rather, the data suggest that the new judicial system has been structured so as to have a broad impact on both urban and rural residents of the district with significant limits on access in regard to civilian complaints against civil servants.

The question therefore arises: What kinds of civilian-civilian cases do and do not get heard in court? Let us take a brief look at cases of two major kinds.

THE COURT AND INHERITANCE CASES

Our data did confirm the presence of a factor mentioned by Stirling: the reluctance of villagers to settle inheritance cases through the courts, because of, according to Stirling, the undue speed and finality with which courts handled what ought to have been a flexible and gradual matter (Stirling 1957:26–27). As reflected in the Bodrum docket, inheritance cases were indeed handled faster than—more than twice as fast as—all cases put together. The median inheritance lasted twenty-nine and one-half days from first hearing to last, while the median of all cases lasted sixty-eight and one-half days. (About fifteen to twenty days usually passed between hearings in a case). Nevertheless, inheritance cases were by far the most numerous. In inheritance cases, judges were often confronted with problems relating to multiple scattered plots that needed to be divided among a score or more of relatives. There might have been no dispute or quarrel among the kin. Rather the issue was to find equivalency: what was the fairest division (among seven kin) of one irrigated tangerine orchard, three nonirrigated fields, and a plot of dry grazing land? A further complication was that kin may have differing rights to the land. Under the new inheritance law, a widow of the deceased was accorded one-fourth of the estate, the remainder to be divided among children, regardless of sex. When three generations were asserting claims, outside assistance was frequently needed. Litigants in inheritance cases were almost always kin, and it was not unusual for one sibling to be living elsewhere, in another city or outside Turkey. The case was postponed until all could assemble for the court hearing, or at least could communicate with the court.

Formerly, Turkish settlers did not hold land as private property but received land and lots as members of kin groups. Under the new Civil law system, land is held individually. The transition between the two different land holding systems meant that many householders in 1965 did not have a state-recognized title to land. The court was awarding title to farm land or house lots to any person who could bring two witnesses in an uncontested suit to demonstrate that he had lived in a particular house or farmed a certain field for twenty years. A person could also provide proof of ownership by demonstrating tax payments for eleven years. In addition to the district courts, a government cadastre team was awarding title to the tobacco fields to the east of Bodrum. Five villages had been completed in two-years' time (Starr 1985).

WOMEN'S USE OF THE COURTS

There were one hundred thirty-eight divorce and twenty-seven adultery cases heard by the Bodrum courts out of the 3,350 cases in our records. Given the extreme dishonor males suffer from wives' adulterous behavior and given the custom of dealing with such behavior directly (Starr 1978a:154–57), even this number (of which 80 percent were brought against wives) must be considered substantial. Although some scholars might think that a cuckolded husband now has greater sanctions to use against his adulterous wife since he can have her jailed, I argue that taking her to court is more humane than the traditional remedy of beating her into submission. Furthermore, in court he needed to bring charges against the wife and her lover. Usually in the course of five to seven hearings stretched out over six months' time, the husband's temper cooled and he dropped charges. Although he wanted to have her lover jailed, he frequently came to realize he needed his wife's services. Thus we concluded that the district courts were providing greater opportunity for women to obtain their legal but often withheld rights and privileges (Starr and Pool 1974:552). (This is analyzed more closely in Starr 1984, 1985b, 1989, and in press).

Women file twice as many "routine" suits in the Bodrum courts as do men. While only 4 percent of the women filing such suits failed to appear when their cases were scheduled, 8 percent of the men filing routine cases failed to appear. Women not only filed more, but they won more. Of "routine" suits which reached decisions, 98 percent of the ones brought by women were won, as opposed to 93 percent of those brought by men. Of 138 divorce cases heard from 1965 through 1967, almost half were brought by wives. With the exception of adultery, the types of cases brought by women against men did not differ greatly from those brought by men against women or between members of the same sex, except that women sued men more often for child support.

If these statistics suggest that women recognize the courts as one of their few protections, it was also clear that the willingness to act upon this recognition had been growing gradually through the 1950s and 1960s. If we assume that actual offenses by men against women did not appreciably decrease during that period, we see that complaints by women in the Middle Criminal Court constituted twice as large a proportion of all cases in 1967 as in 1950 (see Table 5.3).

CONCLUSION AND FUTURE PROSPECTS OF SECULARISM

The reception of European law in Turkey, which was judged only partially accepted in 1955, had indeed become a reality by the late 1960s in western

Table 5.3
Sex of Principal Complainant and Principal Defendant in Middle Criminal Court Cases*

Cases Involving:	1950	1957	1965	1966	1967
M against F	5	4	11	8	4
M against M	12	24	37	40	32
F against F	2	3	4	9	5
F against M	3	9	12	21	16
F against M, as % of all above	14%	23%	19%	27%	28%
Total of above cases	22	40	64	78	57

*Reprinted from Starr and Pool 1974:553.

Turkey, as this regional study of social control demonstrates. The length of time during which aspects of European law had been "received" in Turkey, commencing in 1839, suggests a comparatively gradual process of change, until Ataturk's radical reforms of the 1920s. An immensely popular leader, Ataturk was wholeheartedly endorsed by Western-oriented political, economic, and legal elites. His ideas were supported by a well-trained, loyal, army, the civil bureaucracy, the intelligentsia, and the youth. His charisma and willingness to use coercion to achieve desired ends were aspects of Turkish politics that are noticeably lacking in the 1950s, 1960s, and 1970s.

To begin to suggest an answer to the question of the future of secular law, it is necessary to widen the inquiry and review briefly the political realities in which secular law has functioned since the early 1970s.

Increasing outbursts of violence, and antagonisms between rival political groups gained public attention from the early 1970s.[4] From 1978 to mid–1980 mob violence was the hallmark of urban street life in much of Turkey. University campuses were in turmoil or closed. Although individual criminal acts from mob or terrorist violence were processed through the courts and punished, the courts had no real effect in dampening public terrorist activities. Much of the violence has been traced to extremist political groups, characterized as Marxist-Leninist leftists and Islamic rightists (Yalman 1973:156). The latter appear to be long enduring in their protest. Ataturk's efforts to establish a loyal opposition, for example, continually failed because of Islamic fundamentalist groups.[5] By 1970 the memory of the treachery of Islamic leaders at the end of the Ottoman Empire had faded, and many "yearned" for Islam to become a part of political life again (Yalman 1973:155).

Much of the attempt to revitalize Islam by the right had involved secret organizing. For example, from about 1970 onward, reports surfaced of a "Colonel" Turkes who was training a clandestine rightist army of twenty thousand men near the city of Adana in south-central Turkey. Known as the Gray Wolves, they claimed responsibility for the major killings and bombings by the right between 1968 and 1980 (Kifner 1980a: 1, A8).[6] In a bloodless coup in 1971, the Turkish army took control of the Parliament and attempted to create stability by destroying the coherence of the left. But this allowed rightist groups like Turkes's to gain and consolidate power.[7] The Gray Wolves hope to return to an Islamic state and to develop pan-Turkish unity. During the 1970s they emerged as active organizers among Turkish workers in Europe, using techniques of terror and assassination against opponents and informers.

An even more important association of Islamic fundamentalists was the National Salvation Party (*Milli Selamet Partesi*), headed by Erbakan. The NSP emerged from the 1973 election as the third most important political party. These election results demonstrated that religious issues did influence voter choices, and according to B. Toprak, that religion "can be a political issue and yet invite no cause for alarm" (Toprak 1981: 96). In addition to its theological emphasis, the NSP stressed rapid industrialization. Between 1973 and 1978 the NSP played a part in Turkey's coalition governments.

Between 1978 and September 1980 the intensity of the violence between rightist and leftist groups increased, despite the imposition of martial law in most districts throughout Turkey. Estimates stated that between 2,000 and 5,000 people died in terrorist bombings, assassinations, and gun fights among extremist groups in the first nine months of 1980 (New York Times Index: 1446). For six months prior to the military take-over in September 1980 (the third in thirty years since free elections began in 1950), the government had been at a virtual standstill. The Turkish army considers itself the "guardian" of Turkish democracy. After taking control in 1960 and 1971, its leaders soon returned power to civilian politicians by holding free elections.

In 1980 the Demirel government became paralyzed because its coalition government depended upon the support of an Islamic fundamentalist party, the NSP, which was "agitating for a shift in policy away from the West and toward the Muslim world" (Gwertzman 1980:1). On September 12, 1980 General Evren, four other generals, and one admiral seized power in a bloodless coup and formed a cabinet with Evren at its head. Martial law was declared nationwide. The parliament and all political parties were disbanded.

Under Evren's government, a National Security Council was set up. A new Constitution was drafted. Published on October 18, 1982, three weeks later, on November 7 the Turkish people voted for this constitution and also supported General Evren as president of the Republic. In the next year new laws governing the formation of political parties and elections were enacted. Only new political parties would be recognized, and no former politicians were allowed to run for public office or play a role in a party. To avoid the fragmentary, splinter group politics of the 1970s, a party needed to have an established organization in thirty-four of the sixty-seven provinces of Turkey and at least thirty founding members (*Turkey Today*, Oct. 1983:3). To be seated in parliament, a party needed to receive 10 percent of the national vote. For example, to obtain a three-seat constituency, a party must reach 33 percent of the vote, in a four-seat constituency 25 percent and so on. Without 10 percent of a national vote, no member of their party would be seated (*The Economist* 1988:8). Enacted as a safeguard against the need of the party in power to form unwise coalitions, most scholars of contemporary Turkish politics accepted it as a necessary way to protect civilian government from anarchy on the one hand and military rule on the other.

Three parties ran in the 1983 election: the Populist party, the National Democratic Party and the Motherland Party. The leader of the conservative Motherland Party (ANAP), Turgot Ozal, won a majority in Parliament in the general elections held November 6, 1983 (Howe 1983: A3). His platform stressed giving "new momentum to the nation's stagnant economy." Although Ozal was not the choice of President Evren, the army did not interfere in election results. Ozal's party won 212 of 400 seats in the National Assembly, and Ozal was asked to form a government and to assume the position of prime minister.

Democratic processes are evident in many areas of Turkish life now. For example, in early autumn 1987 the public was offered a chance to vote on a nationwide referendum to allow former politicians to create political parties and stand for election. Ozal's party campaigned against the referendum; all the other newly formed parties campaigned for a "yes" vote. On September 7 by a very narrow margin the political ban was lifted, thus marking only a small defeat for Ozal (49.5 percent against, 50.5 percent for). This allowed former Prime Ministers, Suleyman Demirel and Bulent Ecevit, to run for political office, an event not possible since 1980 (Cowell 1987:3). Ozal quickly announced general elections, and the leading contenders were Ozal's ANAP party, Demirel's True Path party (NYP), and the son of Ataturk's successor, Erdal Inonu's Social Democratic party (SHP). The election was held soon thereafter, and Ozal was restored to power.

With 99 percent of the twenty-six million votes counted, Ozal's centralist Motherland party won 36.3 percent and 292 seats in the expanded 450 member National Assembly. The Social Democratic populist party received 24.8 percent of the vote, thus winning 99 seats in parliament and doubling its strength to become the main opposition; the True Path party won 19 percent and 59 seats, while four other parties failed to meet the 10 percent minimum requirement and thus placed no candidates in the National Assembly (Demirsar 1987:33). This vote was an affirmation of public confidence in Ozal's economic and political policies.

Since the election inflation has run wild, even though Ozal and Rusdu Saracoglu, head of the Turkish Central Bank, took strong measures to curb it in February 1988 (*The Economist* June 2, 1988:11).

In pondering whether Turkish political life will be stable in the future, astute observers are uneasy. They note that an escaped criminal, a known member of the Grey Wolves, shot Ozal in the hand as he was making a political speech in June 1988, and that the gunman probably did not act alone, because voluntary associations are extremely strong in Turkey. Also significant is the coalition formed in June 1988 between the Islamists in parliament, and right-wing nationalists. This coalition of Islam and the far right gained a large majority of seats on the decision-making body of the National Assembly (*The Economist* June 25, 1988:51). It suggests that values of the right and Islamic fundamentalists will continue to be influential in contemporary Turkish politics.

Turkish democratic practices are once more in place although human rights are not yet a significantly developed notion in Turkish democracy. Similar to the uneasy relationship between Ataturk's government and Islamic groups during the period of one party rule (1923–1950), the compromises that are likely to develop will show at least the implicit mark of Islamic fundamentalists who demand a return to Islamic law in an Islamic nation.

NOTES

This chapter was conceived and written in 1980. It was briefly updated in February 1986 and June 1988, based mainly upon field research in Turkey during summers of 1985 and 1987 respectively.

1. The regularized process was governed by written rules and codes of procedures. There were established ways of opening cases, assessing evidence and arriving at decisions. There were also established ways of rejecting cases and/or terminating cases before decisions were reached. A regularized process governs the training and certification of judges and public prosecutors. It involves yearly checkups to see judges are hearing and deciding cases by the standards, set by the Ministry of Justice. For instance, an Inspector spent ten days at the Bodrum courts in July 1967 looking over records.

2. Some writers report on the effectiveness of councils and the village headperson in resolving village disputes (Kudat 1972; Frey and Roos, 1967:8–9 et passim; Scott 1968). Others suggest they were ineffective (Stirling 1960, 1953:42, 1965:254–57; Yasa 1957:150). I found the village council ineffective; in fact, it did not function. The village head was an effective administrator, but he did not perform his dispute-settling role.

3. Also see Starr (1978b, 1978c, 1984, and 1985b) and Abel (1979).

4. For discussions of secular-Islamic clashes, see Davison (1968:16) and Leder (1976: n.8, n.9, n.10). For discussions of incidents which started this current round of violence, see references to the incident at Maras in December 1978 (Kifner 1980a:A8).

5. Concession to Islamic groups include: *muftis* (Islamic jurists) and *vaiz* (Islamic teachers), salaried by the state, and sent to county seats throughout Turkey (Leder 1976:29), as well as an extensive government-financed rural mosque-building program. Between 1950 and 1964 it is estimated that about 21,000 mosques were built (Landau 1974:174–75; see also Starr 1978a:19). Religious education as an elective subject was restored in primary schools after 1946. Religious schools offered a Turkish high school education but spent nearly half the curriculum in study of Arabic and the *Quran*. These religious schools were opened by the state and state financed (Landau 1974:174). The faculty of theology at Ankara University was founded in the late 1940s and received considerable state assistance in its building and hiring program in the early 1950s. One of its functions was to prepare qualified religious teachers for state schools (Landau 1974:172). Arabic call to prayer was restored. Muslim tombs were reopened to the general public for worship. In 1979 Prime Minister Demirel allowed

prayer once again in an annex of the Hagia Sophia, something which had not occurred since 1935 when Ataturk decreed the world-famous mosque a national museum (Howe 1980:3).

6. Two of their secret assignation groups are called the "Turkish Revenge Brigade" and "The Liberation Army of Inflamed Turks" (Kifner 1980a:A8).

7. For a penetrating analysis of the political parties and their politics in the 1960s and early 1970s, see Landau (1974).

REFERENCES

Abel, Richard L. 1979. "The Rise of Capitalism and the Transformation of Disputing: From Confrontation over Honor to Competition for Property." *UCLA Law Review* 27: 223–55.

"Ambassador Visits Six Cities on Major Speaking Tour. Speeches, Interviews March 12-day Trip." 1983. *Turkey Today* (Oct.) 54:1–3.

Austin, Anthony. 1980. "Soviet's Muslims: Quietly Rising Tide of Uncertainty." *New York Times* (13 Jan.), p. 14.

Cowell, Alan. 1987. "Slim Vote Ends Turkish Political Ban." *New York Times* (13 Jan.), p. 14.

Davison, Roderic. 1963. *Reform in the Ottoman Empire, 1856-1876*. Princeton: Princeton University Press.

———. 1968. *Turkey*. New York: Prentice-Hall.

Demirsar, Metin. 1987. "Turkish Vote Gives Premier Fresh Mandate." *Wall Street Journal* (1 Dec.):33.

Feroze, Muhammad Rashid. 1962. "Family Laws of the Turkish Republic." *Islamic Studies: Journal of the Central Institute of Islamic Research* 1: 131–47.

Findley, Carter. 1986. "Mahkama." *Encyclopaedia of Islam*, VI (new ed.), pp. 1–11.

Frey, Frederick W. and Leslie L. Roos. 1967. *Social Structure and Community Development in Rural Turkey: Village and Elite Leadership Relations*. Report No. 10. Rural Development Research Project. Center for International Studies. Cambridge: Massachusetts Institute of Technology.

Gwertzman, Bernard. 1980. "Military Takeover in Turkey Reported: No Sign of Violence." *New York Times* (12 Sept.), p. 1.

Howe, Marvine. 1980. "Turkey Faces Dilemma Over the Sacred and Secular." *New York Times* (31 Aug.), p. 3.

"Islam More Firmly Entrenched than Ever in Iran." 1985. The *New York Times* (Oct.), p. 1.

Kandiyoti, Deniz. 1975. "Social Change and Social Stratification in a Turkish Village." *Journal of Peasant Studies* 2 (2): 206–19.

Kanun Turkiye Cumhuriyeti Anasasi (Turkish Constitution). 1982. Ankara: T. C. Resmi Gazete.

Karpat, K. H. 1959. *Turkey's Politics: The Transition to a Multi-Party System*. Princeton: University Press.

Kifner, John 1980a. "New Turkish Regime Takes into Custody a Rightist Leader." *New York Times* (15 Sept.), p. 1.

———. 1980b. "Turkish Coup Chiefs Make Vow to Bring Stability to Nation." *New York Times* (13 Sept.), p. 1.

———. 1980c. "Turkey's Military Rulers Plan Civilian Cabinet This Week." *New York Times* (17 Sept.) , p. 3.

Kili, Suna. 1969. *Kemalism*. Istanbul: Robert College, School of Business Administration and Economics.

Kubali, H. N. 1957. "Modernization and Secularization as Determining Factors in Reception in Turkey." *International Social Science Bulletin* 9(1):65–69.

Kudat, Ayse. 1972. "Images of Power." *American Anthropologist* 74(3): 639–57.

Landau, Jacob M. 1974. *Radical Politics in Modern Turkey*. Leiden: E. J. Brill.

Leder, Arnold. 1976. *Catalysts of Change: Marxist versus Muslim in a Turkish Community*. Austin, Texas: Center for Middle Eastern Studies.

Lewis, Bernard. 1966. *The Emergence of Modern Turkey*. London: Oxford University Press. First published 1961.

Mardin, Serif. 1973. "Center-Periphery Relations: A Key to Turkish Politics?" *Daedelus* 120 (1): 169–90.

New York Times Index. A Book of Records. *Current Series*, vol. 68:1444–48.

Ostrorog, Count Leon. 1927. *The Angora Reform*. London: University of London Press, Ltd.

"Ready for Europe? A Survey of Turkey." 1988. *The Economist* (2 June):1–30.

"Reception of Foreign Law in Turkey." 1957. International Social Science Bulletin, vol. 9:7–81.

Rustow, D. A. 1957. "Politics and Islam in Turkey 1920–1935." In R. N. Frye (ed.) *Islam and the West*. The Hague: Mouton & Co.

Scott, Richard B. 1968. *The Village Headman in Turkey: A Case Study*. Institute of Public Administration for Turkey and the Middle East. Ankara: Sevinc Matbassi.

Starr, June. 1978a. *Dispute Settlement in Rural Turkey: An Ethnography of Law*. Leiden: E. J. Brill.

———. 1978b. "Negotiations: A Pre-Law Stage in Rural Turkish Disputes." In P. H. Gulliver (ed.): *Cross Examinations: Essays in Memory of Max Gluckman*. Leiden: E. J. Brill.

———. 1978c. "Turkish Village Disputing Behavior." In Laura Nader and Harry F. Todd, Jr. (eds.). *The Disputing Process—Law in Ten Societies*. New York: Columbia University Press, pp. 122–151.

———. 1981. "Strengths of the Anthropological Method in the Study of Law." *UCLA Law Review* 28(3): 591–604.

———. 1984. "The Legal and Social Transformation of Rural Women in Aegean Turkey." In Renee Hirschon (ed.). *Women and Property/Women as Property*. London: Croom Helm, pp. 92–116.

———. 1985a. "*Adliye. The Ethnography of a Rural Turkish Law Court*" Color video. Available from the author.

———. 1985b. "Folk Law in Official Courts of Turkey." In *People's Law and State Law: The Bellagio Papers*. Anthony Allott and Gordon R. Woodman (eds.). Dordrecht, Holland: Foris Publications, pp. 123–141.

———. 1989. "The Role of Turkish Secular Law in Changing the Lives of Rural Muslim Women, 1950–1970." *Law and Society Review* 23(3):497–523.

———. in press. "Law as Metaphor: From Islamic Courts to the Palace of Justice." Albany: State University of New York Press.

———. n.d. "Indian Agrarian Hierarchies and Land Reform Policies, 1948–1979." Paper presented at Third World Development Seminar, Warwick University, England, spring 1982.

Starr, J., and Pool. 1974. "The Impact of a Legal Revolution in Rural Turkey." *Law and Society Review* 8(4): 533–560.

Stirling, Paul. 1953. "Social Ranking in a Turkish Village." *British Journal of Sociology* 4: 31–43.

———. 1957. "Land, Marriage and the Law in Turkish Villages." *International Social Science Bulletin* 9 (1): 21–33.

———. 1960. "A Death and a Youth Club: Feuding in a Turkish Village." *Anthropological Quarterly* 33: 51–75.

———. 1965. *Turkish Village*. New York: John Wiley and Sons.

———. 1974. "Cause, Knowledge and Change: Turkish Village Revisited." In John Davis (ed.): *Choice and Change: Essays in Honour of Lucy Mair*. London: Athlone Press, pp. 191-229.

Timur, H. 1957. "Civil Marriage in Turkey: Difficulties, Causes and Remedies." *International Social Science Bulletin* 9: 34–36.

"Turks Gave Assurances Before the Coup." 1980. *New York Times*. (13 Sept.), p. 5.

Tyabji, Badr-ud-Din. 1979. "Islamic Resurgence." *New Delhi* 2(7) (9 July): 8–11.

Yalman, Nur. 1973. "Some Observations on Secularism in Islam: The Cultural Revolution in Turkey." *Daedalus* 120(1): 139–168.

Yasa, Ibrahim. 1957. *Hasanoglan: Socio-Economic Structure of a Turkish Village*. Ankara: Public Administration Institute for Turkey and the Middle East, Yeni Matbaa.

6

REINSTATING ISLAMIC CRIMINAL LAW IN LIBYA

Ann Elizabeth Mayer

One of the most consistent manifestations of Westernizing influences on Middle Eastern societies since the mid-nineteenth century has been the adoption of laws of European inspiration. First to experience the military and economic expansion of nineteenth century Europe, Egypt and Turkey were also the first Middle Eastern countries to adopt laws on the European model.[1] Although progress elsewhere was uneven, by the 1950s Westernization had proceeded to the point that codified laws from continental Europe had come to predominate throughout the Middle East. The Arabian Peninsula constituted the chief exception since it alone had escaped Western domination and influence.

The law that was the official norm in the Muslim world at the time of the importation of Western codes was Islamic law or *shari'a* law. While *shari'a* law was theoretically supreme and controlling on all legal questions, in application it was in fact often supplemented or even supplanted by laws derived from custom or administrative practice. However, traditional governments were careful not to challenge the basic premise of the *shari'a* system: the law-making function belongs exclusively to Allah and Muslim rulers are bound to follow faithfully what Allah once laid down as rules for human conduct.

The adoption of laws of Western origin was opposed and criticized on religious grounds by many Muslims in the Middle East. Islamic clerics, learned in the traditional Islamic sciences, were particularly attached to *shari'a* law and hostile to a development that threatened to end their long domination of the study of law and the control of legal institutions. That the provenance of these newly borrowed laws was European exacerbated the negative reaction. Europe had not only shown itself hostile to Islam over the centuries; from the time of Napoleon's invasion of Egypt the Middle East had experienced Western imperialism, so that there were political grounds for objecting to the appropriation of European law. In contrast to the negative reaction of traditional Muslims, Westernizing elites in Middle Eastern societies saw the importation of European law as a necessary part of an overall attempt to modernize their societies.

Imported European law was adopted in areas where there was in the official perception the greatest need for law reform and where *shari'a* law was least developed. Commercial law, procedural law, and penal law were therefore among the first areas to reflect the reception of European law.[2] Partly because they were less crucial to the initial stages of modernization and also because the relevant *shari'a* rules were particularly firmly grounded in the Quran and the *sunna* (accounts of the Prophet Muhammad), other spheres of activity continued to be subject to *shari'a* law. Among these the most important was the area of personal status, which remains regulated by *shari'a* rules, albeit sometimes modified ones, everywhere in the Middle East but Turkey.[3]

The general pattern in the Westernizing process was to move from a *shari'a*-based system to a dual one; certain subjects remained reserved for the traditional courts while others were allotted to courts run along Western lines and in which Western law was controlling. This stage was followed in most countries by one in which the legal system was unified into a single system of courts from which the special jurisdiction of the *shari'a* courts was eliminated.

The resentments and antagonisms caused by Westernizing the content of the law, displacing the *shari'a* courts, and retiring the religiously trained scholars who had staffed them have been channeled into many Islamic opposition movements which have advocated a return to Islamic values and revival of *shari'a* law.[4]

Until the success of the Libyan and Iranian revolutions, however, the advocacy of restoration of *shari'a* law was limited to opposition groups. Governmental and professional elites remained committed to the secular legal systems. After the revolutions in Libya and Iran one saw a new phenomenon. The revolutionary regimes in these countries were critical of the European borrowings and sponsored campaigns to revive *shari'a* law.[5] Colonel Mu'ammar al-Qaddafi made much of his commitment to reinstate Islamic law after he came to power on September 1, 1969, and to abrogate such existing law as was in conflict with it. In the process he won an international reputation as an Islamic fundamentalist. However, as this chapter indicates, upon examination of the accomplishments of his official policy of reinstating Islamic law and contrasting these with what has happened in Iran since 1978, one is tempted to conclude that Qaddafi's regime has been less interested in seeing *shari'a* rules implemented than in acquiring political legitimacy and popularity by espousing the cause of Islamic law. It seems that reinstating Islamic law was not an end in itself in Libya but a product of an attempt to become associated with goals that were meaningful to the masses.[6]

LIBYA: THE HISTORICAL BACKGROUND OF THE REVOLUTION

Why there was a particular need for Qaddafi to present himself in the role of the restorer of Islam can be traced to the country's peculiar background and the nature of the regime Qaddafi was replacing.

In the 1950s Libya was still one of the poorest and most backward countries in the world. There was widespread illiteracy and a lack of an infrastructure for development (Golino 1970: 339). Tribal organization remained strong, and a large portion of the populace lived as impoverished pastoral nomads. Aside from a small European Christian population in the urban centers, the population consisted of Arabs and Arabized Berbers who were virtually all Sunni Muslims, and large numbers of these were fervently devout.

Libyans, especially those in the eastern half of the country, were very much under the influence of the Sanusiyya, a religious organization which became a vehicle for political action. The Sanusi fraternities were headed by descendants of the founder of the order, Muhammad ibn 'Ali as-Sanusi (1787–1859), and they played an important role in the resistance against the Italian invasion of 1911 and Italy's later colonial presence. The Sanusiyya espoused what might be loosely called "fundamentalist" Islamic doctrines.

The Italian era brought great suffering to the majority of Libyans, who welcomed Italy's withdrawal from Libya in the throes of World War II. King Idris, the exiled leader of the Sanusiyya, emerged as the most viable leader for the new state when Libya attained independence in 1951. An austere and pious figure, King Idris called upon a combination of political and religious loyalties bound up with his leadership of the Sanusiyya.

In the 1950s the great oil boom in Libya began to have an impact, first slowly and then at a rapidly accelerating pace in the 1960s. With it came the disruption and dislocation that accompany a sudden, vast influx of wealth and foreign technology into a traditional society. Once one of the poorest countries in the world, Libya became the world's third largest oil producer, taking in revenues that its rudimentary economy and small population could not readily absorb.

In this turbulent period, a small group of "Free Officers" under Qaddafi's leadership overthrew the monarch and established a republican regime imbued with Nasserist ideas. Qaddafi, an army officer from a Bedouin tribe in the Gulf of Sirte, and his fellow officers were unknown to the public. They were therefore faced with the need to establish their legitimacy. Moreover, unlike such rulers as King Farouk of Egypt or the Shah of Iran, both of whom had forfeited Islamic legitimacy by the time they were overthrown, King Idris had maintained his legitimacy in traditional terms. Against this background the revolutionary regime sought to prove itself more Islamic than the monarchy it had supplanted.

As part of its first steps toward modernization, Libya under King Idris had imported codified laws from Egypt that were based on French law. These were applied within a dual system of courts in which *shari'a* courts retained their special juridiction over cases still arising under Islamic law (U.S. Government Printing Office 1973: 150). *Shari'a* law of the Maliki law school continued to be applied by these courts in matters of personal status. Qaddafi took the position that this importation of European law by King Idris meant that *shari'a* law had been abandoned by his regime. By promising to reinstate *shari'a* law and to abrogate the European laws that violated Islamic principles, Qaddafi was able to associate his regime with the defense of Islamic values.

Qaddafi then exploited opportunities that allowed him to pose as the defender of *shari'a* law. For example, it was largely due to Qaddafi's pressure that the October 28, 1971 Constitution of the Federation of Arab Republics (which was not implemented due to a political falling out between the prospective members) included a provision that *shari'a* law was to be the main source of legislation in the Federation. When Egyptians, whose country was showing some hesitation about the union, proved nervous at the prospect of reviving Islamic law, Qaddafi personally undertook a mission to Egypt to lobby publicly for his program.[7] On the occasion of the much-publicized Islamo-Christian Dialogue in Tripoli during February 1976, Qaddafi emphasized the virtues of Islam as a religion that also provides guidance in worldly affairs and made the claim that Libya is a state based on religious law (Borrmans 1976: 142–44).

Qaddafi also promoted *shari'a* law within Libya in various ways. When he launched the Cultural Revolution in his famous speech at Zuara on April 15, 1973, Qaddafi announced that all legislation was suspended in order to remove legal impediments to the revolutionary surge. While existing legislation was in abeyance, the law of the land would be *shari'a* law. In the course of this speech he took the position that there was no state which sponsored Islam, adopted the essence of Islam, and achieved Islam as God wanted it as did the Libyan Arab Republic. This being the case, no one was entitled to speak against the government on behalf of Islam.[8]

These and other actions contribute to the impression that Libya had reimposed Islamic law under Qaddafi's leadership. In fact, when one turns from official rhetoric to the specifics of his actual accomplishments, one finds that these are very modest.

Article II of the postrevolutionary constitution promulgated on December 11, 1969 provides that Islam is the state religion, a provision commonly found in the constitutions of Muslim countries. Article III provides that the family is the basis of Libyan society and that its values are religion, morality, and nationalism. It was some time, however, before legislation of religious inspiration was enacted.

The first legal enactments that can be related to the Islamization trend did not revive specific *shari'a* rules. Rather, they were designed to enforce a public morality that was consistent with the conservative mores of Libyan society.

On September 2, 1969, the day after the revolution, an order was issued absolutely prohibiting consumption of, transport of, and commerce in alcohol, on pain of criminal sanctions. This law is different from the previous law, which had treated the sale and consumption of alcohol leniently and instead concentrated on alcohol-related abuses such as the sale of alcohol to minors or to mental defectives and incidents of public drunkenness. Consumption of alcohol had become common in certain Libyan milieus, despite Islamic condemnation of the practice. The September 2 order made it clear that the regime was supporting values consistent with Libya's Islamic heritage and rejecting the values that had been imported from Europe, but it did not purport to be derived from *shari'a* law.

A law of similar character, banning indecent or immoral performances in public places, was enacted on May 5, 1970. The law was mainly concerned with eliminating lewd performances in night-clubs. The prohibition coincided with the general concern of *shari'a* law for the preservation of female modesty and public decency. By enacting the law, the Qaddafi regime was publicly taking a stance disapproving the more liberal sexual mores associated with Europe and associating itself with more puritanical morals of traditional Libyan and Islamic culture.

Qaddafi's commitment to reinstate Islamic law was not formalized until October 28, 1971, in a law which established a committee entrusted with the task of Islamization of Libyan law.[9] The committee was charged with ascertaining where in existing Libyan laws there were conflicts with the fundamental principles of the *shari'a* and preparing new legislation to eliminate these conflicts. The new Islamic legislation was to be fashioned by choosing the most lenient rules from the different schools of Islamic law with regard for the public welfare and prevailing custom. The law did not envisage a wholesale repudiation of the secular law. Rather, *shari'a* law was repeatedly referred to as "a primary source" of law, not "the primary source" of law. Moreover, the *shari'a* law that the committee was to concern itself with was not the *shari'a* law of the classical works of Islamic jurisprudence like the *Mukhtasar* of Khalil ibn Ishaq and the numerous commentaries thereon by Maliki jurists with their detailed regulations covering all varieties of transactions, but only the fundamental principles of *shari'a* law. The decision as to what was or was not fundamental was left to the discretion of the committee. According to the explanatory memorandum accompanying the law, *shari'a* law lays down general and flexible principles that may be varied as time, place, environment, custom, and the public welfare dictate—with the single exception of the area of matters of creed and ritual worship, where the details of *shari'a* law are immutable.

With these very accommodating guidelines in place, the committee was able to be responsive to secular considerations that militated against rigid insistence on application of *shari'a* rules that were least suited to the contemporary environment. Because the majority of members of the committee were not Muslim clerics, these secular considerations seem to have weighed heavily with them.[10] The committee prepared the following new Islamic laws.

CRIMINAL LAW

The Committee's most notable achievement was the drafting of new criminal laws based on criminal law set forth in the Quran. The sources of Islamic law generally provide scant guidance in the criminal area, but the crimes (*hadd* crimes) set forth in the Quran enjoy the distinction of having scriptural authority for principles regarding substantive offences, rules of proof, and applicable penalties.[11] Further, because they are singled out for explicit treatment in the text of Divine Revelation, these crimes tend to be regarded by Muslims as particularly blameworthy and serious. For this reason many Muslims remain convinced that the severe punishments which the *hadd* laws call for (such as amputation of the extremities, crucifixion, lapidation and flogging) are justified. However, other Muslims, especially those who have been subjected to Westernizing influences or who have been trained in Western law, find the continued application of such punishments unacceptable because they have adopted other notions of what constitutes appropriate criminal punishment.[12] At least in part because of a widespread distaste for physical chastisement, the *hadd* laws were readily abandoned by the legal systems of Middle Eastern countries when Western law was imported. Only in the Arabian Peninsula have they been regularly applied until this day.

The resurrection of these penalties in Libya in the 1970s was bound to cause a stir. To many Muslims it signalled that fidelity to Islam superseded any concern for modernity with its connotation of imitation of Europe and European thought. Indeed, it was easy to be led to the assumption—incorrect as it proved—that since Libya had been willing to take such drastic steps as reviving the penalty of amputating the thief's hand, Islamization had gone far. Enactment of *hadd* laws also enabled the Libyan regime to claim that it had taken measures to reinstate Islamic law that no other modern state had taken.

The first of the new *hadd* laws, reviving the crimes of theft and brigandage, was enacted on October 11, 1972. Laws reviving the *hadd* crime of fornication and false accusation of unchastity were enacted on October 2, 1973 and September 16, 1974, respectively. A law prohibiting the consumption of alcohol was enacted on November 20, 1974. The explanatory memorandum that was appended to the first law noted that God, as man's Creator, was the wisest Legislator, that abandoning the *hadd* laws was a departure from the Quran and the Prophet Muhammad's teachings, and that the Libyan Revolution aimed at reestablishing penal law based on the true principles of Islam.[13]

Theft and Brigandage: The *hadd* crime of theft is very narrowly defined in the new Libyan law, in a manner roughly approximating the definition of the offense under traditional *shari'a* rules. For example, in order to constitute a theft for which amputation could be imposed, both *shari'a* law and Libya law require that the item taken be licit (not pork, alcohol, or other forbidden substances), that it have a certain minimum value (here set at ten Libyan dinars), that it be an item to which the thief has no colorable claim, and that the thief be sane and adult. Otherwise, only the penalties applicable under the secular law can be imposed. Libyan law also provides that the penalty should not apply to a person who steals out of need. In the explanatory memorandum the fact that the Caliph 'Umar waived punishment for theft in a year of famine is broadly taken to mean that in general the *hadd* is excused where the thief steals out of need. The memorandum acknowledges that this view of need as a mitigating circumstance is more generous than the legal excuses accepted in the traditional law.[14]

The explanatory memorandum does not try to clarify why the Libyan law is more lenient in its treatment of the needy offender, but this change would seem to be mandated by the socialist philosophy of the regime. Qaddafi's position has been that Islam is in no way a reactionary ideology but a progressive and revolutionary one (al-Qaddafi 1971: 116–18). His stated conviction is that when a person steals out of need, society is to blame and the amputation penalty should not be applicable (Bianco 1974: 172). The traditional rules have thus been readjusted, one assumes, to fit the socialist tenets of the regime.

The rules concerning how punishment is carried out have also been modified. Traditionally, punishments were executed as public spectacles, the gruesome aspects of which were often deliberately highlighted to enhance the sobering effect on witnesses. Just as the bloody corporal punishments and public executions that were so much a part of the practice of implementing criminal penalties in Western societies fell into desuetude and disfavor in this century, so such public punishments and executions have come to be seen as outmoded and barbaric in the Middle East. Qaddafi himself has made statements reflecting this attitude. He has indicated his personal hope that an interpretation of the Quranic verse on theft could be reached that would obviate the need to cut off the thief's hand (Ibid. 172). The new law on theft evinces a corresponding malaise and ambivalence on the part of its drafters. Thus, the amputation of the hand is hedged about with many preconditions unknown in the traditional law. The amputation must be preceded by a medical examination. It must be delayed where it could prove dangerous to the health of the prisoner by reason of an ailment or pregnancy. It must be carried out as a regular surgical procedure under anesthetic in a hospital, and all precautions must be taken during the recuperative stages to ensure recovery. Clearly the intention is that this procedure should be carried out in private with minimum physical impairment to the criminal. The law altogether dispenses with the further amputations that were called for in the traditional rules for successive convictions of the same offense.[15]

The crime of brigandage is dealt with in the same law and is treated much as it was in the traditional *shari'a*, again with exceptions regarding the penalties imposed. The traditional rules imposed the following penalties: banishment or imprisonment for obstructing travelers' passage and frightening them; amputation of the right hand and left foot for the above when accompanied by a taking of property; and crucifixion when the brigand also killed a traveler.[16] For the same offenses the Libyan law applies, respectively, imprisonment, the amputation of the right hand and left foot, and the death penalty. The memorandum fails to explain why the penalties of crucifixion and banishment were eliminated. However, it seems that the drafters of the law found the prospect of public crucifixions distasteful and that of banishment to other countries embarrassing. Again, many precautions are detailed concerning the amputations, but the punishment of successive amputations for repeating offenders that was found in the classical law is eliminated.

In contrast to the many modifications the law introduces in the traditional rules affecting penalties, the *shari'a* rules of proof have been retained. These rules, set forth in the Quran, differ strikingly from the rules in modern codes of evidence and have the effect of reducing the chances of conviction. The testimony of women is absolutely excluded. So, too, is the testimony of a victim of brigandage unless he is giving testimony regarding the charges as they affect other parties. Male witnesses may only testify if they are Muslims and possess the technical standard of moral rectitude, meaning that they have committed no major sins and few minor ones. For conviction there must be at least two such eyewitnesses to the crime, unless the accused makes a confession, which he is privileged to withdraw up to the time of judgment.[17]

Article XXVIII provides for a mandatory appeal from all convictions under the theft-brigandage law. The appellate court is required to review both the legal and factual bases of the conviction on the mandatory appeal. As there were no appellate courts in the *shari'a* system, this provision appears to have been dictated by the wish to insure the greatest possible opportunity for reversal of all convictions obtained under this law and to avert wherever possible the application of *hadd* punishment.[18]

The law indicates which legal sources are to be used in the event of questions not dealt with in its provisions. Article XXIII provides that the prevailing doctrine of the Maliki school is to be consulted and that reference should be made to the Libyan Penal Code if Maliki sources fail to provide a suitable answer. On all procedural matters not covered in the law, reference is also to be made to the Libyan Code of Penal Procedure. This again points to efforts to restrict the law's enforceability. If the law permitted reference to Islamic jurisprudence generally, instead of just to the doctrine of the Maliki school, potentially more traditional rules would have been revived by the law. Since the memorandum indicates that the drafters felt free to base the provisions of the law on rules from many *shari'a* schools, the limitation to Maliki doctrine seems not to have been mandated by a loyalty to that school but rather by a wish to limit the number of *shari'a* rules that could become applicable under this law.

Fornication: The next of the *hadd* crimes to be treated by new legislation was fornication. In Law 70 of October 2, 1973 the offense is defined as that of a man or woman engaging in sexual intercourse with a member of the opposite sex to whom he or she is not married. The penalty for such conduct is set at 100 lashes. This law defines fornication more narrowly than did the traditional *shari'a* jurisprudence and preserves only the milder punishments. In classical Islamic jurisprudence, fornication included punishment of homosexual intercourse and differentiated between offenders who were *muhsan*—those who were or had been married—and those who were not. The *muhsan* offender was punished by stoning to death in accordance with the "missing verse" of the Quran on the subject.[19]

No explanatory memorandum accompanies this law, but one can hypothesize reasons for the changes that have been made. The abandonment of lapidation is probably due to the same reluctance to institute excessively cruel and barbaric penalties that led to the abandonment of the crucifixion penalty for brigandage. It may also be tied in with Qaddafi's personal attitude on the subject: in the face of overwhelming evidence to the contrary he has denied that *shari'a* law ever had a lapidation penalty for fornication. With regard to the exclusion of intercourse between males in the definition of the crime, an explanation would seem to lie in the real purpose of these new "Islamic" laws, which seems to be to show the regime's respect for values that are recognized as being specifically Arab and Muslim. The major difference between Arab-Muslim culture and that of the West as regards sexual conduct lies, of course, in the seriousness with which deviations from the norms of female chastity are treated and their critical implications for family honor in the former. In Arab-Muslim culture neither of these considerations is involved in male homosexual conduct. Thus, by narrowing the definition of fornication to intercourse between a man and a woman who are not married to each other, the law is better able to convey the impression that values indigenous to Arab-Muslim culture—concern for female chastity—have been revived and that Western values are being rejected.

Unlike the theft-brigandage law, the fornication law completely abandons the *shari'a* rules of proof. Instead, the Libyan Code of Penal Procedure applies. *Shari'a* law required that there be testimony by four male Muslim eyewitnesses to actual acts of copulation for conviction.[20] Where the *shari'a* standard of proof was not met, anyone who had testified to the guilt of the accused was himself subject to punishment for false accusation of unchastity (see below). As a result, convictions were extremely difficult to obtain.

The Libyan legislators seem to have wanted this law to have greater effect than it could have had if the stringent Quranic proof standards were preserved. It will be recalled that the regime had already adopted a puritanical stance regarding sexual conduct via the earlier law on public morality. The authors of the fornication law may have been carrying out a mandate to draft the law so that it could be used to further that policy. Furthermore, since they had eliminated the harsher form of punishment for the *muhsan* offender, they may have felt obliged to make the crime easier to prove to make up for their leniency on the former point.

To insure that the flogging penalty would not be too harsh in actual application, the law set down a number of conditions for its administration. The flogging could not proceed until there had been a medical examination establishing that the flogging would not endanger the offender, a physician had to be in attendance throughout the flogging, and he had to interrupt it in the event that it was endangering the culprit. These precautionary conditions are not found in the traditional *shari'a* law.

More *shari'a* law is also potentially applicable under this law than in the case of the theft-brigandage law. Reference is to be made to the pertinent doctrine of the most lenient school of Islamic law, not just the doctrine of the Maliki school, on questions not covered in the law. If no answer is found in *shari'a* rules, the Libyan Penal Code is to be consulted.

The law also made many changes in the previous Libyan law regarding sexual offenses, changes that are too numerous and technical to be covered in detail, although some representative examples can be cited. While private consensual intercourse between adult partners not married to each other was not previously criminalized, the changed law makes such conduct punishable by five years' imprisonment. Private, consensual sexual conduct other than intercourse between adults not married to each other is also made criminal by the new law. Certain previous Libyan laws that reflected the sexual mores of the Latin countries of Europe were also replaced. Formerly a wife's adultery was treated more harshly than a husband's; this unequal treatment was eliminated under the new law. Adultery is also no longer treated as an offense against an innocent spouse for which prosecution can be halted if the complaining spouse has committed adultery within the preceding five years. Under the former law punishment was also reduced if the accused spouse had been abandoned without justification by the complaining spouse or when they were legally separated. By contrast, the new law treats adultery as a violation of the laws of society. The spouses' attitudes, conduct, and legal status cease to affect the prosecution of the offense. These changes reflect an overall policy of prosecuting all sexual misconduct between persons not married to each other and are further evidence of the regime's public posture of condemning and punishing lax sexual mores.

Slanderous accusation of unchastity: The third *hadd* law was enacted as Law 52 of September 16, 1974 and had the slanderous accusation of unchastity as its focus. This law follows the pertinent *shari'a* provisions much more closely than do the other laws. It sets a penalty of eighty lashes and subsequent unacceptability of court testimony by anyone convicted under the law. The rules of proof reproduce the *shari'a* standards: the confession of the accused or the testimony of two male Muslim eyewitnesses possessing the technical legal requirements of rectitude.

The law on false accusations of unchastity is indirectly affected by the new fornication law. Under *shari'a* rules the defendant refuted the charge that he had falsely accused someone of unchastity by proving that fornication had taken place, a virtual impossibility under the traditional proof standards. Now, it is much easier for a person accused of slander to defend himself. The change in the proof standards in the fornication law also removes a strong deterrent that existed under the traditional *shari'a* rules: the fear that an unsubstantiated charge of fornication would result in punishment for false accusation of unchastity.

The special *shari'a* rules on interspousal accusations of adultery have been incorporated in the new law.[21] These provide a way for a husband to establish that his wife has committed adultery and to disavow the paternity of any child that has resulted from his wife's illicit relations by following a ritual of oath-swearing in lieu of producing four male Muslim eyewitnesses. They also allow the wife to escape the adultery penalty by employing ritual counteroaths. This was always a rare procedure, and it is likely to remain rare under the new law. The reason for these rules was to put the husband of an unfaithful wife in a better position than others who were trying to prove a charge of adultery. With the elimination of the requirement of testimony of four qualified witnesses, there will be even less cause than before to resort to such oaths.

Supplementary legal sources to be used in default of provisions in this law are like those in the fornication law, as are the conditions under which flogging is to be carried out.

Alcohol use: The last of the *hadd* laws enacted in Libya is the law prohibiting the consumption of alcohol, Law 89 of November 20, 1974. Like the first of the *hadd* laws it has an explanatory memorandum which provides an insight into the official policies behind the law.

While traditional *shari'a* laws were concerned with the drinking of alcohol, the 1974 law is much broader, covering such activities as acquisition, possession, manufacture, and trading alcohol, and offering it or giving it to someone. It was obviously an outgrowth of the policy established immediately after the Revolution prohibiting alcohol use.

The law sets the penalty for consumption of alcohol at forty lashes for a Muslim. Unlike the other *hadd* penalties, this penalty is not explicitly set forth in the Quran, and jurists have differed as to whether the penalty should be forty or eighty lashes, based on analogies to other *hadd* crimes.

Regarding proof, either the *shari'a* rules or the standard rules of evidence of Libyan law may be applied. It seems that the drafters of the law may have wanted to include the *shari'a* rules to give the new law an Islamic character but that there was a reluctance to limit the means of proof to those rules, which would allow many offenders to escape punishment. Additional evidence that the government sought to enhance the prospects for conviction under this law lies in the statute of limitations for prosecutions, which has been set at three years. The *shari'a* required the prosecution to commence while the accused was still in an inebriated state or had the smell of alcohol on his breath.

The alcohol consumption law also establishes penalties ranging from flogging to fines and imprisonment for Muslims and non-Muslims convicted of a variety of alcohol-related offenses: the manufacture of alcohol, public drunkenness, selling alcohol, and the like. Certain legal disabilities are imposed as penalties for persons convicted under these laws, including disbarment from public office, exclusion from giving court testimony, and the loss of driving privileges. In accordance with *shari'a* rules, non-Muslims are not penalized for acquiring, possessing, or privately consuming alcohol, although it is difficult to see how alcohol could be lawfully obtained in an environment where the restrictions of this law apply.

Because so many of the provisions of this law are not taken from *shari'a* rules, the accompanying memorandum necessarily lacks the extensive references to Islamic sources that characterized the memorandum accompanying the theft-brigandage law. Much of the memorandum is a treatise on the social, political, and cultural ills caused by alcohol consumption. For example, alcohol is condemned as an alien vice introduced by Western imperialism to undermine Libyan society by fostering crime and corruption. The public drunkenness of non-Muslims is equated with manifestations of disrespect for the traditions of Islamic society.[22] The law is thus portrayed as reflecting both the regime's fidelity to Islam and its nationalist commitment to respect indigenous culture.

LIMITED SCOPE OF ISLAMIZATION

It is important to consider why the *shari'a* law regarding *hadd* offenses was revived in Libya, albeit with modifications, while *shari'a* rules affecting subjects like contracts, commerce, and property languished. Legislation to revive such rules has been extremely spotty. The collection of the Islamic alms tax was placed under governmental regulation by laws in 1971 and 1972, thereby allowing the government to enforce what was previously an obligation binding only on the believer's conscience. In 1972 a law prohibiting interest in loan transactions between natural persons was enacted, purportedly to reinstate the Quranic prohibition of usury. However, the prohibition of usury is generally understood by Muslim fundamentalists to apply to all interest-bearing transactions, so the fact that the Libyan law is limited to the relatively unimportant field of loans between natural persons means that it falls far short of reinstating *shari'a* rules. In 1972, a law was also enacted outlawing some types of aleatory contracts on the grounds that they contravened the *shari'a* rules prohibiting wagering. The prerevolutionary law already contained some restrictions on such contracts, however, and the new law only extended them to certain new categories so as to ban activities such as lotteries, the sale of life-time annuities, and the sale of inheritance rights before the size of individual shares is determined. The law specifically exempted insurance contracts from the ban.

Not all legal changes were consonant with Islamization. Some steps were taken to reduce the scope of Islamic law in the legal system. In 1973 Libya abolished the private Islamic trust, a venerable *shari'a* institution. The official justifications for this measure were a history of mismanagement of trusts and their negative economic effects. In 1973 a law unifying the legal system was also enacted, terminating the special jurisdiction of the *shari'a* courts over cases arising under *shari'a* law. In doing so, Libya followed the example of most other Muslim countries, which have integrated the *shari'a* courts into a larger, Western-style court system.[23]

It is clear from these examples that the Libyan regime has shied away from reinstating *shari'a* law where it would threaten orderly economic development and the modernization of its institutions. The reinstatement of *hadd* laws, by comparison, threatens no such disruption. Much of the conduct affected by *hadd* laws was already covered under prior criminal laws, was deterred by the threat of civil action for damages, or was inhibited by powerful social constraints. That the major accomplishment of the Islamization campaign was to enact these laws with their very limited effects indicates that reinstating *shari'a* law is far from being the regime's main concern.

THE LIBYAN AND IRANIAN CONTRAST: IMPLEMENTATION POLICIES

In 1974 the process of Islamizing Libyan law ground to a halt. While the scope of alterations to previous laws was certainly modest, the implementation of the new laws seems to have been even more restricted. While no reliable statistics on the application of *hadd* penalties have been forthcoming from Libya, it is striking that no publicity about the infliction of Quranic punishments followed the Islamization measures. The contrast between this situation and the application of *hadd* penalties in revolutionary Iran is noteworthy: the official media in Iran feels that photographs and reports of the application of *hadd* penalties or of even harsher penalties for "crimes against Islam" are worthy of widespread dissemination.

This difference in official attitude is a result of significant differences in the nature of the two regimes and their respective commitments to reinstating Islamic law. In Iran Quranic criminal law has been revived as part of a revolution that derived much of its cohesion and strength from popular Islamic sentiment and from a network of patronage and institutions controlled by a prestigious clergy. The reinstatement of Islamic law thus was a rallying cry in the period of prerevolutionary ferment. Clerics who specialized in Islamic law were among the strongest ideological and political leaders of the revolution, and even the laymen who assumed prominent positions in the revolution included persons noted for their contributions to modernist Islamic thought. Mehdi Bazargan and Abol Hassan Bani Sadr are two apposite examples of the latter trend. Moreover, the restoration of Islamic law was not only the ideological rationale for the revolution; Iranian clerics also had personal and professional reasons for wanting to see the Shah's Western-oriented legal system with its Western-trained personnel replaced by one which required training in Islamic law. The clergy was sufficiently powerful to dismantle Iran's secular legal system and to establish the supremacy of Islamic law in short order. Having taken over the legal system, the clerics had no qualms that the restoration of physical chastisements might seem barbaric or reactionary by Western standards. It was these very standards that they were pledged to repudiate, and the imposition of *hadd* penalties symbolized their triumph.

In Libya, by contrast, no group or individuals affiliated with the clergy or lay Muslim movements came to power by virtue of the 1969 revolution. On the contrary, a regime with Islamic affiliations was being replaced by young army officers of the middle rank who constituted the Revolutionary Command Council. They were imbued with the ideas of Nasserism and Arab Nationalism, which are basically secular ideologies. Although the popular symbolism of reinstating some well-known Islamic criminal laws apparently appealed to Qaddafi as a device for demonstrating the regime's fidelity to Islam, the implementation of *hadd* penalties could not be easily reconciled with the regime's basic policies, which aimed at rapid development and modernization.

Vital is the matter of implementation. Despite its reforms of substantive law, the Qaddafi regime manifested no desire to return to a traditional system of *shari'a* courts administered by Muslim clerics. Instead it preferred to retain the Western system inherited from King Idris and to eliminate the remaining jurisdiction of *shari'a* courts. The result is that Islamic laws came to be administered by a judiciary trained along Western lines in a system permeated by Western values. In this context, *hadd* penalties were bound to strike a sharply discordant note. It is a well-established juridical phenomenon that when judges view penalties as excessively harsh, they are less likely to convict offenders. Whether or not the Libyan leadership specifically envisaged these results when *hadd* penalties were enacted, the regime subsequently has countenanced the judiciary's failure to apply the penalties. Moreover, it seems that the government actually sent out signals implying that restraint in implementation was officially favored. After all, the commission charged with drafting the new Islamic laws included few clergy, original *shari'a* penalties were significantly watered down, and the commission's mandate expressly charged it with finding "the most lenient" rules from among those potentially applicable. Moreover, Qaddafi himself made known his strong distaste for the harsher forms of punishment required by *hadd* rules and a readiness to accept a revisionist view that no such punishments are actually called for under Islamic law.

The gap between the much-heralded official policy of Islamization and the very modest practical achievements of the program for reinstating Islamic criminal law is a natural result of the inherent conflicts between Qaddafi's desire to exploit Islamization as a legitimation device and his commitment to the realization of a revolutionary, socialist society. He seems personally ambivalent about whether the values of a medieval criminal justice system are suited to the demands of the new order that he envisages. While the Islamization program has resulted in the symbolic revival of a number of criminal penalties borrowed from Islamic models, it is natural in the circumstances that the steps that would be needed to ensure the faithful and rigorous application of *shari'a* rules in the criminal sphere have been neglected.

NOTES

1. Algeria, as a colony of France, is a special case. There French law was not adopted by a Middle Eastern government but imposed by the country's Western conquerors.

2. This pattern was not accidental. Islamic law placed many restrictions on commercial transactions that made it illsuited to regulate the institutions of the developed, European variety which modernizing Middle Eastern societies imported. The *shari'a* rules of procedure had many archaic and cumbersome features, and the *shari'a* sources gave only limited guidance on criminal matters.

3. Turkey remains the only country of the Muslim Middle East which has a completely secular legal system.

4. One of the most powerful of these was the Muslim Brothers, a dissident group that proved especially effective in marshalling support for the Islamic cause among the

more traditional and disadvantaged sectors of the Egyptian urban population. Another example was seen in the National Salvation Party, which appealed to sentiment in favor of reversing the secularization of Turkish law effected under Ataturk in the 1920s: it has been able to garner a significant share of the vote in Turkish elections since 1970. During the ferment that presaged the Iranian Revolution of 1979, the demand for the reinstatement of the *shari'a* proved to be a particularly popular and effective rallying cry. These and other movements revealed that it was possible to win a large political following by appealing to the masses' loyalty to the *shari'a.*

5. This is not to say that such movements were only supported because of their commitment to revive the *shari'a*, but it is clear that appeals to the residual attachment of the populace to the *shari'a* were both effective and perceived as such.

6. Qaddafi is not the only Middle Eastern leader to use this kind of "political religion." See Hudson (1977).

7. There is an interesting account of a discussion of the reinstatement of Islamic law between Qaddafi, posing as the champion of restoring the *shari'a*, and prominent Egyptian intellectuals, who frankly expressed their unease at the prospect, in *Ruz al-Yusuf*, 48 (1973): 4-10, 54-57. Qaddafi's discussions with Cairo journalists on this subject are reported in *BBC Summary of World Broadcasts*, ME/4335/A/3, June 30, 1973.

8. See *BBC Summary of World Broadcasts*, ME/4273/A/16, April 17, 1973.

9. The head of the committee wrote a book about his view of its task. See Mansur (1972).

10. Of the nine members of the original committee, only two were members of the *'ulama.*

11. In fact, the penalty for consuming alcohol was not set forth explicitly in the Quran but was considered to be implied by analogy to other *hadd* penalties.

12. To people accustomed to the values embodied in Western criminal law, the severity of *hadd* penalties is likely to seem out of proportion to the seriousness of the offenses involved. For example, a victimless crime like consensual sexual intercourse between adults not married to each other may be punished by stoning to death under *shari'a* rules. Murder, in contrast, is regarded as a private injury, so instead of punishing a murderer, the victim's relatives may choose to accept appropriate monetary compensation for their loss.

13. See *al-Jarida ar-rasmiyya* [the official gazette of Libya] (1972), pp. 3024-25.

14. *Ibid.*, pp. 3037-38.

15. The explanation offered in the explanatory memorandum is that the drafters of the law were following the authority of 'Ata'. See *al-Jarida ar-rasmiyya* 1972: 3044-45. 'Ata' was a representative of one of the ancient schools of Islamic law which has been defunct for many centuries. Why his isolated and unusual opinion is followed on this issue and not on others is not explained.

16. The law preserves the traditional *shari'a* rule, that a brigand who surrenders to the criminal authorities before suspicion focuses on him as the perpetator is not subject to the *hadd.*

17. The traditional *shari'a* allowed retraction up to the time of the actual execution of the penalty. Perhaps because the Libyan law allows for such a substantial delay between the time judgment is rendered and its actual execution, it may have been seen to be appropriate to depart from the traditional rule.

18. In fact, in the published sources that are available there is no indication that an amputation has ever been carried out.

19. In Pakistan, there has been debate over whether lapidation is the proper penalty for the *muhsan* offender or whether it should be 100 lashes. In a controversial ruling, since reversed under pressure from conservatives, the Pakistani Federal Shariat Court decided that 100 lashes, not lapidation, was the penalty for fornication. The second ruling overturning the 1980 decision, can be found in *Federation of Pakistan v. Hazoor Bakhsh*, 1983 PLD Federal Shariat Court 255. Had clerics, who have exercised great influence over Pakistan's Islamization campaign, enjoyed comparable influence in Libya, the Libyan law mandating 100 lashes would have been similarly challenged for failing to follow *shari'a* rules. Just after the 1980 Pakistani ruling, Libyan and Pakistani laws on fornication briefly dovetailed; now they embody two conflicting interpretations of the *hadd* penalty requirements.

20. These rules are set forth in the Quran at iv, 24, and they are referred to again at xxiv, 4.

21. These are set forth in the Quran at xxiv, 6-9.

22. See *al-Jarida ar-rasmiyya* (1972), p. 2941.

23. In what seems to be an ingenious rationalization of this step, the official Libyan newspaper, *al-Fajr al-jadid*, stated on February 14, 1974 on its first page that it did not make sense to retain the dual system of *shari'a* and secular courts since all law in Libya was based on the *shari'a*.

REFERENCES

al-Qaddafi, Mu'ammar. 1971. *As-Sijill al-gawmi, bayanat wa ahadith al-'aquid Mu'ammar al-qadhdhafi*. Tripoli: Marakiz ath-thanqafiyya al-qawmiyya.

Area Handbook for Libya. 1973. Washington, D.C.: U.S. Government Printing Office.

Bianco, Mirella. 1974. *Kadhafi, messager du desert*. Paris: Stock.

Borrmans, Maurice. 1976."Le Seminaire du Dialogue Islamo Chretien de Tripoli (Libye) 1–6 Febrier 1976)." *Islamo-Christiana* 2: 135–70.

Golino, Frank. 1970. "Patterns in Libyan National Identity." *Middle East Journal* 24: 338–52.

Hudson, Michael. 1977. *Arab Politics: The Search for Legitimacy*. New Haven: Yale University Press.

Mansur, Ali Ali. 1972. *Khutwa ra'ida nahwa tatbiq ahkam ash-shari'a al-islamiyya fi'l-jumhuriyya al'arabiyya al-libiyya*. Beirut: Dar al-fath.

7

LEGAL POSTULATES IN FLUX: JUSTICE, WIT, AND HIERARCHY IN IRAN

Michael M. J. Fischer

The Iranian Revolution of 1977-79 and the institution of an Islamic republic provide an appropriate and important moment to reevaluate the evolution of law and justice in Iran. The initial slogan of the revolution was constitutionalism, specifically the implementation of the 1906 Constitution, and more generally the call was for social justice. In time, the slogan became the abolition of the monarchy and the institution of a new Islamic constitution, including the controversial formula "guardianship by the clergy" (*vilayat-i faqih*). The formula was defended as merely a strengthening of the right of veto accorded a board of five clerics in the 1906 Constitution, a provision which had been ignored.

The furor and controversy sparked by the notion of guardianship by the clergy, out of fear of theocracy, aired basic questions about the nature of law and justice. The terms of reference are like those of classical Greek jurisprudence and those of Thomism. Defenders of the guardianship by the clergy formula referred to Islamic efforts paralleling those of Aquinas to harmonize Plato and Aristotle and the divine law. Such defenders invoked Islamic interpretations of the Platonic philosopher-king, philosophically grounded in gnostic notions of illuminationism, and institutionally elaborated through notions of an ideal leader (the Imam) and an ideal state or utopia. But this is the twentieth century, not 1274, and a horrified (and paralyzed) middle class looked on with fear. As one of them, exaggerating somewhat, put it:

> Of far greater long-term consequence, if they succeed, are the designs to desecularize Iran's judiciary; to demolish the secularized judiciary system that, despite all its imperfections, constitutes arguably the greatest institutional achievement of the generation of Westernized intellectuals of the 1920s and '30s (Arani 1980: 23).

Clearly the Pahlavi state (1925-1978) cannot be considered a model liberal system, as the Arani quote might imply. It was a patrimonial monarchy using modern police state methods, inefficient by Soviet standards, and not as brutal as Idi Amin, Adolph Hitler, or the recent military rule in Argentina but nonetheless relying on terror, torture, informants, censorship, closed trials, and rigged elections, as well as the less blatant inducements of cooptation through bribery and patronage. It is for this reason that lawyers and judges were among the leaders of the secular faction of the revolution to oust the shah.

The invocation of a Platonic-Islamic republic as a possibility for modern Iran, therefore, should not be reduced to simply a reactionary atavism. The Islamic idiom of the revolution not only confronted the utopia and ideology of modernization, based upon a bourgeois legal language, with an older, medieval utopia of social harmony and justice. It also pointed out the contradictions between bourgeois legal notions of individual freedom and bourgeois economic notions of expansion as naturally ensuring social welfare. The Islamic idiom of the revolution, thus, might well serve (and did so serve among the more progressive elements in the early days of the revolution) as a vanguard effort to reconsider the moral basis of the rules by which society is regulated.

That this potential of the Islamic heritage has been increasingly vitiated by the course of the revolution should not blind us to the contributions to notions of justice made by Aristotelian-cum-scholastic jurisprudence (in either its Christian, Jewish, or Muslim versions). Sociologically, furthermore, there are too many Muslims whose belief is too deeply seated to dismiss Islam as too simple, too ambiguous, or too flawed a basis for reform. Rather, one must stress what is progressive and just in the Islamic heritage and expose interpretations which so easily have led in the past and continue to lead to political and psychological repression and injustice. Such an endeavor leads toward dialogue and persuasion rather than to confrontation and mutual withdrawal.

This chapter attempts to sketch the competing reform efforts of clerics and secular lawyers over the past century in Iran, to provide a historical sociology of punishment and of conflict-resolution procedures, and to pose the issue of the relation between power and judicial systems. This chapter, attempts to contribute to the struggle for both Muslims and non-Muslims to achieve a critical social consciousness, as well as to formulate the philosophical questions embedded in historical experience. While it would be possible to collate bits of information from Amnesty International and other sources on human rights violations and the penal system,[1] and from press reports on various other aspects of the legal system during the 1981–89 period, this has not been pursued here partly because detailed case material from the several levels of society analyzed here is not available, and partly because these bits seem to provide little ground on which to modify the sociological, historical, and philosophical analysis. In this sense, 1981 remains a strategic historical moment for both looking back at the Pahlavi period, and forward at a very slowly emergent post-revolutionary Iran.

IRAN AND ISLAMIC JUSTICE

Three initial caveats. First, many of the acts of the Islamic revolutionary courts in Iran have more to do with being revolutionary than with being Islamic. It is possible to concede to those who argue for the establishment of institutions of Islamic justice that there may be a distinction between what is necessary in the fight to establish Islam and the procedures or due processes of law which must be observed once an Islamic society has been established. The question remains open as to when the means used vitiate the ends sought. Part of this discussion in the Islamic context revolves around the critical Shi'ite notion of *taqiyya* (dissimulation, keeping one's cards close to one's chest) as well as the use of force.

Second, in its history Islam has rarely, if ever, served as the sole source of law or judicial authority. There has almost always been a tension between sources of authority vested in royal courts or governments and those derived from the Quran and *sunna*. Furthermore, Islamic law itself recognizes a distinction between *shari'a* (the law derived from the Quran and *sunna*) and *'urf* (the law derived from local custom). Islamic jurists historically have had to negotiate their way among sources of law grounded in the Quran, local custom, and royal or government decrees, all of which may in varying degrees be Islamically valid.

Third, the Islamic tradition itself, as distinct from both royal and *'urf* sources of law, is pragmatic, more of a common-law tradition than a rationalized legal code tradition. Neither the stereotype of arbitrary *qadi* justice nor the stereotype of rigidity in how Islamic courts function is correct. Efforts to deny this are usually politically motivated. Portrayals of rigid codes mandating the stoning of adulteresses, amputation for theft, or specified numbers of lashes for other crimes, although deriving from the Quran (the so-called *hadd* provisions of the penal law) reveal only part of the required due process. Ignored are the rules of evidence which must be met before such punishments can be applied. These rules, which can provide considerable protection for the accused, have been suppressed by both antagonistic Western writers and Muslim, would-be fundamentalist, fanatics.

ISLAMIC REVOLUTIONARY JUSTICE

On April 1, 1979 an Islamic republic was declared in Iran. It was the culmination of three distinct but reinforcing struggles: the fourteen-month-long struggle to oust Muhammad-Reza Pahlavi from the throne; the century-old struggle to institute a constitutional form of government; and the age-old struggle to establish a utopia of social justice, as represented for Shi'ite Muslims by the example of the first Imam, the son-in-law of the Prophet, 'Ali ibn Abi Talib.

The revolution itself can be analyzed in stages, much as Crane Brinton suggested could be done for popular democratic revolutions in Europe (Brinton 1938). The fourteen months from November 1977 to February 1979 constitute the first stage, the sweeping away of the old regime. This is followed by a stage of dual sovereignty in which there exists a weak public government, in conjunction with a secret government with more power. There are also a terror and a series of political crises which narrow the base of the ruling factions. Eventually, a third stage emerges, a long period of reconstruction which, if the revolution is successful, should create a stronger state with greater popular participation, mobilization, or loyalty. The 1980s was dominated by the Iran-Iraq War, which functioned domestically to maintain revolutionary discipline. With the end of that war and the death of Ayatollah Khomaini, Iran is now (1990) presumably entering into a reconstructive third stage in the 1990s, the contours of which only time will tell. At the time of the initial writing of this article (September 1981) Iran was still in the midst of the second stage. The terror, which has included some three thousand executions, has proceeded in phases paralleling the political crises and the narrowing political base. The attempt to reconstruct a political arena, so that decisions may be taken about the economic and social agendas of the revolution, has not yet been completed and is likely to be subject to several more major preliminary shifts in power alignments. This remains true in 1990.

The fate of justice and law during the second stage needs to be recounted briefly, although it says relatively little about what can be expected in the future. Immediately upon his return to Iran, Ayatollah Khomaini directed the Minister of Justice that all decisions should be swift and final and there should be no appeal processes in either civil or criminal cases. He reiterated that criminals had no right to lawyers. In part, he was reacting to the interested slowness of the Pahlavi regime's administration of justice, which allowed graft. In part, full investigations were felt to be a luxury, and executions had to be done swiftly in order to protect against a counterrevolution. According to an Amnesty International report, nearly two-thirds of the first 350 to be executed whose occupations are known were police, military, or SAVAK personnel. Charges against them included Islamic phrases equivalent to the Nuremberg indictment for "crimes against humanity," as well as the specific crimes of murder, torture, theft, and misuse of public office.

As the number of executions rose without either public trials or consultation with the public government, protest was heard from many quarters, from the clergy, as well as from the middle class which had fought against the police state of the shah in favor of civil liberties and due process. On March 14, 1979 (by which time sixty-eight people had been executed), then Prime Minister Mehdi Bazargan delivered a major speech denouncing the executions as "irreligious, inhuman, and a disgrace to the country and revolution." Sayyid Mahmud Taleghani (d. 1979), one of the most popular of the clerical leaders of the revolution, also dissociated himself from the executions. On March 15, as former Prime Minister Amir Abbas Hoveyda's trial began, Khomaini bowed to the outcry against summary executions and halted the trial until a code of procedure could be established. That code, however, allowed Khomaini to appoint prosecutors, obligated sentences to be carried out within twenty-four hours, and denied the need to provide criminals with lawyers. Hoveyda's trial resumed, and he was executed April 7.

Thereafter, trials became slightly more public. Witnesses were called against the accused, and the accused was allowed to speak in his own defense (although

Hoveyda was denied his request to prepare a full defense). In early May, Khomaini announced that executions were to be limited to persons who were proven to have killed people, who had issued orders for killing, or who had committed torture resulting in death. But executions also continued for sexual deviance, pornography, prostitution, political dissent (in the case of the Kurds), contact with Israel (in the case of several prominent Jews), and religious belief (in the case of the Bahais). "Ayatollah" Sadegh Khalkhali ran for election to the Assembly of Experts, which drew up the new constitution, proudly claiming as his qualification that he personally had condemned to death two hundred former "enemies of Islam" and "corrupters of the earth." He was rejected by the electorate but was eventually elected to the new parliament.

Several preliminary observations may be hazarded about the give-and-take of these events. First, the revolutionary courts served as a highly visible arena for power struggles. An increase in the rate of executions, noted *Times of London* correspondent Tony Alloway (May 1980), often presaged political struggles between clerical and secular forces. In May 1980, for instance, during the second round of elections for the first parliament under the new constitution, and as struggles for control of the new government intensified, there was a flurry of executions, including the first woman cabinet minister under the shah, seven Bahais, a woman accused of selling girls into prostitution, and a corrupt businessman. These occurred despite a repetition of a Khomaini directive issued only two months earlier against further executions of former officials except for charges of murder and torture. Presumably it was a flexing of fundamentalist clerical muscle. It was also accompanied by other antiminority gestures (the trial of a family of prominent Jewish hotel keepers; the murder of the Anglican bishop's son) and by the pointed flouting by Sadegh Khalkhali of President Bani-Sadr's directive that the destruction of Reza Shah's tomb cease.

Second, increases in due process procedures occurred in a period of greater quiescence. By December 1979 death sentences were not carried out immediately but were subject to review. Khomaini issued directives to limit executions. And a special court was established to consider complaints against the clergy.

Third, there was a continuing recognition of the power of accusation and the need to protect revolutionary leaders from "exposure." At first there was a rule against criticizing Khomaini or the Islamic republic. A running battle with the press followed over the acceptable limits of criticism. When accusations were made by militants against Bazargan's National Freedom Party and a member of the Revolutionary Council in January 1980, tighter controls on such slander were imposed. Accusations of complicity with imperialism had become effective political devices for discrediting rivals.

The primary casualties of such accusations have been moderate middle class secularists and their religious allies. This includes the lawyers and writers who helped spearhead the revolution against the shah in 1977. In May of that year fifty-three lawyers sent a telegram protesting the decision to degrade the Supreme Court to the status of an ordinary court and demanding the legal profession be consulted in major constitutional changes. In July 1977 sixty-four lawyers signed a manifesto reaffirming the telegram and adding demands for an independent judiciary, free elections, and freedom of speech. An Association of Jurists was formed to monitor the law. In September another letter was signed by 164 sitting and retired judges. Somewhat parallel to this activity in the legal profession was activity among writers. In the fall of 1977 meetings sponsored by the Iranian Writers Association turned into antishah demonstrations which proved to be foreshadowings of the growing demonstrations of the following year. The leading members of the Committee for the Defense of Freedom and Human Rights—Abdul Lahiji, Hasan Nazih, Rahmatullah Moghaddam, and others—were all forced underground or abroad by the political crises of the second phase of the revolution (March 1979–present). Both Ayatollah Taleghani and Ayatollah Shariatmadari, who tried to protect these activists, were silenced. By summer 1981 the political crises had intensified with the forcing from office of President Bani-Sadr and his liberal Islamic associates, with the execution of the poet Said Sultanpour who had led the antishah meetings in the fall of 1977, and with the assassination by the Islamic leftist Mujaheddin of over a hundred members of the ruling Islamic Republican Party. Executions now became a daily event: over 1000 occurred within an eleven-week span. Pretenses to due process of law, Islamic or otherwise, were all but abandoned.

As the lineup of protagonists demonstrates, what we are witnessing is a revolutionary political process, which only nominally goes under the name of Islam.

Finally, a comment should be made about the revolution and the international legal system. On November 4, 1979, Islamic militants seized the American Embassy in Tehran and held fifty-three Americans hostage. It was a spectular ploy, brilliantly catering to the international media for magnified effect. It helped oust the Bazargan government and squeeze out of the political arena moderates who were already beginning to talk about accommodation with the United States and with the global economic order. The 1989 call by Ayatollah Khomaini for the death of novelist Salman Rushdie functioned in parallel fashion, with parallel intent and equal effectiveness. It blocked talk of normalizing relations with the United States, and helped channel whatever normalization in trade and aid with the West to Western Europe rather than to the United States. The seizing of the American Embassy in 1979 stifled criticism of the controversial new constitution about to be submitted to a popular referendum. And, as Roy Mottahedeh (1980) points out, it was a bid to extend the revolution into the international arena. Seizure of hostages is illegal by Islamic law as well as international law, although it is not without precedent for rulers to seize hostages from among those whom they fear may otherwise attack them. The act, however, was portrayed as one of "civil disobedience" against an international legal order which condoned unequal relations between states. Great powers could contravene or bend international law with impunity. Witness the red-tape obstructions to Iranian demands for the return of the shah and his money, argued Iranian spokesmen, as well as the participation of the United States in the 1953 coup which returned the shah to power. At the time, there were hopes in the Islamic world and the Third World at large that Iran might provide the leverage for renewed nonaligned movement with moral credibility between East and West. Such hopes rapidly faded with the handlings of the hostage affair and the continuing course of the Iranian revolution.

CLERICAL VERSUS SECULAR LAW

Secular lawyers and clerics cooperated in a tactical alliance during the first phase of the revolution. Thereafter their paths separated. Both had argued over the past century that the Iranian judicial system needed reconstruction. The lawyers saw their efforts as restructuring a premodern society, one which in the nineteenth century had an arbitrary monarch and a fragmented judicial system administered variously by clerics, state officials, local elders, landowners, bandits, and even the self-help procedures of tribal feuding. This anarchic "system" employed medieval forms of corporal punishment and was liberally greased by bribery. For their part, the clerics saw their efforts similarly as an attempt to restructure the same judicial system under their supervision, an attempt which began in the sixteenth century and again in the nineteenth century.

CLERICAL INITIATIVES AND CLAIMS

The 1906 Constitution, whose implementation was the unifying slogan of all parties to the 1977–79 revolution, granted a body of five *mujtaheds* (experts in religious law) the right to veto proposed legislation which they found contrary to Islam. This supervisory role was based on the claim that Islam provides a complete, infallible, and divine law. Originally this law could be applied with perfection by the Imams, successors to the Prophet. Since the withdrawal of the twelfth Imam from the world in the ninth century, the clerics claimed that as professional students of the law they were in the best position to interpret it. This claim was easier to uphold in the days of restricted literacy when schools were largely in clerical hands. The clergy have no claim to infalliblity, despite hopes that their piety will cause God to guide them. The best they can do is for a number of well-trained clerics to come to the same conclusions (the principle of *ijma'* or consensus) or for all believers to trust the scholarship of a supremely well-educated person. The followers of Khomaini thus treated him as their "Imam." Others, however, disparaged his scholarship and therefore his claims to leadership.

Apart from the problem of who should interpret the law, instituting Islamic law entails other practical problems. Different parts of Islamic law have been worked out over the centuries with different degrees of detail, and the development of law has not kept pace with changes in modern society. These are not new problems. The Syrian scholar Riyad Maydani, for instance, says of '*uqubat*, the penal law of both torts (where the remedy is to the individual) and crimes (where the remedy is to the public):

> No other parts of the *shari'a* are as inadequately worked out by Muslim jurists as the law of *'uqubat*. As a result, the caliphs and their viziers had more freedom in this field than in others to enforce their own executive decrees, based on custom and precedent (1955: 221).

This disjunction between religious and royal court law was reinforced to the advantage of the latter by medieval political theorists, who composed political manuals or "mirrors for princes." The famous *Siyasat-nama* of the Seljuk vizier Nizam ul-Mulk, for instance, advocated the strengthening of one-man rule, leaving the welfare of the general population as a residual category to be taken care of by the *shari'a*. Both the Safavid and Qajar dynasties attempted to bolster state courts and downgrade *shari'a* courts.

The activist clerical tradition, which Ayatollah Khomaini espoused and which tried to counter the tendency towards accumulation of state hegemony over the judicial system, can be traced back to the eighteenth century founder of the Usuli school of Shi'ite clerics, Aqa Muhammad Baqir Bihbihani (1705–1803) (Algar 1969), and perhaps even to a sociologically distinct faction of Shi'ite immigrant clerics in the sixteenth century which achieved dominance under the leadership of Muhammad Baqir Majlisi (d. 1699) (Arjomand 1978). Now see also the parallel case of Usuli clerics in Awadh, 1722–1859 (Cole 1988).

When the Safavids (1501–1722) established Shi'ism as the state religion of Iran, they invited Shi'ite clerics from present-day Lebanon, Iraq, and Bahrain to come to Iran to staff new theological colleges and to become *shaykhs ul-Islam* of various cities. Large numbers of clerics immigrated. Arjomand argues that they became competitive with the native Shi'ite clerics who had been integrated in the regional and state administrations as *qadis* and administrators of endowments. Many of the native clerics were landed and espoused a mandarin culture with catholic interests in philosophy and *'irfan* ("high sufism" or gnosticism). The immigrant clergy had to depend upon their religious scholarship to carve out a competitive position. Arjomand calls them dogmatic religious professionals who attacked all rivals, not only Sunnis, but Sufis, philosophers, and popular *shaykhs* or *pirs*. Particularly in the last half century of Safavid rule, under weak shahs, this group exercised increasing power and claims to be above the monarch as representatives of the twelfth Imam. Majlisi, the most prominent of this group, became *Shaykh ul-Islam* of the capital city, Isfahan, in 1687. It is particularly out of his formulations of Shi'ism, Arjomand suggests, that we get an exclusivist, dominance-seeking interpretation of the role of the clergy. The attraction of Arjomand's account is that it can accommodate three otherwise puzzling features of Iranian religious competition to the present: (1) the decline of the formal office of *qadi* during the Safavid period and the rise of the role of *mujtahed* or *faqih*; (2) the extreme hostility of clerics to the enduring interest of Iranians in philosophy, specultative mysticism, and the practices of sufism; (3) the ambiguity between insistence on scholastic rational argumentation and proprietary appropriation of scholastically suspect popular mythology and belief as part of the preaching canon. Popular mythology is sanctioned if it is under clerical auspices.

The fall of the Safavids caused the clerics to withdraw into quiescence until Bihbihani, a grandson of Majlisi, re-energized their activist claims. His most militant student, Seyyid Muhammad Baqir Shafti, wrote a treatise on *The Incumbency of the Huddud* (punishments explicitly mandated in the Quran) *upon the Mujtaheds during the Occultation of the Imam* and then imposed the death penalty on some seventy to a hundred persons. Inaugurating the first such death penalty, it is said, Shafti could find no one willing to execute the sentence and so had to strike the first blow himself. After reciting the funeral prayers, he did so and promptly fainted with emotion. By the end of the century, clerical courts sentenced many Babis and Bahais to death as heretics without any sign of emotional strain. A few activists, such as Mullah Ahmad Naraqi, went so far as to call for a theocracy of the clergy.

But clerical activism did not go unchallenged. The leading scholar of the late Qajar period, Shaykh Morteza Ansari, rejected the tradition of direct political activism. While Arjomand overstates Ansari's quietism, saying he held a pious antipathy to all worldly activity and tried to refrain from issuing judicial opinions (*fatawa*)—after all, he wrote what is still the classic commercial code of Shi'ite law, the *Makaseb*, and he is known for many *fatawa*—there was indeed a sharp contrast between the pious clerics and the political ones. Many of the latter acquired estates and fortunes. (Shafti, mentioned above, was one of the richest men in Isfahan.) *Akhund-i siyasi* (political cleric) remained a term of abuse until the followers of Khomaini turned it into a virtue.

By the time of the early twentieth-century struggles leading to the Constitutional Revolution, the clerics divided into roughly three groups (Kasravi 1952). There were those who argued that after the withdrawal of the twelfth Imam in the ninth century, Muslims had to live by the Quranic injunction to do good and prevent evil as best they could, and this meant a European-style constitutional democracy. A second group said that Iran was not ready for democracy, but a check needed to be placed upon the despotic tyranny of the Qajar monarchs. The third, most conservative, group said it would go along with the contemporary fashion for constitutions, but one "conditioned" by the Quran, punning on the Arabic root of the word for constitution (*mashrutiyeh mashru'e*). Such a constitution would be quite different from the European models, rejecting the European system of taxation in favor of the Islamic ones, rejecting the equality of non-Muslims and Muslims, and rejecting any absolute freedom of press or education (nothing anti-Islamic must be permitted). It was the champion of this interpretation, Shaykh Fuzlullah Nuri, who helped author the clause in the constitution giving a panel of five *mujtaheds* the right to veto legislation they found contrary to Islam. Nuri's interpretation became the standard clerical position throughout the twentieth century.

Until 1979 the line between the clerics' claim of the right to guide society morally and the right to participate directly in political affairs remained vague. Ayatollah Borujerdi, the leader of Iran's Shi'ites in the 1940s and 1950s, objected to daily political activism by clerics of the sort engaged in by Ayatollah Kashani, the leader of the religious faction supporting Mosaddegh's National Front. At that time the future Ayatollah Khomaini was an aide to Borujerdi, and although close to Kashani, he also criticized Kashani's activism. Khomaini's 1943 book, *Revealing the Secrets*, still took the traditional line that bad government was better than no government, and that the duty of true Muslims was to encourage governments to be more just and more Islamic. Even in his 1970 book, *Islamic Government: Guidance by the Clergy*, there is ambiguity. The European notion of the three branches of government (executive, legislative, and judicial) is adopted, but instead of checks and balances between the three, the judicial is raised above the other two. Clerics, it is argued, should hold the judicial position. Furthermore, there are no grounds for excluding them from involvement in political affairs. Whether this meant involvement along the lines of the constitutional panel of five *mujtaheds* or more day-to-day involvement was not specified. Thus, when the 1979 Constitution incorporated the phrase "guardianship by the clergy" as meaning leadership through a supreme cleric or council of clerics, plus several lower level supervisory councils of clerics, it caused considerable dismay among a number of leading clerics who objected that the technical meaning of guardianship by the clerics in Shi'ite jurisprudence was being abused and that clerics should restrict themselves to moral guidance, lest day-to-day responsibilities for political events destroy their claim to higher moral authority.

SECULAR INITIATIVES

Clerical activism was only one attempt at reform over the past century. Secular reforms to systematize the premodern judicial anarchy and corruption were begun in the Qajar period. Though considerably advanced under Reza Shah Pahlavi, they were increasingly vitiated by the overwhelming growth of a police state and a patronage state.

In the nineteenth century, there were attempts to introduce reforms modeled on European, Ottoman, and British Indian law. The vizier Amir-e Kabir (1848–52) sought to promote customary law courts and extend state supervision over endowments. Mirza Husayn Khan (vizier from 1871–80) tried wide-ranging rationalizations of the cabinet and bureaucracy, including the systems of justice. He proposed a unified code of laws and a set of six high courts to replace the decentralized customary law system run by *hakims* and *kadkhodas*, which operated without any written code. He proposed that records be kept of all proceedings, bail be established in all cases except murder and grand robbery, warrants be issued for arrests, the gubernatorial right to impose the death penalty be revoked (reserving this for the king), private individuals be prohibited from trying their subordinates, and the punishing of mere suspects be banned. A box for public complaints was also established but was so flooded that it was shortly removed. Another proposal which would have given some supervisory control over religious endowments and *shari'a* courts was opposed by clerics and governors and was dropped (Nashat-Mirdamad 1973). In 1889 there was an abortive move to translate both the Napoleonic Code and the British Muhammadan Code for India for use in Iran.

Just how far any of these and similar reforms made an impact remains obscure. Curzon (1892) claims that *shari'a* courts were in decline under Nasir ud-Din Shah Qajar, while Banani, also giving no evidence, claims that "the unstable governments of Iran had defaulted nearly all judicial authority to the shari'ah courts" (1961: 68). The two systems, in any case, overlapped. The *shari'a* courts had little means to execute their judgments and theoretically were dependent on state officials (*kadkhodas*, *kalantars*, and *daroughas*) for this. On the other hand, governors and customary court officials often asked *mujtaheds* for opinions and rulings. Curzon comments that dread of crude justice and bribery was sufficient to deter most people from submitting cases to the courts whenever possible. They preferred arbitration in the councils of merchants, village elders, or by a *mullah* they knew and trusted.

With the introduction of the new legal codes of 1911, the Civil Code of 1926 (ratified 1928), the Penal Code of 1925–26, and subsequent judicial reforms, the authority of the *'ulama* was severely and systematically restricted, and the state courts were rationalized on European models. The codes themselves were partial translations of European codes, modified to Islamic and Iranian circumstances. In 1932 the registry of documents, a source of much clerical income, was taken out of the jurisdiction of the *shari'a* courts, which were now limited to marriage, divorce, and appointment of trustees and guardians. Further, they were limited to determining innocence and guilt, with sentencing being reserved to the state courts. In 1936 it was decreed that all judges must hold a degree from the Tehran University Faculty of Law or an equivalent degree from a European law school or must pass a qualifying exam, thus effectively disbarring clerics from the bench. After 1940 there was further state legislation in divorce and marriage statutes. The most important was the 1967 Family Protection Act. Among other things, it made polygamy a possible ground for divorce and eased the initiation of divorce proceedings by women. This act raised the ire of the clergy and their students.

By 1976 Iran had eighty-two high courts (each composed of two to five judges), 220 district courts, 2,053 judges (of whom 45 were women), 9,000 village Houses of Justice (see below), and 240 urban arbitration councils. All judges and prosecutors were royal appointees through the prime minister, and all courts except military courts were under the Ministry of Justice. Since the 1953–57 period of military law, however, there was a steadily increasing use of military courts, including SAVAK officers who were empowered as military magistrates. Military tribunals dealt not only with military personnel but also with political dissent, armed robbery, smuggling, and narcotics.

An insight into the ideology of the lawyers who helped introduce legal reforms in the 1920s and 1930s can be gained from their *theses pour le doctorat*. Particularly, those done at French and Swiss universities generally begin with a section on Shi'ite law and the attempts to reform the "judicial anarchy" of Qajar Iran. There is then a discourse on one of the major divisions of the law and how it could be reformed. This is elaborated by comparisons between the categories of European law and those of Iranian and Shi'ite law. Such comparisons served as stimuli to systematize and rationalize the national legal system. The second generation of secular lawyers were among the leaders of the protest against the usurpation of the judicial system by the military courts and arbitrary royal directives. Khomaini and the clerics joined in the cry against graft and injustice in the legal system, but it was the legal profession which most vigorously called for respect for due process of law, the limitation of secret military trials, and the use of legal procedures to protect individual rights rather than as an instrument of state domination.

PUNISHMENT AS SOCIOLOGICAL INDEX

Nineteenth-century punishments in Iran remind one of the seventeenth and eighteenth centuries in Europe. As Foucault (1977) has phrased it, pain was publically inflicted on the body as a kind of corporeal inscription of a theory of law and crime. This contrasts quite sharply with the theories of reforming the character or soul of more modern days. Rusche and Kirchheimer (1939) pioneered the effort to correlate such differences in modes of punishment with changes in social structure and economic formations: slave economies utilize penal slavery; feudal systems use capital and corporal punishment; mercantile economies introduce workhouses; industrial capitalism employs technologies of behavior modification and re-education.

> In late Qajar Iran condemned criminals were crucified, blown from guns, buried alive, impaled, shod like horses, torn asunder by being bound to the heads of two trees bent together and then allowed to spring back to their natural position, converted into human torches, flayed while living (Willis, quoted in Curzon 1892: 457).

Robbers and thieves were treated with mutilation of a finger, or a thumb, a hand, or an ear. Flogging was used to gain information as well as to punish. Willis distinguishes three kinds of prisons in Tehran: the one under the citadel, which held in its subterranean cells criminals and persons convicted of conspiracy and treason; the town prison which held vulgar criminals wearing iron collars, their feet in stocks and bound together with chains; and private guard houses.

The use of corporal punishment as a public spectacle may be seen in the torture visited upon Bahais, who were often condemned as heretics and foreign agents by clerical courts and then executed by city governors:

In 1901 two Abarghu Bahai peasants were condemned by local clerics in consultation with Aqa Najafi of Isfahan. They were led around town, their hair cut off and goat skins nailed to their heads. They were then beaten to death, and their bodies burned with kerosene.

In 1892 in Yazd there was a ritual slaughter of seven Bahais on the order of five clerics, with the concurrence of the Governor, Zil us-Sultan. The ritual involved processions and killings in many of the major public spaces of the town. First a 19 year old was strangled, and Jews were made to drag the body from the citadel to the central square of the bazaar. There, the Governor seated himself on a roof to watch a 60 year old have his throat cut, his belly ripped open and stones thrown at the corpse, which was finally burned. The procession then went to another square where a 30 year old was decapitated, the head put on a spear and the corpse stoned. On the parade went to a space by a mosque where a 45 year old was dismembered with a spade and burned. In Bazaar-e Sadri a 42 year old was killed. They then returned with knives, pulling out his intestines, and bringing his heart, lungs and head to the Governor who paid a reward. The head and lungs were then nailed to a tree and people threw stones at them. A feast was proclaimed: the bazaar was decorated with lights; tea and sweets were served.

In 1903 in Yazd, to try to calm the public frenzy during the Aqa-Najafi incited massacre of Bahais, the Governor had one man blown from a cannon in a public square and another's throat cut.

Part of the public display is explicitly a political demonstration of clerical power and anger at the crown (see Fischer 1973: Appendix I). But why such torture at all? Confession is one element. Part of the aim is recantation and admission that the socioreligious order of the clerics is correct. It is a public struggle of knowledge and conviction in which "truth" must be demonstrably more powerful. Compare Plato's judgment that if you cannot reform an offender, including an atheist, execution is justified in order to deter others and protect society (Sorabji 1980: ch. 18).

Under the Pahlavi dynasty, both public torture and public execution by hanging or being blown from a cannon disappeared. As the exercise of power became more secure, a dual system of punishment gradually was established: civilian offenders were put in prisons modeled on the reformatories of the West; political offenders were subjected to modern methods of secret or private interrogation and torture. Although done in private rather than as public spectacles, interestingly enough a photographic record was kept of these "inscriptions on the body," as if this were some kind of bureaucratic necessity. In the terms proposed by Rusche and Kirchheimer (1939), just as the state was a mixed industrializing-capitalist one and a fascist one, so the punishments were an increasingly technological mixture of reform and return to capital punishment. Thus a European observer could note the introduction of a model juvenile center in Tehran with a staff of psychiatrists and an expanding program of open prisons, simultaneous with the increase of torture and military justice (Butler and Levasseur 1976). As Rusche and Kirchenheimer had said regarding the fascist penal legal systems in the

1930s, "The law of procedure loses its function as a guarantee of the rights of the individual and takes on the character of a legal instrument for the realization of the punitive aims of the state" (p. 181).

Revolutionary Iran, having suspended the technological state, also abandoned reform and returned to capital punishment alone. In the early days of the revolution public hangings and public firing squads were also re-introduced as were floggings, occasional stoning, and, more rarely, mutiliation. Whether public or private, the executions are explicitly tied to a totalizing vision of justice and morality.

LAW AND ISLAMIC MORALITY

Shi'ite morality, like ancient Greek morality, revolves around two ideas: justice (*'adalat*) and ingenuity-prudence-cunning-dissimulation (*zerangi*, *taqiyya*). The first term, *'adalat*, is a criterion of being an office holder (whether king or religious leader). It means the equipoise of Greek philosophy: finding compromises between conflicting interests. It also means never having committed any major sin such as adultery and trying to avoid the minor sins such as shaving or dressing like a non-Muslim. It also involves knowledge: the first three caliphs are not regarded as evil (except insofar as they deliberately usurped the leadership of the community). By the series of faulty decisions that they made, however, they are shown to be unsuited for leadership.

The second set of terms is more subtle and open to debate, and is best illustrated by two parables about the first Imam, Ali, the legitimate successor to the Prophet. They parallel the Greek discussions about *metis* (cunning intelligence which upsets the relations of force), *kairos* (the ability to seize an opportunity), *sophie* (cleverness), *dolos* (cunning), *kerde* (tricks), *deinotes* (cleverness), and *phronesis* (prudence). Because of the moral ambiguity of these forms of intelligence, Plato wished to downgrade the entire practical world in favor of pure knowledge. Aristotle, however, reintroduces them in his discussion of the prudent man (Detienne and Vernant 1974/1978). The key parable of Ali about truth and justice is the story of the death of the Caliph Omar. Very briefly, Omar is killed by the Persian slave-artisan, Firuz, when Omar fails to provide a remedy for Firuz's just complaint against his master. Firuz runs out of the mill where the deed is done, passing Ali, who happens to be sitting at the entrance. Ali gets up and shifts his seat. When Omar's retainers ask Ali if he has seen Firuz, Ali replies, "As long as I have been sitting on this spot, I have not seen Firuz." The Persian tag to this parable is the famous line from the poet Saadi: *durush-i maslahat amiz beh az rasti fitna-angiz* (a calming lie which brings social good is better than truth which brings calamity).

It is the stress on the socially just end which makes the parable one of justice. Omar's death is contrasted with Ali's quite explicitly. Omar cries: "Seize that Magian (Persian), my end is near." Ali, slain by Ibn Muljam, says instead that he will be closer to God, that Ibn Muljam should be treated fairly, and his family should not be molested. Such contrasts are multiplied. The key parable of Shi'ism, the story of the Battle of Karbala, involves the refusal by the forces of Yezid to allow the thirsty followers of Imam Husayn (including children and women) to get water. Ali, in an analogous battle situation, allows his enemy to get water. Ali uses deceits in battle, but his moral purposes are pure. A foe tricked into defeat, lying prostrate, spits into Ali's face. Ali walks away until his passion cools, and only then does he give the opponent a last chance to convert or die. The latter asks why Ali had not cut off his head the first time, and Ali replies that he only kills for the protection of Islam. Had he killed in the heat of anger it would have been partially for personal revenge.

Ali's ethics, then, is a morality of just ends. But he is also the model of just procedures in court and is often contrasted with Omar:

> One day Ali sees a youth being led away and is told that Omar had ordered the boy to be bastinadoed because he had called a certain woman his mother. Ali finds it strange that this should be cause for lashes and stays the sentence. He asks Omar to explain. Omar says the lad called the woman his mother, but she claimed to be a virgin. The lad had lied and insulted the chastity of the woman and so was to be punished with eighty lashes. Islam protects the reputation of Muslims, and an idle tongue is a sin.
>
> The woman's brothers then testify to Ali that they had been unable to marry off their sister. Ali has a solution: he will marry the woman to the youth. He, Ali, will supply the dowry. The woman should go to the baths and prepare herself. The woman now speaks up: she fears the fires of hell and will tell the truth. She had married and became pregnant, but her husband died and her brothers refused to raise the child. They forced her to leave it in a pit. Secretly, she watched over it and saw it rescued by some tribesmen. As it grew up, she kept watch from afar. Somehow the lad learned his origin, but she, fearing her brothers, did not acknowledge him. Omar at this point cried out, "Oh, how without Ali would Omar have caused justice to miscarry!"

The moral legacy of Islam, as evidenced in popular preaching as well as doctrinal writings, is a complex, pragmatic, but also totalizing one. Islam is a teleogical structure of the form: if everyone behaved according to the divine laws, society would be just and equitable. As a moral platform from which to criticize injustice, Shi'ism provided a powerful critique of Pahlavi politics, economics, politics of the family, and general morality (see Fischer 1980: 147–70). As an ethical framework for reconstituting society, this critique has not yet evolved into pragmatic programs. Rather the totalizing vision has been used to justify morally ambiguous strategies (terror, executions, misleading promises).

The Greek and medieval Islamic theories about justice are worth reconsidering here, for it is ironic that Ayatollah Khomaini and the members of the Islamic Republican Party who follow him should have fallen into precisely those traps identified by the sources they discuss and teach. Plato worried about the nature of punishment, about the potential inflexibility of written law codes, and about power relations in applying the law. The purposes of punishment, he thought, are to compensate the victim and reform the offender. If reform is impossible (including cases of pollution), the offender is to be executed so as to deter others and protect society. In an ideal utopia, one might be able to rely on a true philosopher-king and dispense with laws. Aristotle, by contrast, preferred having written laws as norms, which could then be applied by judges to particular cases using their discretion to ensure equity. Khomaini's title "Imam" is often compared to Plato's ideal philosopher-king. Islamic interpretations of Plato, like indeed many Western ones, however, ignore Plato's practical efforts to incorporate the best of both democratic-populist and aristocratic-elitist courts of his day into an elaborate system of checks and balances intended to prevent abuse of power either by elites or by the tyranny of the majority (Morrow 1971). Islamic theorists of the medieval period, building both on Greek heritage and on observations of their own societies, clearly identified the effort to impose utopias in this world, whether on Plato's model or on idealized visions of the justice of Ali or other early Islamic figures, as major sources of unrighteous tyranny. All one could or should do in this world was to encourage governments to behave more justly and thereby more Islamicly (Laroui 1981). Ibn Khaldun, for example, after attempting to educate rulers in Fez and Granada in the ways of an Islamic philosopher-king, decided that the only defense against tyranny in this world is a body of laws and judicial procedures above the arbitrariness of any individual (Mahdi 1957).

Behind the executions, floggings, and complaints of "corruption of the earth" in the early days of the Iranian revolution, one could discern the detritus of Hellenic ethical concerns with reform of individual character (or the impossibility thereof), degrees of punishment to effect reform or deterrence, and notions of pollution. The concerns with power relations and abuse of legal procedures, which were such an important part of the alliance between lawyers and clerics in phase one of the revolution, have in phase two been overwhelmed by the retributive procedures of summary revolutionary courts. Khomaini's warnings against yielding to the simple passions of revenge have been issued half-heartedly and have been all but ignored in the calls by various clerical leaders of the Islamic Republic Party for revenge on those who oppose their consolidation of power.

CONFLICT RESOLUTION IN THE PAHLAVI STATE

Just as punishment forms were of a mixed genre in the Pahlavi state, so too was conflict resolution. Sociologies of law at the turn of the century made much of a general pattern of evolution from status to contract, from Gemeinschaft to Gesellschaft, from mechanical to organic integration, from community to society. This pattern began to be seriously questioned with the rise of fascism in Germany and Italy; it was recognized that liberalism could be rolled back. Sociologies of law in the Third World perforce are complicated by the combination of what liberals can view as progress and authoritarian forms of government which seek to control the judicial processes and use litigation as an instrument of domination. The Pahlavi state was no exception.

Two sets of real estate disputes illustrate the use of litigation by parties of unequal power: the state against the clergy over the control of religious endowments (*awqaf*) and religious minority owners versus religious majority renters in disputes over land and water. Two further sets of local level disputes illustrate the inutility of the state court system for peasants who lack powerful social ties and the greater utility of traditional mediation procedures, including ostensibly ritual forms.

The Pahlavi government used litigation to regulate religious endowments. The basic policy was to try to incorporate all endowments under the Office of Endowments and then to maximize the endowment income. All possible loopholes in endowment deeds were litigated to establish the Office as administrator or at least supervisor. The rationale for this shift in control was that many of the endowments were being allowed to decay, were being misused or converted into private holdings, or that the income was not being maximized or put to optimal use.

The religious establishment, as well as nonclerical administrators, countercharged that the Office of Endowments was absorbing the religious endowments and using the income for purposes not intended by the original deeds. The Office replied that endowment deeds are indeed inviolate, but that increase in the endowment's value within the deed's terms are permissible under the principle of *tabdil* (substituting something better). It was said, for example, that a small mosque in the middle of Tehran, unused, in ruins, of no particular architectural or historical value, with no endowments for its support, but itself still an endowment property, could properly be razed and an office building put in its place, the rents from which could be applied to hospitals, schools, and other community services. The counter argument by opponents of the Office's control was that the intent of the endowment was for a mosque, not an office building. Part of the argument also involved the dispute whether turning property into market capital with the intent of capitalizing on rent and interest contravenes the Quranic injunction against usury. Opponents of the Office's control invoked the usury prohibition, but in fact opinion among the clergy about the legality of interest and rents was divided. More importantly, at issue were two other items: the right of the administrator to 10 percent of the income and control over how endowments and their income are used.

Government regulation of endowments was not simply autocratic but operated through a set of negotiable bureaucratic and litigation procedures. The former included the use of bribes to remove or insert documents.

Case 1

> The court confirms two men as joint *mutavalli* (administrators) of some land as well as several shops endowed as support for a mosque. The Office of Endowments appeals by asking: how do we know the deed

in hand is the original one? (There is a gap of four hundred years between the deed and the present claimants.) How do we know the present claimants are entitled? The deed says they are administrators of the mosque, not of the lands endowed to support the mosque. Only a photocopy of the deed has been presented: where is the original? The original claim was that a certain Sayyid Abdul Husayn was the donor; the photocopy says the donor was a certain Abdullah. Even though there is a *sanad mahalli* (a document signed by locals confirming the two men as the rightful administrators), the issue is unclear. Under the law, endowments over which rights to administer are unclear fall under the jurisdiction of the Office of Endowments. Although the case is still under appeal after five years, the Office of Endowments signs and administers the rental contracts.

Case 2

Since 1804 there has been a dispute over a small piece of land originally donated by Shah Sultan Husayn Safavi (1694–1722) for the upkeep of a small shrine, Imamzada Khak-i Faraj, in Qum. In 1804 Muhammad Kak-i Faraj, the descendant of the original administrator, complained to Fath 'Ali Shah Qajar that the administrator of the great shrine of Hazrat-i Ma'suma was trying to take over. The shah confirmed Muhammad Kak-i Faraj's right. Beginning in 1955 the Endowments Office decided to contest the claims of Muhammad Khak-i Faraj's descendants on the grounds that it was never specified in any of the documents that the position of administrator was a hereditary job. The court ruled in favor of the Endowments Office, but as late as 1975 the case was still being appealed.

Other cases might be cited involving the regularization of documents and rights, as well as offers by the Office of Endowments to take over management of endowments. An administrator appeals to the Office for aid in forcing a lessee to pay his rent, for example; the Office replies that it should be appointed the representative of the administrator. A man is sued for taking over an endowment property as his private property, he has sold some of the land to a third party, and he asks if he may substitute an equivalent piece of land elsewhere; new documents need to be drawn up. Nor is the Office of Endowments always unhelpful. The administrator of a *madrasa* (religious school) says that his students' expenses far exceed the income of the school and asks that some of the 2 percent tax on endowment properties, which normally goes into a general fund for the support of *madrasas* and mosques, be given to him; he gets some financial aid.

These cases (see Fischer 1980: 118–20 for others) illustrate, I think, both the systematic expansion of state control over endowments and the regularization of registration and administration. The latter was part of a more general effort at rationalization of land rights and may be thrown into further relief by a second set of cases, from the town of Yazd, this time not from written records but from oral accounts by farmers of a religious minority. Religious minorities face problems in addition to the general problems of registering land due to their weak power relations.

In the process of introducing modern private property registration, whether in the last century or recently, it was the literate and powerful who understood the need to register and the ruses by which they might maximize their holdings. Peasants and lower-class urbanites have often been disinherited because they feared registration would only mean increased taxes; therefore they allowed lawyers, headmen, nobles, *shaykhs*, and merchants to register their land in the latter's names. This sort of fraud has been reported all over the Middle East. It happened in the 1930s in urban and suburban land in Yazd; it also happened as late as the 1960s during land reform in some parts of Iran. Among the ruses used was for a merchant, say, to claim a stretch of unused land and then donate a portion of it for a park, a graveyard, or some other municipal purpose. By accepting the land, the municipality ipso facto gave legal acknowledgment to the merchant's claim of ownership. Thereafter, he could develop and sell the land. For land which was in use, the government attempted to introduce some laws which protected those actually working the land.

These laws and the laws of endowment exacerbated problems for Zoroastrian villagers. Much Zoroastrian land is nominally held in the form of endowments because, it is claimed, in the nineteenth century and earlier this was the only way to protect it from Muslim usurpation, which occurred either through outright encroachment or through alienation of entire family lands when one member converted to Islam. In the nineteenth century, land deeds were notarized by Muslim clerics who, Zoroastrians say, had to be supplied with a constant flow of gifts to prevent forgery and other foul play with legal papers.

One source of foul play was the old system of documenting sales; another was the method of documenting ownership when no written deeds were extant. At a sale, a new deed would be drawn up for the new owner, but the old owner would retain the old deed, now presumably cancelled, but available for use in fraudulent claims. When no deed existed, ownership would be attested by having locals sign a statement that in local memory so-and-so had always owned or was entitled to the property. Thus, a convert to Islam could claim rights to his family land, or if he had taken the family deeds, he could have them rewritten or testified to by his new co-religionists. (By clerical law in the nineteenth century, converts to Islam were entitled to the entire property of their family, thereby disentitling other family members who had not converted.)

Zoroastrians claim that Muslims recognized religious endowment lands as sacred, and so they turned entire family or village holdings into this legal form for protection. Although such holdings supported certain Zoroastrian rituals called *gahambars* (see Fischer 1973), in a sense making them legitimate religious endowments, much of the land was considered private heritable land within the community. Under changed legal conditions, however, it was somewhat tricky to convert the holding back into private land, especially if there was some family or community member who wished to dispute a claim. Since much of the land was undivided for two or three generations, such disputes were not infrequent. Recourse to the courts was feared lest the Office of Endowments simply seize the property. Whether or not this was a legitimate fear, it reinforced the distrust of a court system in which someone who was not powerful, who did not have connections, and who was of a minority community was felt to be disadvantaged.

These disadvantages can be seen in the following two cases:

Case 3

Muhammad, a Muslim from another village and something of a troublemaker, demands written receipts for his payment of rent on a piece of land owned by Sohrab, a Zoroastrian villager. Sohrab is afraid to issue receipts because they would provide legal proof of Muhammad's tenant status. Should Sohrab wish to sell the land, the law gives the tenant the option to buy if he claims it is his livelihood. Not only does this limit Sohrab's ability to sell to whomever he wishes, but Muhammad might be able to get the land at government-assessed values below the free market price. In a village which is already half Zoroastrian and half Muslim, this is a likely eventuality and a further encroachment on the Zoroastrian community's ability to hold onto land.

Case 4

Rustam, another Zoroastrian of the same village, bought a piece of village land which he wants to farm. The land, however, already has a tenant on it, the same Muhammad. The law has a provision that a cultivator must be compensated for investments in the land, an amount called *dastrangi*, which varies according to the preparation of the land, including the previous crops sown which affect present fertility. Rustam is willing to pay more than the government-assessed *dastrangi*, but Muhammad still refuses to leave and sows a wheat crop. Rustam files suit in court and gains a judgment that he may harvest and take the wheat. Muhammad files a countersuit and gets a second judge to rule against the first judgment and that Muhammad is entitled to damages. A broker intervenes and gets the two parties to agree to a settlement of 1200 *tomans*. Rustam writes out a check in return for a written statement, signed by Muhammad, that there is nothing on the land and it is Rustam's to possess. Muhammad then has second thoughts, and taking both check and the signed statement, says they had better make the transaction legal in court. A new court date is set, but Muhammad fails to appear. Rustam cancels the check. The case is likely to have one of two conclusions: either Rustam will have to pay still more to get Muhammad to abandon the land, or Muhammad will claim a right to buy the land at the government assessed price which is far below market value. Indeed at this juncture, Muhammad makes a new move in Case 3: he says he will not pay Sohrab any further rent, nor will he give back the land; instead he is claiming the land as his own. It is socially, if not legally, important that Muhammad is a Muslim from another village, and that the village in which the land is located is half Zoroastrian, half Muslim.

It is also relevant that the village is increasingly becoming a suburb of Yazd and that the land will rise in value as urban rather than agricultural land. The conflict between two defensible legal principles—protection of property rights and protection of tenants' rights—is socially skewed in these cases against the socially weaker group. The realization of this reality often keeps cases from reaching the courts. In the same village, a Zoroastrian water pump operator who had trouble collecting rates from a number of Muslims, was warned by the water board authorities and the police that it is better to write off some rates as a loss or to give "discounts" to troublemakers than to go to court, stirring up trouble in a small, divided community. Such realities of unequal power and access cause villagers to avoid government legal systems entirely when possible and to rely on ritual mediation or the arbitration of powerful personages in reaching a judgment.

Ritual procedures are relatively weak techniques, depending for efficacy on the closed nature of the community. A trivial sort of ritual procedure is *tir-i-Imam Abbas*, a device for detecting a thief, usually a child or servant. The Quran is read while two persons seated facing each other hold four rods, one in each hand, aligned in two parallel lines, the rod ends touching. Suspects are asked to place their arm between the two lines. The rods will move inward to pinch a thief; the rods will not move, or will move outward, for an innocent. Child or servant, frightened by the attention, solemnity, and the sacredness invoked by the Quran, will often confess and burst into tears.

Less trivial but less effective is the following attempt to use the *yasht dowr-i dakhma* ritual to help solve a Zoroastrian endowment dispute.

Case 5

During the dry pre-World War II years, many people left the village as the water gave out. Ardeshir moved to another village, leaving his brother's son, Hormuzdiar, to struggle with the family lands and some rented lands in the better-watered neighboring village. The latter were soon taken back by their owner, leaving Hormuzdiar destitute with wife and children. He went to Bombay to raise money to refurbish the village fire temple and to utilize the endowed land for its support. Returning to the village as manager of the temple and its endowments, he managed to make ends meet. After the war, when the water supply began to improve, Ardeshir returned to claim his share of the lands. Hormuzdiar refused, saying Ardeshir had forfeited his rights by leaving the village. The dispute continued to Hormuzdiar's deathbed. Ardeshir threatened him: "If you die without giving me my land, I will not bless your corpse, and it will putrify in the tower of silence, but it will not go away" (i.e., neither will the vultures touch the body nor will the soul be able to cross over into the next world). Hormuzdiar, angered, replied, "Get out; I am not going to die." Hormuzdiar died. Ardeshir did not bless the body.

Rustam, a son of Hormuzdiar, returned from Bombay and learned of the dispute. Half-gullible, he went to the tower of silence watchman, who affirmed that the corpse was still there, bloated and putrifying. Rustam asked to verify this for himself but was denied. Rustam then decided, whatever the truth of the matter, a compromise should be reached. He called upon the aged Ardeshir and agreed that if he could get six people to sign a statement that they remembered the land to be rightfully his, he, Rustam, would sign over the deed. The land would revert legally to Ardeshir, but since Ardeshir did not live in the village, Rustam would farm it and pay rent. This was done. Rustam then took Ardeshir to a ritual bath and then to the tower of silence where the old man blessed Hormuzdiar's soul, and a *yasht dowr-i dakhme* (an all night ritual) was held. After a few days Rustam was informed that the corpse was gone.

But the dispute continued. Rustam's brothers did not agree with his initiative and did not recognize Rustam's signature on the deed to Ardeshir's share of the land, saying it was not Rustam's to give away. Since the land in question had been rented out to third parties, their opposition blocked Rustam's ability to pay the agreed rent to Ardeshir.

There are a number of complications in this case. For three generations inheritance had not been divided. Hormuzdiar, in whose hands all the land was held at one point, had ten children, a brother, and two uncles. There were a death, a cousin marriage, and several other status changes among the heirs, complicating their claims. In the 1930s when land was being registered by the government, Hormuzdiar had all the land registered as private land (*melki*). His brother and uncle objected that most of the land was a family endowment (*vaqf-i oladi*) which was to support three family *gahambars*. Others in the community point out that the *gahambars* are celebrated in the fire temple, indicating that the lands are not family endowments but communal religious endowments made up of a number of lands entrusted to Hormuzdiar in his role as fire temple administrator. Of course, much of the land is now in the hands of tenants who also have rights. Clearly then, while the *yasht dowr-i dakhma*-associated folk beliefs and practices (cursing and blessing of a soul) were sufficient for Rustam, they could not solve the problems. Some parties to the dispute vaguely talked of taking the case to court, but others (and a judge informally) said families should solve their own disputes.

Of more general importance are the Houses of Justice (*khana ensaf*), which also illustrate the problem of villagers' power relations and lack of access to the courts as a viable device for resolving local conflicts. The Houses of Justice were a White Revolution program for streamlining the national legal system and taking pressure off urban courts by trying to resolve local problems in the villages. Fundamental problems arose. The villages already had their informal conflict resolution procedures centering on one or another of the village elders. More importantly, the Houses of Justice were tied to the national system so that appeals could be made to gendarmes, to town doctors for medical opinions, and to bureaucratic structures over which villagers had no leverage. Craig (1974) analyzed sixty-nine cases adjudicated in the village of Emadabad over four years. Over time the Houses of Justice were used less and less. There was a decline in written complaints, testimonies, number of adjudicators, number of cases in which doctors' certificates were secured, and number of cases in which gendarmes were involved. Among the reasons for abandoning the Houses of Justice were lack of efficient guidance, inability to control the extravillage procedures, and availability of a better alternative. Fines collected had to be sent to Shiraz, for example, and after the following incidents, the head of the House of Justice in Emadabad saw no reason for such transfer payments:

Case 6

An engineer working on a canal cut off the water to some fields. The peasants protested and got an order from the engineer's boss to restore the water flow. He refused. The House of Justice wrote a letter in support of the peasants to the gendarmerie. The engineer bought off the gendarmes. Eventually the head of the House of Justice was able to find a higher rank gendarme officer in Shiraz to restore the flow. Faith in the gendarmes as an impartial force was shattered.

Case 7

Several persons were injured in a fight. The House of Justice sent them to doctors to certify the extent of injuries. Documentation of the severity of injury proved to be a direct function of the amount of money paid to the doctor. Faith in the doctors of Shiraz was undermined.

Case 8

Two brothers disputed claims to a piece of land. At the time of land reform, one brother had been in the army, and the other had registered the land in his own name. Upon the return of the soldier, the two worked the fields together, and the soldier invested ten thousand tomans in a pump. They then quarreled. The House of Justice wrote a brief to be presented in the Shiraz court (as the amount at issue was over the two thousand *toman* limit for House of Justice adjudication) which affirmed the right of the soldier to half the land. The court tried to refuse the case, saying brothers should settle their dispute out of court and that the court would have to go by the title to the land. The case went to court nonetheless, and the court disinherited the soldier, against all local sense of justice. Further, since the soldier had no right to the land, the court also ruled that the claim to reimbursement for the irrigation pump was invalid.

The alternative to the House of Justice was the traditional procedure of mediation by a third party more powerful and of higher status than either disputant. By the sixth six-month period of the operation of the House of Justice, 77 percent of the verdicts were being given by the head of the House of Justice alone, and increasingly written documentation was being abandoned in the small face-to-face community where people do not want formally to testify against one another. Similar techniques of justice are to be found in the bazaar. The credit structure of the bazaar is the main enforcement mechanism. Since one's moral as well as business trustworthiness is measured by one's credit rating, this mechanism can be powerful. Bankruptcy is the limiting case; creditors share out and discount whatever assets are left. But one should never declare bankruptcy if one can possibly avoid it, because it makes decent credit almost impossible to get again. Rolling over debts at higher and higher interest rates, even if crippling, is preferable. Powerful bazaaris have enforcers and in the past operated openly under the Islamicly sanctioned principle of self-help (*tayassul 'ala'l haqq*). Seizure of a debtor's property sometimes resulted. Harrassment was also employed in the nineteenth century: *sayyids* (whose persons were inviolate from attack) were hired to follow the debtor in public crying loudly for payment and justice. If this did not work, a debtor could be arrested, flogged, tortured to tell where hidden assets might be, or subjected to a court of arbitration with either a leading merchant or a religious figure presiding (Floor 1977).

Hiring of *sayyid* criers and public floggings are things of the past, but the notions of honor and justice involved are very much alive. The role model of the *luti*, the neighborhood enforcer of morality, is a frequent subject of popular films and discussions of employer-employee (or middle-class patron/lower-class worker) relations. His no-nonsense paternalism, helping the poor and weak and teaching the rich and powerful humility, is often invoked as the proper style of running a factory or business. Films also explore the breakdown of self-help procedures, especially the tragedy of becoming duty-bound to avenge a sexual dishonor by murder. In Aristotle, anger (and lust), while not constituting legal excuses of involuntary action (such as force or ignorance), yet may be pardoned (Sorabji 1980: ch. 16). In Persian folk morality, anger and lust are very close to involuntary action. Cases of revenge for sexual dishonor thus carry tragic overtones. To kill in a matter of *namus* (that honor which men lose through attacks on their women), although pardonable among men, makes one religiously unclean as well as bringing one into conflict with the modern justice system. It cannot restore the status quo ante. True honor is preventing injury from the outset. Many films, such as the very popular *Qaisar*, explore the tragedy of feeling compelled to take justice into one's own hands before the state judicial system swallows it in meaningless, impersonal, and distant red tape, knowing full well that to kill will destroy one's social relations, one's religious purity, as well as one's legal status.

Such moral dilemmas seem no longer to exist in phase two of the revolution for those clerics who claim to be the guardians of utopian morality and justice.

CONCLUSION

Iran poses almost paradigmatically the problems of constructing a modern state in the late twentieth century without slipping into externally dominated, internally authoritarian forms. The availability of oil revenues and the increased literacy ought to provide flexibility and opportunity for Iranians to mold their own destiny. Yet, oil revenues under the Pahlavis, particularly in the last years, allowed the state to be financially independent of and unresponsive to its citizenry. People at various levels of society thus resorted to a variety of devices to avoid the state or parry its demands: among these were the patronage system, the inward turning to traditional social control mechanisms of the peasant and bazaar communities, dissimulation, and the moral ideologies of both Islam (with its emphases on social justice and situational ethics) and constitutional law (with its espousal of due process and representative government). The revolution of 1977–79 drew on both the Islamic and constitutional ideologies as well as on the network and patronage modes of organization of the villages and bazaars.

The Islamic legacy, like the Jewish and Christian legacies, is rooted in part in the engagement with Greek moral philosophy. Moral philosophy is not an easy set of answers, not even in the writings of the most rationalized of the scholastics, but involves constant debate about justice, ingenuity, and social order or hierarchy. The debate over the role of the clergy has today a new sociological ground. In the past, restricted literacy gave a certain power and control to the clergy. Now, the young generation of Iran is largely literate.

Thus one might well expect that part of the revolution in Iran will prove to be a change in attitude toward interpreting Islam: one of denying specialized judicial authority to the clergy, since laymen can read the sources as well as they. This was the call of Dr. Ali Shariati, enthusiastically taken up by large segments of the young revolutionaries. Ayatollah Shariatmadari, at the time of Khomaini's return to Iran, reiterated the warnings of Islamic scholars through the ages that attempts to impose utopias by force and without sincere consultation lead to injustice and tyranny. He warned that Khomaini's long-term legacy was likely to be the destruction of the clergy's claim to moral authority. Sayyid Mahmud Taleghani insisted that only through consultative cooperation could a society be built worthy of the name Islamic. This is not the place to consider appropriate tactics and strategies of revolutionary and reform efforts, but rather to stress that the legacy of Islam is rich and multivocal. Among the voices of Islam, Khomaini's is but one. That of Mullah Nasiruddin is another:

> Mullah Nasiruddin had a donkey. The donkey fell into a ditch. A passerby helped by pulling on the tail. The tail came off. Mullah took the man to court. There, two other cases were heard first. To the man who claimed his daughter had been spoiled by another, the *qadi* said: Go bring proof your daughter was a virgin. To the man who claimed another had blinded him in one eye, the qadi said: Go bring proof your eye was sound. When Mullah Nasiruddin's turn came, he cried: "*Hici baba! Khar-e ma-az-kurigi dom nadosht*! (Never mind, baba! Our donkey, since infancy, has had no tail!)

Khomaini insisted on playing *qadi*; Iranians perforce continued playing Mullah Nasiruddin.

NOTES

1. See Amnesty International (1987) on the creation and provisional implementation of the new statutory Islamic Penal Code of Iran.

REFERENCES

Abdoh, Djalal. 1937. *L'element psychologique dans les contrats suivant la conception iranienne*. Paris: University of Paris.

Akhavi, Shahrough. 1980. *Religion and Politics in Contemporary Iran: Clergy-State Relations in the Pahlavi Period*. Albany: State University of New York Press.

Akhoundi, Mahmoud. 1961. *De l'influence de la tradition religieuse sur le droit penal de l'Iran*. Neuchatel: University of Neuchatel.

Algar, Hamid. 1969. *Religion and State in Iran 1785–1906: The Role of the Ulama in the Qajar Period*. Berkeley: University of California.

Alloway, Tony. 1980. Column on Iran. *London Times*. May 8. Amid, Moussa. 1939. *Le divorce en droit iranien*. Paris: University of Paris.

Amir-Soleymani, A. 1936. *Etude comparative sur la formation et les effets des contrats entre le droit iranien et le droit français*. Paris: University of Paris.

Amnesty International. 1987. *Iran: Violations of Human Rights*. London: Amnesty International Publications.

Arani, Sharif. 1980. "Iran: From the Shah's Dictatorship to Khomaini's Demagogic Theocracy." *Dissent* 27(1): 9–26.

Arjomand, Said Amir. 1978. "The Shi'ite Hierarchy and the State in Iran under the Early Qajars 1785–1848." Unpublished paper.

———. 1983. "The Office of Mulla-Bashi in Shi'ite Iran." *Studia Islamica* 57: 135–46.

Banani, Amin. 1961. *The Modernization of Iran, 1921–1941*. Palo Alto, Cal.: Stanford University.

Baraheni, Reza. 1977. *The Crowned Cannibals: Writings on Repression in Iran*. New York: Vintage.

Bassidju, Ahmed. 1936. *La situation juridique de la femme*. Paris: University of Paris.

Brinton, Crane. 1938. *Anatomy of Revolution*. New York: Random House.

Butler, William J., and Georges Levasseur. 1976. *Human Rights and the Legal System in Iran*. Geneva: International Commission of Jurists.

Cole, J.R.I. 1988. *Roots of North Indian Shi'ism in Iran and Iraq*. Berkeley: University of California Press.

Craig, Daniel. 1974. *A Return to Tradition: Conflict Management in Emadabad since the White Revolution 1970–73*. B.A. Thesis. Harvard University.

Curzon, George N. 1892. *Persia and the Persian Question*. London: Longmans, Green.

Detienne, Marcel, and Jean-Pierre Vernant. 1974/1978. *Cunning Intelligence in Greek Culture and Society*. Brighton, England: Harvester Press.

Docteur-Zadeh, Ibrahim. 1939. *De la validité des contrats sur la chose d'autrui en droit positif iranien*. Paris: University of Paris.

Fischer, M. M. J. 1973. *Zoroastrian Iran between Myth and Praxis*. Ph.D. diss. University of Chicago.

———. 1980. "Iran and Islamic Justice." Washington, D.C.: *Middle East Executive Reports*.

———. 1980. *Iran: From Religious Dispute to Revolution*. Cambridge: Harvard University Press.

Floor, W. M. 1977. "Bankruptcy in Qajar Iran." *Zeitschrift der Deutschen Morgenlandischen Gesellschaft* 127(1): 61–76.

Foucault, Michel. 1977. *Discipline and Punish*. New York: Vintage.

Hairi-Yazdi, Mehdi. 1980. "Shia Jurisprudence." Talk given at the Harvard Law School.

Heyayat, Sadegh. 1937/1957. *The Blind Owl*. New York: Grove.

Kasravi, Ahmad. 1330 (1952). *Tarikh-i Mashruta-i Iran*. Tehran: Amir Kabir.

Khochbine, Gholam-Hossein. 1938. *Etude sur l'organisation judiciaire civile de l'Iran*. Paris: University of Paris.

Laraoui, Abdallah. 1981. "Classical Islamic Theories of State". Lecture, Center for Middle East Studies, Harvard Univ., February 24.

Mahdi, Muhsin. 1957. *Ibn Khaldun's Philosophy of History*. London: George Allen and Unwin.

Maydani, Riyad. 1955. "'Uqubat: Penal Law." In M.Khadduri and H.J. Liebesny, eds. *Law in the Middle East*. Washington, D.C.: Middle East Institute.

Mohebbi, Manoutchehr Khodayar. 1958. *L'influence religieuse sur le droit constitutionnel de l'Iran*. Paris: University of Paris.

Morrow, Glen R. 1971. "Plato and the Rule of Law" in Gregory Vlastos, ed., *Plato II*. Notre Dame, Ind.: Notre Dame University.

Mossadegh, Mohammad. 1914. *Le testament en droit musulman*. Neuchatel: University of Neuchatel.

Motahhedeh, Roy. 1980. "Iran's Foreign Devils." *Foreign Policy* 38 (Spring).

Nader, Laura, and Harry F. Todd, Jr., eds. 1978. *The Disputing Process: Law in Ten Societies*. New York: Columbia University Press.

Nashat-Mirdamad, Guity. 1973. *Beginnings of Modernizing Reform in Iran 1870–80*. Ph.D. diss.: University of Chicago.

Nassiri, Mohammad. 1937. *La donation en droit iranien*. Paris: University of Paris.

Rusche, George, and Otto Kirchheimer. 1939. *Punishment and Social Structure*. New York: Columbia University Press.

Sabi, Musa. 1973. *The Civil Code of Iran*. Tehran.

Sorabji, Richard. 1980. *Necessity, Cause, and Blame: Perspectives on Aristotle's Theory*. Ithaca: Cornell University Press.

8

WORKING THE LAW: A LEBANESE WORKING-CLASS CASE

Suad Joseph

The legal process for the Lebanese working class in the early 1970s, was a mazeway of face-to-face encounters channeled along the lattice of the Lebanese class structure. The powerless worked the law by linking themselves to the powerful through patron-client relationships constructed from kin and associational networks. Recognizing that the law responded more to the pressures of personal relationships than the logic of jural rules, they personalized interclass alliances by legitimating the patron-client ties in the idioms of intimate relationships. They worked the law by manipulating kin morality to cross class lines. Their method was successful because interclass relationships in Lebanon drew upon kin morality and the legal process is an expression of the structure of class relationships.

THE PROBLEM: LAW AND CLASS IN LEBANON

In this chapter, I use the case study method to demonstrate relationships between law and class in Lebanon. The case details a Syrian Sunni man's successful mobilization of personal networks—including me—to obtain papers from the Lebanese government for the release of his son from Syrian military service. As a reflection of the interlocking of law and class in Lebanon, the ordeal of this long-term, working-class resident of Greater Beirut, in many respects represented the legal experience of those living in Lebanon in the early 1970s regardless of sect or citizenship. The first part of the chapter outlines a theoretical framework for analyzing the relationships of law and class; the second part details the case. The chapter concludes with a discussion of the theoretical implications of the case study.

THEORETICAL FRAMEWORK

A number of political sociologists have argued that Middle Eastern polities conform to Max Weber's patrimonial model (Hermassi 1972; Bill and Leiden

1974; Waterbury 1970; Gellner 1969; Vatikiotis 1957). In patrimonial systems, a state administration takes over specialized functions from kin-based patriarchies, but the ruler and the populace remain connected through personalized networks woven through the state bureaucracies. In rational legal systems, on the other hand, law comprises consistent systems of consistently applied abstract rules; persons in authority—obeying only law—occupy offices governed by an impersonal order; and obedience to persons in authority is obedience to the impersonal order, not the person (Weber 1947).

The application of Weber's patrimonial model to Middle Eastern polities is, in certain respects, productive. The distinction between the rule of abstract principles and personal-moral obligations is particularly useful; rational legal systems, indeed, are not operative in much of the Middle East. However, the model, by focusing on the political leader—king, caliph, shah, or sultan—neglects the operative force of class relationships. I suggest that the descriptive insights of the patrimonial model need to be conjoined to the heuristic power of class analyses. I argue that personal-moral obligations underpin legal systems in many Middle Eastern countries because they uphold the structure of class relationships.

The class relationships relevant to working the Lebanese law were manifested in patronage ties and legitimated in personal-moral terms. The law neither protected individuals automatically nor operated independently by formal rules. To make the law "work," individuals needed *wasta* (brokerage connections to persons in power). By exchanging services, manipulating identities, and evoking moralities, individuals created short- and long-term, horizontal and vertical alliances to build *wasta* networks. Like star constellations, the networks wove through the class structure, connecting laypersons to successively more powerful leaders.[1]

Such patronage networks constructed from personal ties drew upon and were imbued with the moral and emotional content of primordial relationships. Strangers, connected through mutually known primary relationships, temporarily addressed each other as siblings, cousins, or the like. The stranger, then, could be asked to carry out the moral obligations of the primary relationship even when those obligations contradicted the formal responsibilities of public office. The "impersonal order" thus was personalized through kin idioms and its "abstract rules" particularized through primordial morality.

Personal intervention in the legal process was possible because the law in Lebanon was not morally compelling. Individuals responded to neither the law nor the state directly. Rather, for them the morally compelling relationships were primordial. The tension between rational and patrimonial orders occurred, in large part, because the ruling class constructed its power on the basis of personal control over law, state, and populace.

The political leaders, *zu'ama'*, maintained power by personalizing it. Rather than building autonomously operative government agencies or rationally organized (in Weber's terms) political institutions, they retained personal control over the allocation of public resources and services, decision making, and the implementation of law and government regulations. They each intervened with such regularity in government agencies to make exceptions for their clients that the norm of operation was intervention—so much so, that government agencies had difficulty working at all without the personal intervention of political leaders. Their methods pervaded the entire society. Alliances within and between class lines, therefore, were necessary to work not only the law, but all aspects of political, economic, and social life in Lebanon.

The case of Abu Mufid details the story of one man working the Lebanese legal system, revealing the relationship between law and class on many levels. In 1972, about one third of Lebanon's three million residents did not have citizenship. Of these one-half million were Syrian. Most of these people were urban working class. Certain aspects of Abu Mufid's case were specific to that alien population. In general, however, his case speaks to the difficulties with the law experienced by the Lebanese working class as a whole and, in varying degrees, the Lebanese populace as a whole. Abu Mufid's story demonstrates that working the law in Lebanon required a tremendous amount of time, energy, persistence, critical questioning, and skepticism—and many hidden financial and nonfinancial costs.

The urban working class entered the legal process with handicaps: lack of time, money and resources, the likelihood of illegal statuses, and negative past encounters with public officials. They often received incomplete and incorrect information, as well as careless or abusive treatment, from state officials. Such abuse reinforced their need for *wasta* and their activist and instrumental attitude toward the law. They used primary relationships to link themselves with the power structure behind the law. Generating networks from horizontal and hierarchical relationships, they bonded themselves normatively and instrumentally to short- and long-term ties. They used any relationship available to work the law—crossing ethnic, sectarian, class, gender, regional, and national boundaries. Attributing situational meanings to social categories, they used the categories as vehicles to transactions. In constructing such complex networks nested in the idioms of intimate relationships, these working-class individuals reinforced and reproduced the very structure of class relationships which exploited them. The success of Abu Mufid was, then, on the one hand, a testimony to his intellect and endurance and, on the other, a demonstration of the manner in which class relationships in Lebanon were expressed and reproduced.

THE CASE: WORKING THE LAW

In 1972, Muhammed Rafik—addressed in the neighborhood as Abu Mufid (father of Mufid) after his eldest son—was a forty-seven-year old Syrian Sunni who had worked for fifteen years, off and on since he was thirteen, in the Greater Beirut municipality of Borj Hammoud.[2] He and his wife had eight children, six sons and two daughters. Their eldest daughter was married, and the remaining seven children lived with them. Abu Mufid and his three oldest sons operated a welding repair shop in Borj Hammoud. Since he had little formal education—five years of Quranic instruction—he capitalized on his own labor and skills and those of his children to achieve mobility. A disciplinarian, he maintained tight control over his family; his family kept a neat and efficient household; his children devoted themselves to the shop and school. As a family, they seemed to be content and to have few disruptive family problems.

Abu Mufid saw the outside world as a place filled with both possibilities and dangers. A self-made man, he believed that one advanced through individual initiative but that advancement was on behalf of one's family. He was generous, yet cautious and serious. Although he was articulate and socially adept, he remained slightly aloof from neighbors, especially as his circumstances improved. Highly respected in the neighborhood as hardworking, enterprising, and peaceloving, he was also envied for his success.

He maintained political independence. Like many in the neighborhood, he was critical of the Lebanese government, the Syrian government, and Western and Arab leaders. He discussed politics with ease and cynicism. Yet in many respects he was an idealist, genuinely believing that society could be improved by conscious human effort and goodwill.

I knew Abu Mufid from 1971 to 1973. He lived in the apartment above mine in the Camp Trad neighborhood of Borj Hammoud. We had become particularly friendly because of my attachment to his four-year old daughter who daily frequented my apartment. In June 1972 Abu Mufid asked me to help him process papers through the Lebanese government to obtain release of his son from the Syrian military.

The Syrian government had begun permitting Syrian youths who had lived outside the country for over ten years to be released from military service. Papers from the host government testifying to the residence and payment of U.S. $1,000 were required for the release. Abu Mufid had become dependent upon his eldest son for the skilled work in the welding shop. He was afraid, also, that should one serve, the others would be called up as well—spelling disaster for the shop. Releasing Mufid from the military was therefore vital to sustaining the family.

However, obtaining the proper papers was complicated by a number of factors. While he had the original residence permits for his family, Abu Mufid had never renewed them. Additionally, he had neither a Lebanese work permit nor a license for his shop. Thus, while he and his family had lived in Lebanon more than the required ten consecutive years, he did not have legal proof. Knowing he would need *wasta*, he asked me to help. During the two months in which I was involved with the case, I kept daily accounts of my conversations with Abu Mufid and my actions on his behalf. The case description summarized below abstracts the key events from my records.

June 1, Thursday: Abu Mufid informed me that his son, Mufid, was conscripted into Syrian military service. He had learned from a Syrian friend that the Syrian government was now permitting release from service for those living for ten consecutive years outside the country. He needed papers attesting to Mufid's residency in Lebanon signed by the Camp Trad *mukhtar* (mayor) in Borj Hammoud, the governor of Mount Lebanon, and the Lebanese ministers of Interior and Foreign Affairs. The papers, with the payment of U.S. $1,000, would be processed through the Syrian government. He also indicated that friends of his, attempting this process, had been misinformed and exploited repeatedly. To avoid wasting time, money, and dignity, he asked me to help him obtain the Lebanese papers. While he had had past difficulties with the *mukhtar* (they had competed years ago selling cooking gas), he said he would be able to get the paper from him. The major problem with which he would need my help, he said, was the Ministry of the Interior. Because of the loss of time and income it would have entailed, he had neither renewed the family's residency permits nor obtained work permits or a license for his welding shop. He therefore had no officially acceptable proof of the family's residence in Lebanon.

He thought he might have a *wasta* in the Ministry of Interior. His son-in-law had fixed the car of a high ranking official—a Mr. Harik—who had given him a work permit in exchange. Abu Mufid conjectured that, through his son-in-law, he might be able to acquire a work permit from Harik. However, since he was uncertain of this *wasta*, he asked if I had contacts. I told him I would talk to the Ramzis, family-like friends of mine and a part of Lebanon's intellectual elite, well-connected to the political elite, especially the Christian *zu'ama'*.

June 4, Sunday: I saw the Ramzis in the morning and explained Abu Mufid's needs. They suggested I bring him in the evening. At 8 p.m. I took Abu Mufid, and he retold his story in detail. Rafik, the oldest son, explained that they had connections with the governor of Mount Lebanon, but not the minister of Interior. He also pointed out that the Syrian government instructions, which Abu Mufid had brought with him, did not require a signature from the minister of Interior. Abu Mufid then related the story of a friend whose papers had been rejected because he did not have the minister's signature. Rafik suggested we begin with the *mukhtar*'s paper, and they would help as they could from there.

Returning to Borj Hammoud, Abu Mufid expressed concern about the *mukhtar*'s papers. I offered to go with him. I had a cordial relationship with the *mukhtar*: his daughter had befriended me, and my contacts within the Armenian Dashnag Party which had placed him in office led me to believe that I might be of some service.

June 5, Monday: I visited the *mukhtar* and told him a friend of mine needed residency papers to release his son from Syrian military service. He said he would help.

June 6, Tuesday: At 8 a.m. Abu Mufid and I visted the *mukhtar*. After Abu Mufid indicated what he needed, the *mukhtar* told him that his assistant, Khawaja Hanna, would help him after lunch. That afternoon, Abu Mufid spoke with Khawaja Hanna. Shortly after, he told me that Khawaja Hanna had refused to do the papers because he was not registered with their office. He had offered to bring a *malik* (property owner) to testify to his residency.[3] Khawaja Hanna had agreed to do the paper only if the *malik* would accept full responsibility for the statement. Abu Mufid brought a *malik*. Khawaja Hanna told Abu Mufid to return with him the next morning.

June 7, Wednesday: I visited the *mukhtar* in the morning to ask about Abu Mufid's papers. He told me that it was risky, but, nevertheless, Khawaja Hanna would do the paper that day. In the evening Abu Mufid related the day's events. He had taken the *malik* to the *mukhtar*'s office in the morning. The *mukhtar* told him to return at 3 p.m. since Khawaja Hanna does not work there mornings. Returning at 3 p.m., they found Khawaja Hanna with the completed paper. The *malik* and *mukhtar* each signed. Khawaja Hanna's charges included the cost of the government stamps, LL5 for the *mukhtar* and LL2 for himself. Abu Mufid had given Khawaja Hanna an additional LL3, requesting that he obtain the signature of the *qa'im-maqam* (governor) of Mount Lebanon. Khawaja Hanna took the money and told him to return Thursday.

Abu Mufid informed me that the services of the Ramzis were no longer necessary. I told him that the Ramzis and I had decided that should he need further help, I would consult with a mutual family-like friend, Sheikh Jamal, who had extensive government experience. His father had been in parliament, his brother had held several government posts, and he frequently was a *wasta* for friends and clients.

June 8, Thursday: Abu Mufid showed me the *mukhtar*'s paper. I took the paper to Shaykh Jamal. He found the paper inadequate, noting that it only affirmed the signature of the *malik*, rather than the truth of the statement. When I returned the paper to Abu Mufid in the evening, he confessed that he had suspected it was inadequate. I volunteered to see the *mukhtar* the next morning.

June 9, Friday: In the morning I reported to the *mukhtar* that a government official had told me the paper must indicate his testimony to Abu Mufid's residence. Reading the paper, he agreed and asked me to return in the afternoon to see Khawaja Hanna. In the afternoon Khawaja Hanna was alone in the *mukhtar*'s office. I pointed out that the paper was insufficient and detailed again what was required. Despite my reasoning, he refused to do anything further, contending the responsibility was too great. The *mukhtar* entered to see a man who had come for him. After he and Khawaja Hanna had conferred in Turkish about Abu Mufid's case, Khawaja Hanna repeated what he had said earlier and added that, even if the *mukhtar* was willing, he would refuse to do the paper. The *mukhtar* agreed that he could not accept such responsibility. I replied that, given the many people willing to attest to Abu Mufid's residency, no responsibility was entailed. Raising his voice, the *mukhtar* questioned me if I wanted to hurt him or have him hurt me. When I assured him otherwise he said "good" and left with the man who had come for him.

Later at his shop, I suggested to Abu Mufid that he find another *mukhtar* to do the paper. As we were talking, an Armenian friend of mine, Hagop, passed by. We explained the predicament. He said he would call the *mukhtar*. I hoped his good reputation and standing in the local ruling Dashnag Party would help.[4]

He and I went to call the *mukhtar* and Abu Mufid went to find a friend to go with him to another *mukhtar*.

Calling the Armenian *mukhtar* from his office, Hagop suggested that perhaps the *mukhtar* had not understood what was needed. The *mukhtar* shouted back that Abu Mufid had no proof of his residency, that he did not know Abu Mufid, and that he would not do the papers. Attempting to explain the situation to Hagop, I detailed Abu Mufid's previous troubles with the *mukhtar*, conveying Abu Mufid's contention that the *mukhtar* discriminated against Arabs. Hagop countered that he acted the same way with Armenians.

That night, Abu Mufid reported he had taken a Shi'ite friend with him and had obtained the proper residency papers from a Shi'ite *mukhtar* in Nab'a, Borj Hammoud.

June 12, Monday: Shaykh Jamal approved the new *mukhtar*'s paper. I returned the paper to Abu Mufid, conveying Shaykh Jamal's approval. Shaykh Jamal had agreed to act as *wasta* to the Ministry of Interior after the *qa'im-maqam*'s signature was obtained.

June 15, Thursday: Abu Mufid learned from a Syrian friend that he now additionally needed a paper from the *baladiyi* (municipality), attesting to his residency in Lebanon. I told Abu Mufid that I could connect him to Elias Nakhli, the municipal director of health services who, by stretching family names, considered me a distant relative. Abu Mufid refused, explaining that Nakhli had not paid him full compensation some time ago when his son had been run over by a municipal truck. He knew a certain Hanna, a municipal tax collector, who would help him.

June 21, Wednesday: Abu Mufid asked me to see Elias Nakhli. Hanna had demanded LL18 for the municipality paper. Abu Mufid asserted this was too much since he had already fixed a mattress for him, charging him only LL25 for a LL33 job. I left immediately to see Nakhli. Since he was not there, I went to my 9 a.m. appointment. Returning at 10 a.m., I found Nakhli and indicated I wanted to pick up my neighbor's residence paper. He called the municipal secretary who relayed that the papers were with the municipal president and would be done shortly. I told Nakhli I had an 11 a.m. appointment in Beirut, thirty minutes away.

At 10:30 a.m., I asked Nakhli about the papers. He called again and reported it would only be a few minutes. The president's messenger boy, whom I knew from previous visits, passed by and said he would get the paper for me. At 10:45 a.m. I nudged Nakhli again; again he called; again he said it would be a few minutes. I called my Beirut appointment to say I was still coming. As I was leaving at 11:15 a.m., a messenger delivered the paper. Nakhli corrected the grammar and gave it to me. I asked about the fees. Since Nakhli refused to take anything, I later took him a gift at home. As I was leaving I saw Mufid and gave him the paper.

That night Abu Mufid expressed concerns about the municipality paper. The paper was in the name he used to use, Muhammed Tufik. In the mid–1960s, he had legally changed his name in Syria to the original family name, Rafik but had not changed his registration in the municipality for fear of jeopardizing his already-established, but unlicensed, shop. The municipal registration, he revealed, was actually that of his cousin (his father's brother's son) who had the same name. He had used his cousin's name because he had not lived in one place long enough to register his own name with the municipality. However, he added the good news that the *mukhtar*'s paper had been signed by the *qa'im-maqam*.

June 22, Thursday: Abu Mufid reminded me that he had volunteered, long before these events, to fix the dents in my car. He arranged to do it Sunday.

June 25, Sunday: Mufid took the car, promising to have it finished by noon. At 4 p.m. he returned the car, having taken a ride to Jouni, thirty miles away. They had not replaced the bumpers because the repairs were not complete. Since it was illegal to drive without bumpers, I expressed some concern.

June 26, Monday: I took the municipality and *mukhtar*'s papers to Shaykh Jamal. He noticed that the *mukhtar*'s paper claimed Abu Mufid had lived in one place over ten years while the municipality paper listed three different residences, none of which was the same as the one on the *mukhtar*'s paper. I returned the papers to Abu Mufid and pointed out the inconsistency. He said he knew about it but hoped it would pass. We agreed he would make a new *mukhtar*'s paper concurring with the municipal one, but in the name of Muhammed Rafik and indicating that his son was living with him. I mentioned to Abu Mufid that I had been stopped that day by a traffic police because of the missing bumper. He said he would finish the car the next day.

June 27, Tuesday: I took the car to Abu Mufid at his shop. He said it would be done by noon. At 5 p.m. Mufid came to tell me the car was finished. I asked Mufid and Abu Mufid how much the repairs had cost. They both said nothing. Mufid said I had walked in front of them; now they wanted to walk in front of me. Abu Mufid added that I was a sister to him, and he wanted me to know his brotherly affection. Knowing they would not let me pay, I decided to take them a gift later.

That evening as I was talking to a neighbor, Mufid came by on his bicycle. He said my back lights were not working, and he would take the car to fix them. I said I had an electrician, and he could do the work. He insisted it would be easy for him since he was on his way to an electrician to pick up a motor. Thinking that he wanted the car because it would be difficult to pick up the motor on a bike, I gave him the keys. He said he would return in fifteen minutes. He returned a few hours later, having had an accident which knocked out the left fender and light. He assured me he would fix the car on Thursday. Abu Mufid came by shortly after to apologize for the accident. Trying to restore his "face," I said the fault was mine for having given Mufid the keys. He quickly agreed and lectured me that I should have known better. He had to fix the other car involved in the accident for free (a job which would cost a mechanic LL125) and mine.

June 30, Friday: Abu Mufid reported that he had just finished fixing the other car. Through his Lebanese Shi'ite friend he also had completed the new *mukhtar*'s paper which, while not exactly the same as the municipality paper, did affirm his residency in his current apartment for over ten years. However, there was a new development. The *qa'im-maqam* in Jdeidi had refused to sign the new *mukhtar*'s paper, noting that such papers now needed the additional clearance of the *maghfar* (police station) in Jsir Beirut. He had gone there directly but was told he first needed clearance from the district police station in Nab'a and the central station in Borj Hammoud. He had proceeded to the Nab'a station, where officials took the *mukhtar*'s paper and told him he could pick it up the next day in the central Borj Hammoud station. I reminded him that the *mukhtar*'s paper was now in the name of "Rafik" but the municipal registration was "Tufik." He said he was confident the police would not really verify the *mukhtar*'s paper with the municipality. He was so confident, I thought he must have some *wasta, insh' Allah* (God willing)!

July 4, Tuesday: Abu Mufid reported the following events between Friday and Tuesday. Friday, after being told in Jdeidi that the *mukhtar*'s paper would have to be verified by the Jsir Beirut police station before the *qa'im-maqam* would sign it, he had gone to Jsir Beirut. There he was told that he would have to go to the Aminos police station near Borj Hammoud, then to the Camp Trad police, and finally back to Jsir Beirut. At the Aminos station he was told to pick up his papers on Saturday at the Camp Trad station, Saturday he had taken a Lebanese friend known to the local police with him to the Camp Trad station. The officer in the Camp Trad station, after refusing to verify the *mukhtar*'s paper because it had been written by the Nab'a *mukhtar* rather than the Camp Trad *mukhtar*, agreed to certify the paper for the sake of his friend (the *wasta*) but at a charge of LL100. Following some angry negotiations, the price was reduced to LL75, and Abu Mufid was told to return Monday to claim the paper. Monday, the officer told Abu Mufid the paper could not be certified as written. He sent two officers with Abu Mufid to verify in person that the Nab'a *mukhtar* had written the paper. Abu Mufid was then asked to bring two additional witnesses to testify to his residency in Lebanon. The officer wrote a new residency paper according to the testimony of the two propertied Lebanese witnesses. He told Abu Mufid to return Tuesday for the paper. Tuesday (July 4), Abu Mufid picked up the paper, paid LL75, took it to the Aminos and Jsir Beirut stations and the *qa'im-maqam* in Jdeidi to be signed. Signatures completed, he gave me that paper and, with bravado calming some of his anger, also handed me a completed work permit. He had had to pay LL50 for the permit, and his son-in-law had had to repair, at no cost, the car of the official in the Ministry of Interior who stamped the permit. "There is no law (*ma fi kanun*); there is no government (*ma fi hikumi*)," he commented, "there is only brokerage and bribery (*ma fi illa wasta wa bakshish*)."

I took the papers to Shaykh Jamal, who approved them. Since the municipality paper was in a different name, he told me to keep it until and if we needed it.

July 6, Thursday: Shaykh Jamal called me to ask if he could tell the Ministry of Interior officials that the papers were for the release of Mufid from Syrian military service. He had sent his cousin (his mother's sister's daughter) to process the papers through Asad, her son-in-law, in the Ministry. Asad had agreed to process them but needed to know the purpose. I went to Abu Mufid's shop, conveyed the information, and then called Shaykh Jamal to tell him he could answer Asad's question truthfully. He explained that Asad had little time now. Since President Frangieh was in his home village of Zgharta, the Tripoli Ministry of Interior, where Asad worked, was very busy. When Asad was free, he would come to Beirut to do the papers.

July 7, Friday: As I was driving home late at night, a policeman whistled for me to stop. I slowed down; but then, remembering I still had no left light or left fender, I sped away. Disturbed by the affair, I reported the incident to Abu Mufid. He told me that he would fix the car the next day.

July 8, Saturday: Abu Mufid took the car.

July 9, Sunday: Abu Mufid completed the repairs at his expense.

July 11, Tuesday: Abu Mufid asked me to pressure Shaykh Jamal to finish the papers. Mufid had to go to Syria on July 16 for the army physical and could be enlisted on the spot. I called Shaykh Jamal to explain the urgency. He told me that if Abu Mufid were in a hurry, he could go to the Ministry of Interior himself and tell them Asad had sent him to process the papers. I relayed the message to Abu Mufid. He decided he had enough time to wait for Asad.

July 12, Wednesday: Shaykh Jamal called me to bring Abu Mufid to him. That afternoon at his home, Shaykh Jamal instructed Abu Mufid to go to a certain Tony in the Ministry of Interior. Asad had talked to Tony, a friend of his, that very morning from Shaykh Jamal's house, and he knew what to do.

July 13, Thursday: At 9 a.m. Abu Mufid and I went to the Ministry of Interior in Beirut. We were told that their work hours were 11 a.m. to 1 p.m. Since I had an appointment in the afternoon, Abu Mufid returned alone to see Tony. Tony told him to go to another office where he filled out some forms and was sent to two additional offices. At the last office he was given a slip of paper. He returned to Tony who told him that he would contact Asad when the papers were finished.

July 14, Friday: I conveyed Thursday's events to Shaykh Jamal. He said he would call Asad Saturday to tell him to expect a call from Tony.

July 22, Saturday: Shaykh Jamal phoned me to tell Abu Mufid to see Tony Monday or Tuesday. The instructions were from Asad.

July 24, Monday: Abu Mufid went to the Ministry of Interior. Tony sent him to another office. At that office he was sent to a third office. At the third office he was sent to a fourth to find the registration number of his papers. He returned to the third office with the registration number. After searching for his papers, an official there told him to return in one week. He returned to the initial office to which Tony had sent him. The official there, without noting Abu Mufid's name or purpose, told him he would process the papers as soon as he received them. Returning to Tony's office, Abu Mufid was told Tony would contact Asad about the matter. Dismayed by this runaround, Abu Mufid said he feared he would have to start over with another *wasta*. I called Shaykh Jamal to give him the latest details. He said he would call Asad.

July 31, Monday: Abu Mufid picked up the completed papers from the Ministry of Interior. Having finished the legal process for the Lebanese papers, he now had to begin the Syrian process.

August 5, Saturday: Abu Mufid asked me if I knew a good lawyer with strong *wasta*. With these legal papers in hand, he wanted to apply for Lebanese citizenship. With misgivings, I told him I would inquire.

August 9, Wednesday: I visited Shaykh Jamal to bring some gifts. I mentioned Abu Mufid's desire for citizenship. He told me to convey to Abu Mufid his wishes for luck in finding a good soul to help him. I relayed Shaykh Jamal's good wishes to Abu Mufid—and mine as well.

Months later: Abu Mufid informed me that he had succeeded in obtaining the release of his son from Syrian military service.

CONCLUSIONS: LAW AND CLASS IN LEBANON

The details of Abu Mufid's case, which were even more complicated than the events summarized here, demonstrate many aspects of the legal process for the urban working class and, in many respects, for the more privileged in Lebanon. For them, law was a set of externally imposed regulations which often had little rationality, predictability, humanity, or moral compulsion. Their rights derived more from the prerogatives of personal relationships than the protections of legal procedure. It was the power of these relationships which determined the outcome of legal transactions.

In working the law, however, Abu Mufid was working the Lebanese class system. His success came from his ability to mobilize networks across class lines and to motivate powerful individuals to intervene on his behalf. Certain aspects of his case were related to his status as an alien Syrian: the lack of legal residence, work permit, and shop license and the lack of protections from both the Syrian and the Lebanese governments. Abu Mufid's story, however, was reflective, generally, of the legal experience of the urban working class in Lebanon.[5]

The urban working class experienced the law as a series of face-to-face relationships build from *wasta* connections. They learned about the law through kin, friends, neighbors, and associates. Abu Mufid continually talked with fellow Syrians to learn about the requirements for release of his son and with Lebanese to learn about the workings of Lebanese law. He questioned relatives, friends, and contacts for loopholes, new developments, and parallel cases. He lost time because he was misinformed and would have lost even more time had he not been so skeptical of both the information and the law.

The misinformation often came from the very state officials who were processing his papers. They not only misinformed him but also sent him needlessly from office to office, delayed responses, forgot or neglected his case, and insisted on bribes to complete legal procedures. After all this they, at times, had given him papers which they themselves or other state officials rejected or found useless. The carelessness and lack of concern reinforced, for Abu Mufid and the urban working class like him, the recognition that those employed to enforce the law were the ones who least respect it.

Hidden costs confronted Abu Mufid because of this misinformation and the behind-the-scenes bribes and inflated prices for ordinary procedures. He paid a local *mukhtar* for a paper that he ultimately could not use and fixed a municipal employee's mattress for a reduced price for another paper he did not use. He fixed my car twice and those of two other people, which cost him several hundred Lebanese pounds in labor and material. He paid an outrageous price for the police clearance and for the work permit. The hidden costs not only affected him, but those who helped him. I took gifts to the *mukhtar*, to Elias Nakhli, to the Ramzis, and to Shaykh Jamal. Shaykh Jamal had to reciprocate favors to his cousin and her son-in-law at future dates. Asad became indebted to Tony.

Abu Mufid was fortunate to have money to pay bribes, to have skills to use in exchange for services, and to be self-employed so that he could take time to pursue the case. The Lebanese working class often could not take time from work to go from office to office or *wasta* to *wasta*. They often did not claim medical benefits or social welfare, for example, because to do so would have cost them wages. They also often did not have the money to pay or the skills to exchange for services. Their lack of time, money, resources, and information frustrated their legal endeavors. Additionally, their past relationships with public officials compromised their cases more often than not. For example, although Abu Mufid acquired a work permit because of the good relationship of his son-in-law with Harik in the Ministry of Interior, he had great difficulty obtaining a residency paper from the *mukhtar*, in part because of past competition with him. He also feared dealing with Nakhli from the municipality because of a bad past experience.

The abuse Abu Mufid suffered from public officials and the law reinforced his distrust of the state and the law. The urban working class, like Abu Mufid, neither actively internalized the law as a moral force nor passively accepted it as a historical necessity. Abu Mufid, for example, had known that he was supposed to register himself and his family, but had not done so because of the costs. When he finally needed the papers to save his son from military service and his shop from disaster, he aggressively sought out every avenue available to him to get them. He had little respect for the law. It was an external, irrational, and exploitative intrusion which he fought actively when it impinged too oppressively on him and passively when it appeared to matter less.

Abu Mufid realized that the only way to accomplish his objective was to mobilize the most powerful people he knew to help him. He had, over the years, constructed around himself a network of resourceful people: his own family, including his son-in-law; his neighbors, including me; his fellow Syrians; and a number of Lebanese he had come to know through his work and good reputation in the neighborhood. All these people were potential *wasta*. The network of relationships became an instrument to push the case along. He couched the exchanges, however, in the moral idioms of kinship and friendship, real and fictive. His son-in-law became a son. He spoke to me as a sister. He spoke of the *mullak* (property owners) as brothers and friends. His fellow Syrians were addressed as kinfolk.

He was willing to use any *wasta* who would help his case. He used men and women, Muslims and Christians, Syrians and Lebanese. He crossed gender, sect, ethnic, class, regional, and national lines to mobilize *wasta*. The social categories did not stop him from approaching individuals. Rather, he chose which categories to use for the appropriate intervention. He took a Shi'ite friend, for example, to deal with the Shi'ite *mukhtar* of Nab'a. He used me, a Lebanese Christian in his terms, to contact other Lebanese Christians.

Through primary relationships based on kinship and friendship, he built a constellation of connections leading to successively more powerful people. He used his relationship to me, as a neighbor, to activate my connections to powerful people. I used my family-like connections to Elias Nakhli, the Ramzis, and Shaykh Jamal to mobilize locally and nationally powerful individuals. Shaykh Jamal, in turn, called on his cousin and she on her son-in-law and he on his friends to penetrate the Ministry of Interior. Abu Mufid's network escalated to the top levels of Lebanese society. With few intervening steps of brokerage, he connected himself to the political elite.

Drawing on the moral obligations of kinship and friendship, Abu Mufid was able to make socially legitimate demands which superseded the jural implications of the "impersonal" legal order. His *wasta* worked by linking primary relationships to the power structure. He worked the law successfully because he was working, effectively, to reproduce the structure of class relationships in Lebanon.

Interclass relationships in Lebanon drew upon and were legitimated by kin morality. Ernest Gellner (1977) has remarked that patronage systems often borrow the language and linkages of kinships systems. Such political systems, he contends, are likely to emerge in incompletely centralized states, defective market economies, or defective bureaucratic systems.

While Lebanon in the early 1970s qualified on all three counts, the first is particularly relevant to the analysis of the relationship between law and class proposed here. The incomplete centralization of the Lebanese state was in part due to conflicts within the ruling class, conflicts based on competition among ruling families (Khalaf 1977), among ethnic-sectarian leaders (Salibi 1976), and among compradorial, merchant and landlord interests in the ruling class (Farsoun and Carroll 1976). It was due also to the fact that the ruling class had not struggled, as a class, to construct the Lebanese state. The state structure was as much an artifact of foreign imposition as it was a consequence of indigenous developments (Joseph 1978). As a result the ruling class had not constructed a coherent conception of itself as a class. Such a conception would have been necessary to generate a morality superseding primordial values, to legitimate the political institutions of the state. The inter-class conflicts and the external imposition of state structure had deterred the ruling class from building centralized state institutions. Instead, it ruled through informal structure of patron-client relationships recruited from and legitimated by primordial relationships.[6] In building interclass relationships on the bed of primordial social affinities, the ruling class had preempted the development of a public morality which could have legitimated an impersonal legal realm. They undermined the emergence of allegiances to the state and its institutions.[7]

Distinguishing between the emics and etics of patronage, Sydel Silverman (1977) argues that the ideology of patronage can uphold the status and authority of the ruling elite, even though the nonelite recognize the discrepancies between myth and reality. For the elite, the ideology serves to stave off challenges to its rule; for the nonelite, it serves as a way of making claims on powerful and high-status persons. The nonelite in Lebanon were as skeptical of the ideology of patronage as of the state and the law. Nevertheless, it manipulated the morality to make claims on the system. The impact of such use of morality was, as Michael Gilsenan observes, to disguise the "consolidation by the dominant group of shared class position" (1977:182).

Abu Mufid's case, therefore, is instructive beyond the story of one man. It is the story of urban working class vulnerability in the face of a legal system that operates through the manipulation of class-based relationships outside the formal law. Abu Mufid had to operate in the manner that he did not only because he was poor and Syrian but also because this was the way to work the law in Lebanon. For him as well as for others in Lebanon, rights and protections came from personal relationships, and not from the law or the state. Personal relationships ultimately protected individuals, however, ultimately because they expressed and reproduced the class system which upheld the law and the state.

POSTSCRIPT: THE CIVIL WAR

The events described here took place in 1972. Three years later a civil war broke out in Lebanon. I returned to Lebanon to carry out fieldwork in brief trips in 1974, 1976, 1978, and 1980. This chapter was written in 1980. The war in Lebanon continues through the writing of this postscript in March of 1986.

Borj Hammoud has changed in many ways during the war (Joseph 1983). By my 1978 trip I noticed that almost all the Syrians, including Abu Mufid, had left—mostly for Syria. Almost all of the Palestinians had moved, as had most Shi'ite and other Muslims. Many Lebanese Christians had moved into those vacated homes. In addition, I noticed both in 1978 and 1980 the residents in the neighborhood seemed subdued and more reluctant to engage in the extensive social visiting that had been an important source of neighborhood *wasta* networks.

Despite the changes, however, *wasta* still appeared to be important. In some ways it has become even more important during the war. One of the reasons for this is that almost all semblance of state order and control have collapsed. The army has split, the police have little power, and other state institutions are severely crippled. Numerous militias fill the power vacuum and, in varying degrees, provide order.

A multiplicity of militias has developed. Most are based on the styles of political leadership that previously governed the Lebanese polity, that is, they are the personal followings of individual political leaders. Some, popularly described as "boutiques," appear to be made up of a handful of followers of neighborhood "big men." The multitude of militias and the personalistic organization of most of them reinforce the importance of personalized brokerage networks, even exaggerate it. Now life and death issues are often immediately a factor of one's political connections. Militias set up roadblocks. Lack of proper identification or proper connections could spell a death sentence. Finding kidnapped or disappeared relatives or friends requires *wasta*. Protecting a home from seizure by militias or occupation by war refugees requires personal intervention by powerful individuals. Daily necessities like water, sometimes are obtained by networking. One cannot turn to the police or state; one relies mainly on personal ties.

In neighborhoods where several militias operate and compete for control, it becomes important for residents to maintain connections with many or all of them. Beirut as well as Borj Hammoud residents reported to me that, whereas previously they might have had contact with one or a few political groups, they now have to have contact with many. For those living in mixed neighborhoods or who must travel between neighborhoods, this often means having contacts with factions from different ethnic, religious, and political groups. In some areas like West Beirut, the war, to some degree, has spawned more heterogeneous networks.

In others areas, networks were consolidated along more sectarian lines. This consolidation is probably most systematically developed in East Beirut and in the regions solidly controlled by the Christian Lebanese forces. In many village areas more distant from Beirut, individuals' networks are to a large degree unaffected by the war while in those villages which have been more contested during the war, networking has become more politicized. Regardless of whether the specific content and sectarian character of people's networks has changed as a result of the war, what has remained true is that networks matter. Survival in war-torn Lebanon, has, at times, called for an artful manipulation of networks. That art may have been refined during the war, but its practice had begun long before.

NOTES

1. Brokerage networks also crossed ethnic-sect lines, a point which cannot be developed here, but which also raises questions concerning the relationship between ethnic-sectarianism, class, and law in Lebanon. See Joseph (1975, 1978) for the relationship between ethnic-sectarianism and class in Borj Hammoud and Lebanon.

2. The research from which this case study was taken was carried out 1971 to 1973. At that time, Borj Hammoud was a working-class municipality of about 200,000. The

religious and ethnic diversity and the intensity of relationships at the neighborhood level meant that reciprocity networks crossed religious, ethnic, regional, national, and political-ideological categories. The reshuffling of populations during the current war has left Borj Hammoud primarily Christian. For a description of Borj Hammoud in the early 1970s, see Joseph (1975).

3. Property owners, as a class, were considered respectable citizens and their testimony reliable. The landless often had to recruit propertied witnesses to testify. Such requirements reflect the necessity of interclass networks to work the Lebanese law.

4. The Camp Trad *mukhtar* was also a member of the Dashnag Party which controlled the municipality and all the *makhatir* (sg. *mukhtar*).

5. While there is no space to develop the point here, I would argue that his experience was common to rural as well as urban dwellers and to all social classes. For discussions of law and *wasta* in Lebanese villages and small towns, see Huxley (1975), Witty (1980).

6. See Khalaf (1968, 1977) for the relationship among primordial ties, patronage, and politics in Lebanon.

7. Khuri (1975) has presented an alternative argument, that primordial affiliations in Lebanon, such as sectarianism, are stages in the development of national allegiance. I have argued elsewhere that the manipulation of family, sect, and patronage by the ruling class has undermined such balanced development in Lebanon (Joseph, 1984).

REFERENCES

Bill, James, and Carl Leiden. 1974. *The Middle East: Politics and Power*. Boston: Allyn & Bacon.

Farsoun, Samih, and Walter Carroll. 1976. "The Civil War in Lebanon: Sect, Class, and Imperialism." *Monthly Review* 28: 12-37.

Gellner, Ernest. 1969. *Saints of the Atlas*. Chicago: University of Chicago Press.

———. 1977. "Patrons and Clients." In Ernest Gellner and John Waterbury, eds., *Patrons and Clients*. London: Duckworth.

Gilsenan, Michael. 1977. "Against Patron-Client Relationships." In Ernest Gellner and John Waterbury, eds. *Patrons and Clients*. London: Duckworth.

Hermassi, Elbaki. 1972. *Leadership and National Development in North Africa. A Comparative Study*. Berkeley: University of California Press.

Huxley, Fred. 1975. "Wasita Revisited: Social Exchange in a Lebanese Village." Ph.D. diss. Yale University.

Joseph, Suad. 1975. "The Politicization of Religious Sects in Borj Hammoud, Lebanon." Ph.D. diss. Columbia University.

———. 1978. "Muslim-Christian Conflict in Lebanon: A Perspective on the Evolution of Sectarianism." In Suad Joseph and Barbara L. K. Pillsbury, eds. *Muslim-Christian Conflicts: Economic, Political and Social Origins*. Boulder, Colo.: Westview.

———. 1983. "Working Class Women's Networks in a Sectarian State: A Political Paradox." *American Ethnologist* 16:69-90.

———. 1984. "Local Level Development Strategies in Borj Hammoud, Lebanon." In Louis J. Cantori and Iliya Harik, eds. *Local Level Politics and Development in the Middle East*. Boulder, Colo.: Westview.

Kerr, Malcolm H. 1966. "Political Decision-Making in a Confessional Democracy." In Leonard Binder, ed. *Politics in Lebanon*. New York: John Wiley.

Khalaf, Samir. 1968. "Primordial Ties and Politics in Lebanon." *Middle East Studies* 4:3:243 to 69.

———. 1977. "Changing Forms of Political Patronage in Lebanon." In Ernest Gellner and John Waterbury, eds. *Patrons and Clients*. London: Duckworth.

Khuri, Fuad I. 1975. *From Village to Suburb. Order and Change in Greater Beirut*. Chicago: Chicago University Press.

Salibi, Kamal. 1976. *Crossroads to Civil War*: Lebanon 1958-76. New York: Caravan.

Silverman, Sydel. 1977. "Patronage as Myth." In Ernest Gellner and John Waterbury, eds. *Patrons and Clients*. London: Duckworth.

Vatikiotis, P. J. 1957. *The Fatimid Theory of State*. Lahore: Orientalia Publishers.

Waterbury, John. 1970. *The Commander of the Faithful: The Moroccan Political Elite—A Study in Segmented Politics*. New York: Columbia University Press.

Weber, Max. 1947. *The Theory of Social and Economic Organization*. New York: Oxford University Press.

Witty, Cathie J. 1980. *Mediation and Society: Conflict Management in Lebanon*. New York: Academic Press.

INDEX

Abdullah, 132
Abi Talib, 'Ali ibn, 117
Abortion, in Egypt, 18–19
Abu Mufid (Muhammed Rafik), 145–56
Adultery: in Egypt, 17, 19–20; in Iran, 128; in Libya, 108–9; in Turkey, 85, 91
Aggravated assault, in Egypt, 31
Alcohol consumption/transport, in Libya, 102–4, 109–10
Ali, the first Imam, 128–30
Amin, Idi, 115
Amnesty International, 116, 118
Ardeshir, 135–36
Aristotle, 115, 128, 130, 139
Asad, 152, 154
Atatürk, Mustafa Kemal, 77, 79–81, 92, 94, 95
Attempted murder, in Egypt, 31

Bahrain, 122
Bani–Sadr, Abol Hassan, 111, 119, 120
Bankruptcy, in Iran, 138
Bazargan, Mehdi, 111, 119, 120
Bihbihani, Aqa Muhammad Baqir, 122, 123
Borujerdi, Ayatollah, 124
Brigandage, in Libya, 105–7

Child custody: in Iraq, 6; in Jordan, 7
Child support: in Jordan, 55; in Turkey, 91
Class differences: case history, 145–56; in Egypt, 54; in Lebanon, 9–11, 143–57; in Yemen, 67
Committee for the Defense of Freedom and Human Rights (Iran), 120
Conjugal obedience, husband's right to: case histories, 44–50; in Jordan, 39, 42, 44–50, 55, 56
Court system: case histories, 44–53; in Egypt, 10, 54; introduction to, 4–5; in Iran, 116–20, 122, 124–26, 130, 132, 134, 137, 138; in Jordan, 7, 35–39, 42–58; in Libya, 100, 110, 112; in Morocco, 5; in Turkey, 78, 81–82, 88–91; in Yemen, 62, 64–65
Criminal law: in Egypt, 7, 10, 11, 15–33; in Iran, 9, 118–19, 122, 125, 126; in Libya, 9, 99–112; in Pakistan, 9; in Sudan, 9; in Turkey, 77, 79, 82, 88, 89

Dashnag Party (Lebanon), 147, 148
Demirel, Suleyman, 93, 94
Divorce: case histories, 50–53; child custody, 6, 7; child support, 55, 91; in Iran, 125; in Jordan, 2, 7, 37, 50–53, 55, 56; in Morocco, 6; in Tunisia, 3, 6; in Turkey, 82–83, 91; in Yemen, 67
Documents, legal: background of, 61–62; case history, 146–54; document specialists, 66–70, 74–75; exchange of, 65–66; forgery of, 74; holding of, 62–65; in Iran, 132–36; in Lebanon,

146–54; necessity of, 70–72, 74; reinforcement of, 72–74; in South Yemen, 67; in Yemen, 8, 61–75
Drug trafficking: case histories, 27–28; in Egypt, 17, 26–28; in Iran, 125

Ecevit, Bulent, 94
Egypt, 99, 101; abortion in, 18–19; adultery in, 17, 19–20; aggravated assault in, 31; attempted murder in, 31; case histories, 23–25, 27–32; class differences in, 54; court system in, 10, 54; "Crimes Against Honor," definition of, 17; criminal law in, 7, 10, 11, 15–33; drug trafficking in, 17, 26–28; fundamentalism in, 11; homicide in, 17–20, 23–25, 31–32; indecent public exposure in, 17, 21; infanticide in, 17–18, 25; kidnapping in, 21–22, 25; legal status of women in, 7, 10, 11, 15–33; Libya and Federation of Arab Republics, 102; marital rape in, 17; marriage in, 17–20, 23–26, 31–32; polygyny in, 19, 20; prostitution in, 17, 21, 25, 26, 28–31, 33; rape in, 17, 20–22; sexual assault in, 17, 20–22; smuggling in, 25–28; theft in, 26; Western legal influences in, 15–16
Erbakan, 93
Ethnic differences, in Lebanon, 9–10
Evren, General, 93, 94

False accusation of unchastity: in Iran, 129; in Libya, 104, 107–9
Faraj, Imamzada Kak-i, 132
Farouk, King, 101
Firuz, 128
Forgery, in Yemen, 74
Fornication, in Libya, 104, 106–8
Frangieh, President, 152
Fundamentalism, 1; in Egypt, 11; introduction to, 8–10; in Iran, 9, 11, 100, 111, 115–24, 126, 128, 139–40; in Jordan, 11; in Libya, 9, 11, 99–112; in Morocco, 11; in Pakistan, 9; Palestinians and, 11; in Sudan, 9, 11; in Yemen, 11

Gambling, in Libya, 110
Gray Wolves (Turkey), 92–95
Guardianship, in Iran, 125

Hagop, 148–49
Hanna, Khawaja, 147–49
Harik, 147, 154
Hitler, Adolf, 115
Homicide: abortion, 18–19; case history, 31–32; in Egypt, 17–20, 23–25, 31–32; infanticide, 17–18, 25
Hormuzdiar, 136–37
Hoveyda, Amir Abbas, 118–19
Husayn, Imam, 129
Husayn, Sayyid Abdul, 132

Ibn Khaldun, 1, 130
Idris, King, 11, 101, 112
Incumbency of the Huddud upon the Mujaheds during the Occultation of the Imam, The (Shafti), 123
Indecent/immoral performances, in Libya, 103
Indecent public exposure, in Egypt, 17, 21
Indonesia, Morocco compared to, 4
Infanticide, in Egypt, 17–18, 25
Inheritance, 6; case history, 135–37; in Iran, 135–37; in Jordan, 58; in Turkey, 88, 90–91; in Yemen, 64, 67, 69, 71
Injury claims: case history, 137–38; in Iran, 137–38; in Yemen, 67
Inonu, Erdal, 94
Insult, in Turkey, 85
Iran, 77, 101; adultery in, 128; bankruptcy in, 138; case histories, 131–38; clerical involvement in law, historical background of, 121–24, 128–30; Committee for the Defense of Freedom and Human Rights in, 120; court system in, 116–20, 122, 124–26, 130, 132, 134, 137, 138; criminal law in, 9, 118–19, 122, 125, 126; divorce in, 125; documents (legal) in, 132–36; drug trafficking in, 125; false accusation of unchastity in, 129; fundamentalism in, 9, 11, 100, 111, 115–24, 126, 128, 139–40; guardianship in, 125; inheritance in, 135–37; injury claims in, 137–38; Iraq, war with,

118; Islamic Republican Party in, 120, 129, 130; land claims/transfers in, 131–38; Libya compared to, 111–12; loans in, 138; marriage in, 125, 128; mediation in, 138; Mujaheddin in, 120; National Freedom Party in, 119; National Front in, 124; political dissent in, 119–20, 125, 127; polygamy in, 125; pornography in, 119; prostitution in, 119; punishments (severe) in, 115–21, 123, 126–30, 138; religious differences in, 11, 119, 123–24, 126–27, 133–35; robbery in, 125, 126; SAVAK in, 118, 125; secular involvement in law, historical background of, 124–26; sexual assault in, 139; sexual deviance in, 119; slander in, 119, 129; smuggling in, 125; theft in, 135; trusteeship in, 125; U.S. embassy, seizure of, 120; Western legal influences in, 3, 111, 123–26
Iraq, 122; child custody in, 6; Iran, war with, 118
Islamic Government: Guidance by the Clergy (Khomeini), 124
Islamic Republican Party (Iran), 120, 129, 130

Jamal, Sheikh, 148, 149, 151–55
Jordan: case histories, 44–53; child custody in, 7; child support in, 55; conjugal obedience, husband's right to, 39, 42, 44–50, 55, 56; consanguine versus conjugal ties in, 36–38; court system in, 7, 35–39, 42–58; divorce in, 2, 7, 37, 50–53, 55, 56; estrangement in the family in, 38–39; fundamentalism in, 11; implementation officer in, 55–57; inheritance in, 58; maintenance, wife's right to, 39, 42, 46–47, 49–50, 55–56; marriage in, 2, 7, 36–39, 42– 58; marriage payment in, 7, 37–38, 42– 43, 50–53, 55–57; mediation in, 42, 56–57; polygyny in, 44–46, 54–55

Kabir, Amir-e, 124
Kashani, Ayatollah, 124
Khali ibn Ishaq, 103
Khalkhali, Sadegh, 119
Khan, Mirza Husayn, 124–25
Khomeini, Ayatollah Ruhollah: death of, 118; *Islamic Government: Guidance by the Clergy,* 124; Islamic law and, 11, 118–24, 126, 129–30, 140; punishments (severe) under rule of, 118–20, 129–30; *Revealing the Secrets,* 124; rise to power of, 140
Kidnapping, in Egypt, 21–22, 25

Lahiji, Abdul, 120
Land claims/transfers: case histories, 131–38; in Iran, 131–38; in Turkey, 83–84, 88, 90–91; in Yemen, 64–66, 68–69, 71, 72, 74
Law, Islamic: background of, 1–2; court system, introduction to, 4–5; fundamentalism, introduction to, 8–10; personal status law, introduction to, 5–8; sources of, 2–4; variability in, 10–12. *See also individual countries and legal matters, e.g.,* Divorce; Inheritance
Lebanon, 122; case history, 145–56; civil war in, 156–57; class differences in, 9–11, 143–57; Dashnag Party in, 147, 148; documents (legal) in, 146–54; ethnic differences in, 9–10
Libya, 77; adultery in, 108–9; alcohol consumption/transport in, 102–4, 109–10; brigandage in, 105–7; court system in, 100, 110, 112; criminal law in, 9, 99–112; Egypt and Federation of Arab Republics, 102; false accusation of unchastity in, 104, 107–9; fornication in, 104, 106–8; fundamentalism in, 9, 11, 99–112; gambling in, 110; indecent/immoral performances in, 103; Iran compared to, 111–12; loans in, 110; marriage in, 108–9; punishments (severe) in, 104–12; Sanusiyya in, 101; slander in, 104, 107–9; theft in, 104–7; Western legal influences in, 3, 11, 99–101, 110, 112
Literacy in Traditional Societies (Goody), 61
Loans: in Iran, 138; in Libya, 110; in Turkey, 85, 88; in Yemen, 71

Maintenance, wife's right to: case histories, 46–47, 49–50; in Jordan, 39, 42, 46–47, 49–50, 55–56
Majlisi, Muhammad Baqir, 122, 123
Marital rape, in Egypt, 17
Marriage: adultery, 17, 19–20, 85, 91, 108–9, 128; case histories, 23–25, 31–32, 44–53; conjugal obedience, husband's right to, 39, 42, 44–50, 55, 56; in Egypt, 17–20, 23–26, 31–32; in Iran, 125, 128; in Jordan, 2, 7, 36–39, 42–58; in Libya, 108–9; maintenance, wife's right to, 39, 42, 46–47, 49–50, 55–56; marital rape, 17; marriage payment, 7, 37–38, 42–43, 50–53, 55–57, 66, 80, 83; in Morocco, 6; polygamy, 125; polygyny, 3, 6, 19, 20, 44–46, 54–55; in South Yemen, 5; in Tunisia, 3, 5; in Turkey, 5, 80–83, 85, 91; in Yemen, 63–64, 66, 67, 69. *See also* Divorce; Inheritance
Marriage payment: case histories, 50–53; in Jordan, 7, 37–38, 42–43, 50–53, 55–57; in Turkey, 80, 83; in Yemen, 66
Mediation: in Iran, 138; in Jordan, 42, 56–57; in Turkey, 10; in Yemen, 67
Moghaddam, Rahmattullah, 120
Morocco: court system in, 5; divorce in, 6; fundamentalism in, 11; Indonesia compared to, 4; marriage in, 6; water rights in, 2; Western legal influences in, 3
Mossadegh, Mohammed, 124
Motherland Party (ANAP) (Turkey), 94
Mufid, 145–55
Muhammad, 134–35
Muhammad, the Prophet, 100, 104, 117, 121, 128
Mujaheddin (Iran), 120
Muljam, Ibn, 128–29
Mulk, Nizam ul-, 122

Najafi, Aqa, 127
Nakhli, Elias, 149, 154, 155
Napoleon I, 99
Nasiruddin, Mullah, 140
Nasser, Gamal Abdel, 11
National Democratic Party (Turkey), 94
National Freedom Party (Iran), 119
National Front (Iran), 124
National Salvation Party (NSP) (Turkey), 93
Nazih, Hasan, 120
Nimeiry, Gaafar al-, 11
Nuri, Sheikh Fuzlullah, 123

Omar, the Caliph, 128–29
Ozal, Turgot, 94–95

Pahlavi, Muhammad-Reza. *See* Shah of Iran
Pakistan, 77; criminal law in, 9; fundamentalism in, 9
Palestinians, fundamentalism and, 11
Personal status law, introduction to, 5–8. *See also individual legal matters, e.g.,* Divorce; Inheritance
Plato, 115, 127–30
Political dissent, in Iran, 119, 125, 127
Polygamy, in Iran, 125
Polygyny, 3, 6; case history, 44–46; in Egypt, 19, 20; in Jordan, 44–46, 54–55
Populist Party (Turkey), 94
Pornography, in Iran, 119
Prostitution: case histories, 29–31; in Egypt, 17, 21, 25, 26, 28–31, 33; in Iran, 119
Punishments, severe: in Iran, 115–21, 123, 126–30, 138; in Libya, 104–12

Qaddafi, Muammar: Islamic law and, 11, 100–103, 105, 107, 111–12; rise to power of, 100–102
Qaisar (film), 139
Qajar, Fath 'Ali Shah, 132
Qajar, Nasir ud-Din Shah, 125

Rafik, 147
Rafik, Muhammed (Abu Mufid), 145–56
Ramzis, the, 147, 148, 154, 155
Rape: in Egypt, 17, 20–22; marital, 17; in Turkey, 85. *See also* Sexual assault
Religious differences, in Iran, 11, 119, 123–24, 126–27, 133–35
Retail sales, in Yemen, 71

Revealing the Secrets (Khomeini), 124
Robbery, in Iran, 125, 126. *See also* Theft
Rushdie, Salman, 120
Rustam (son of Hormuzdiar), 136–37
Rustam (a Zoroastrian), 134–35

Saadi, 128
Safavi, Shah Sultan Husayn, 132
Sanusi, Muhammad ibn 'Ali as-, 101
Sanusiyya (Libya), 101
Saracoglu, Rusdu, 94
SAVAK (Iran), 118, 125
Sexual assault: in Egypt, 17, 20–22; in Iran, 139. *See also* Rape
Sexual deviance, in Iran, 119
Shafti, Seyyid Muhammad Baqir, 123
Shah of Iran (Muhammed-Reza Pahlavi), 11, 121, 124, 129; conflict resolution under rule of, 130–39; fall of, 101, 116, 117, 119, 120, 139; punishments (severe) under rule of, 115–16, 118, 127; Western influences on, 111
Shariati, Dr. Ali, 140
Shariatmadari, Ayatollah, 120, 140
Slander: false accusation of unchastity, 104, 107–9, 129; in Iran, 119, 129; in Libya, 104, 107–9; in Turkey, 85
Smuggling: case histories, 27–28; in Egypt, 25–28; in Iran, 125. *See also* Drug trafficking
Social Democratic Party (SHP) (Turkey), 94
Sohrab, 134, 135
South Yemen, 62; documents (legal) in, 67; marriage in, 5
Soviet Union, 77
Study of Man, The (Linton), 35–36
Succession, 6
Sudan: criminal law in, 9; fundamentalism in, 9, 11
Sultan, Zil us-, 127
Sultanpour, Said, 120

Taleghani, Ayatollah Sayyid Mahmud, 118, 120, 140
Theft: in Egypt, 26; in Iran, 135; in Libya, 104–7; in Turkey, 85. *See also* Robbery
Thomas Aquinas, Saint, 115
True Path Party (Turkey), 94
Trusteeship, in Iran, 125
Tunisia: divorce in, 3, 6; marriage in, 3, 5
Turkes, Colonel, 92–93
Turkey: adultery in, 85, 91; child support in, 91; court system in, 78, 81–82, 88–91; criminal law in, 77, 79, 82, 88, 89; divorce in, 82–83, 91; Gray Wolves in, 92–95; inheritance in, 88, 90–91; insult in, 85; Islam versus secular state in, 77–85, 88–95; land claims/transfers in, 83–84, 88, 90–91; loans in, 85, 88; marriage in, 5, 80– 83, 85; marriage payment in, 80, 83; mediation in, 10; Motherland Party (ANAP) in, 94; National Democratic Party in, 94; National Salvation Party (NSP) in, 93; Populist Party in, 94; rape in, 85; slander in, 85; Social Democratic Party (SHP) in, 94; theft in, 85; True Path Party in, 94; village headman in, 84–85; Western legal influences in, 78–81

'Umar, the Caliph, 104

Water rights: in Morocco, 2; in Yemen, 2
Western legal influences: in Egypt, 15–16; in Iran, 3, 111, 123–26; in Libya, 3, 11, 99–101, 110, 112; in Morocco, 3; punishments (severe) and, 104; in Turkey, 78–81; in Yemen, 3

Yemen: class differences in, 67; court system in, 62, 64–65; divorce in, 67; documents (legal) in, 8, 61–75; forgery in, 74; fundamentalism in, 11; inheritance in, 64, 67, 69, 71; injury claims in, 67; land claims/transfers in, 64–66, 68–69, 71, 72, 74; loans in, 71; marriage in, 63–64, 66, 67, 69; marriage payment in, 66; mediation in, 67; public prosecutor in, 3; retail sales in, 71; water rights in, 2; Western legal influences in, 3. *See also* South Yemen
Yezid, 129

About the Editor and Contributors

RICHARD T. ANTOUN is Professor of Anthropology at the State University of New York at Binghamton. His research interests focus on peasant societies in the Middle East, mainly Jordan and Iran, and on comparative religion, particularly Islam. He recently co-edited one book, *Religious Resurgence: Contemporary Cases in Islam, Christianity and Judaism* (Syracuse 1987), and just published another, entitled *Muslim Preacher in the Modern World: A Jordanian Case Study in Comparative Perspective* (Princeton 1989).

DAISY HILSE DWYER is a practicing attorney in New York City, with specializations in corporate and transnational law. Prior to entering into legal practice she taught Middle East studies and anthropology of law at Columbia University and also taught at the Columbia University School of Law. She has authored *Images and Self-Images* (Columbia 1978), co-edited, with Judith Bruce, *A Home Divided* (Stanford 1988), and published numerous articles on comparative legal systems and the Middle East.

MICHAEL M. J. FISCHER is Professor of Anthropology and Director of the Center for Cultural Studies at Rice University. His work on Islamic law stems from fieldwork in two culturally vital cities of Iran in the pre-revolutionary period: Yazd, the center of what remains of traditional Iranian Zoroastrian life as well as a city important in Baha'i, Jewish, and Shi'ite life, was the site of fieldwork for the dissertation, *Zoroastrian Iran between Myth and Praxis* (1973); Qum, the seminary town for training the Shi'ite clergy of Iran, was the focus of fieldwork reported in *Iran: From Religious Dispute to Revolution* (Harvard 1980). He is also co-author with George Marcus of *Anthropology as Cultural Critique: An Experimental Moment in the Human Sciences* (Chicago 1986), and with Mehdi Abedi of *Debating Muslims: Cultural Dialogues between Tradition and Postmodernity* (Wisconsin, in press).

SUAD JOSEPH is currently Associate Professor of Anthropology at the University of California, Davis. Her research and publications include studies of women, family, networks, work, local development, politicization of religion and the state in Lebanon and women and work in Iraq. She is co-editor, with Barbara Pillsbury, of *Muslim-Christian Conflicts: Economic, Political, and Social Origins* (Westview 1978).

ANN ELIZABETH MAYER is an Associate Professor of Legal Studies at Wharton School of the University of Pennsylvania. She has written many articles on Islamic law in contemporary Middle Eastern societies and has edited a volume entitled *Property, Social Structure, and Law in the Modern Middle East* (State University of New York 1985).

BRINKLEY MESSICK is a Lecturer in the Department of Anthropology at Brandeis University. He has conducted ethnographic and social historical research in both Morocco and Yemen and has published articles on legal hermeneutics, notarial writing, prosecution, hierarchy and textuality, education, gender discourses and law and political economy. He is currently completing a book on the interrelationship of law, textuality, and history in Islam.

SAFIA K. MOHSEN is an Associate Professor of Anthropology at the State University of New York, Binghamton. Her research and publications on Middle Eastern legal systems include a monograph entitled *Conflict and Law Among the Awlad 'Ali of the Western Desert* (Cairo 1975) and a co-authored volume entitled *Islam: Legacy of the Past, Challenge of the Future* (North River 1984). Professor Mohsen's research interests include comparative legal systems and women and work.

JUNE STARR is Associate Professor of Anthropology at the State University of New York, Stony Brook. In 1979, she published *Dispute Settlement in Rural Turkey*, (Brill 1978), and has written extensively about legal change in that nation. In addition to field research in Turkey, she also completed a year's fieldwork with Muslim populations in India. Professor Starr has been a Fulbright Scholar at the Indian Law Institute in New Delhi, Professor of Sociology of Law at Erasmus University at Rotterdam, and a Fellow at Wolfson College, Oxford.